Bob Dylan

INTIMATE INSIGHTS
from Friends
and Fellow
Musicians

KATHLEEN MACKAY

OMNIBUS PRESS
LONDON · NEW YORK · SYDNEY

Omnibus Press
A Division of Music Sales Corporation, New York

Exclusive Distributors:
Music Sales Corporation
257 Park Avenue South, New York, NY 10010 USA

Music Sales Limited
14 - 15 Berners Street, London W1T 3LJ England

Music Sales Pty. Limited
120 Rothschild Street, Rosebery, Sydney, NSW 2018, Australia

Order No. OP52272
International Standard Book Number: 978.1.84772.134.1

Cover Design: Fresh Lemon

Printed by Gutenberg Press, Malta

Library of Congress Cataloging-in-Publication Data

Mackay, Kathleen, 1948-
  Bob Dylan: intimate insights from friends and fellow musicians / by Kathleen Mackay.
      p. cm.
  Includes bibliographical references.
  ISBN-13: 978-0-8256-7330-6 (hardcover)
  1. Dylan, Bob, 1941- 2. Singers—United States—Biography. I. Title.
    ML420.D98M13 2007
  782.42164092—dc22
  [B]

2006026805

For my husband, David

TABLE OF CONTENTS

God is in the details.
—Mies van der Rohe

FOREWORD

The publication of Bob Dylan's book *Chronicles* in late 2004 was a publishing event. Finally those who had loved Dylan's music throughout the decades could gain insight into this enigmatic, mysterious musician who kept his personal life so closely guarded.

As fascinating an autobiography as *Chronicles* is, however, it does not provide great illumination of Dylan's character, his likes and dislikes, his personality, his highs and lows. Let the songs do that, perhaps he is saying, and he has admitted in interviews that his songs are more "con-fessional than pro-fessional." Yet given the fact that Bob Dylan is probably the greatest songwriter of the twentieth century and certainly one of its most important musicians, readers are naturally hungry for more. What do his friends think? Do they know the *real* Dylan, and if so, can they offer insight into his artistic genius? What anecdotes can they share?

This is a book about Bob Dylan based on interviews with musicians who know him well. It is a direct result of the fact that *Chronicles* is so vague as an autobiography that it leaves a lot of questions about Dylan's life unanswered. If he won't answer them, then let's turn to his friends for insight into his artistic genius and personality. The musicians whose accounts are collected here have known Dylan throughout the years and are longtime friends with whom he has shared a great deal. They range from Pete Seeger, who vividly recalls Dylan's entry into the New York folk scene, and Joan Baez, with whom Dylan had a highly publicized romance that contributed to his rising fame in the early '60s, to Ringo Starr and

Paul McCartney, Dylan's peers in the pantheon of rock 'n' roll stars.

Taken simply, this is a history of a major musician who played a significant role at an important time in America's cultural life. His story is told by the people who were there—who participated in a time of rollicking change, artistic breakthroughs, and ecstatic music and experiences. This book provides a portrait of the friendships and relationships that helped to shape important musicians whose voices have influenced our society as a whole. At the same time, it traces significant moments in our cultural history, from the early '60s civil rights era to the creative promise of the '70s and forward to the confused times we live in today—once again a country at war. In the '60s music was the megaphone of our generation and provided a sense of cohesiveness that united disparate young Americans in their struggles to seek a more racially integrated society and to end the war in Vietnam. The songs spoke our truths; they spoke from the heart. Dylan was the absolute best at capturing these truths, and although he did not seek or embrace it, he wore a mantle as his generation's "spokesman."

This book chronologically traces the friendships that influenced Dylan: From the respect he showed to the dying Woody Guthrie and the energetic, idealistic Pete Seeger in the early '60s, to his loose, comfortable camaraderie today with Bono. It also captures the sense of place that was so important in nurturing the music. The book evokes the heady atmosphere of Greenwich Village in the early '60s, a hotbed of left-leaning political fervor, a magnet for artistic, musical, and bohemian types. It was in contrast to that scene that Dylan enjoyed the quiet, pastoral life in Woodstock, New York in the late '60s. It was only natural that the work he produced at that time, like the album *John Wesley Harding,* resonated with simplicity and contentment.

The musicians reflect on Dylan the man at the same time that they explore his music and influence. They reflect on the times and serve as sensitive barometers of cultural change. They share insights that help to mirror our times and shed light on how great music—like great art— can always inspire and uplift us.

In other words, this is not a traditional biography. If you favor a denser and more detailed work, there are several to sample. The ardent Dylan fan has probably already read *Down the Highway: The Life of Bob Dylan* (Grove Press) by Howard Sounes and Clinton Heylin's *Bob Dylan: Behind the Shades Take Two* (Penguin). If you are of the intellectual bent, you will have appreciated Greil Marcus's *Invisible Republic:*

Bob Dylan's Basement Tapes (Henry Holt). Marcus focuses on how Dylan and The Band breathed new life into songs borrowed from folk, blues, and country musicians in their bootleg Basement Tapes. In Marcus' 2005 book, *Like a Rolling Stone: Bob Dylan at the Crossroads* (Public Affairs), he traces how Dylan's 1965 revolutionary hit "Like a Rolling Stone" transformed rock music. Robert Shelton, the former *New York Times* music critic whose favorable review of Dylan in 1961 is credited with helping him get his Columbia recording contract, wrote the star's biography, *No Direction Home,* which was published in 1986.

Bob Dylan: Intimate Insights from Friends and Fellow Musicians is a different kind of biography because the voices you hear will be the musicians who are friends of Dylan, not the biographer's voice. Too often a biographer, intentionally or not, inserts his or her point of view into the work, and the result can be a distorted look at a life. Albert Goldman's books on John Lennon and Elvis dwell on the darker, druggy sides of their lives. Kitty Kelley's extensively researched biographies on a variety of contemporary figures from Sinatra to the Bush family relish any anonymous source who dishes up the dirt. This book takes the opposite tack: From the highly principled Pete Seeger to the enthusiastic Rosanne Cash, the musicians speak on the record with nothing to hide.

The musicians' own takes on Dylan are pure: Acoustic, clear, and simple. They are unfettered by an outsider's judgment. The interviews with musicians, who are themselves outstanding performers, singers, and songwriters, can also be read as individual essays and self-contained autobiographies. When Joan Baez talks about taking Dylan on the road with her in 1963 when she was playing to huge crowds and he was not yet well-known, we get a glimpse of what was going on in her life and career at that time. When Seeger acknowledges that he was knocked out by Dylan's rough, elementary lyrics, so influenced by his own and Woody Guthrie's music, Seeger admits he was witnessing an artistic evolution. Seeger had written "Where Have All the Flowers Gone," "Turn, Turn, Turn," and other memorable folk songs, and he saw how the genre was being transformed by younger, raw and imaginative songwriters like Dylan. The interviews make the reader feel as though he or she is having a personal conversation with the musicians. With insights from politically engaged artists that range from Baez to Bono, the book shows how music can reach across generations in its appeal. It also tells the stories of folk and rock music through the perspectives of the pioneering artists who spearheaded the musical revolution. Ultimately, it offers a musical journey through American culture and history.

This book does not deal in gossip and recycling old rumors. Leave the stories of drug-dazed nights and marital infidelities to others. To tell the reader that musicians take drugs is like reminding people that the Pope is Catholic—yes, of course, we know... now let's move on. Stories of the libidinous escapades of musicians are not news, either. Rock 'n' roll is inspiring, energetic, and exciting, and the people who have the guts and talent to make it—and make it well—are imaginative, artistic, visionary, and poetic. Yes, they may be prone to excess, and yes, the music scene was fueled by drugs, especially in the '60s and '70s. Yet what feeds the rock imagination, in a musical or literary sense, is far more fascinating than which self-indulgence made someone sick in a hotel room in 1969. Let's focus on history, and let's capture it before the people who witnessed and participated in it are gone.

The musicians provide insight into Dylan's artistry and provide the reader with the "fly on the wall" experience of being there at critical moments. When Paul McCartney took a copy of *Sgt. Pepper's Lonely Hearts Club Band* to play for Dylan at the Mayfair Hotel in London in 1967, what was Dylan's reaction? Such memories are jewels, important to preserve. They contribute to our appreciation for the musicians who provided the soundtrack of the '60s and who were our guides and catalysts on an adventurous cultural revolution.

For my generation, "Where were you when you first heard a Dylan song?" evokes the same immediate response as, "Where were you when you first heard the Beatles?" These memories don't fade; they are strong and still resonate today, especially when they belong to other highly sensitive and talented artists who knew, when they first heard Dylan, that they were listening to music totally original, authentic, stirring, and real. A young, unknown Kris Kristofferson was working as a janitor in a Nashville recording studio when Dylan was recording *Blonde on Blonde* and watched him work at the piano all night long, wearing shades, writing music. Kristofferson did not dare to speak to him. To hear Kristofferson recapture his earliest responses to Dylan's music is to relive our own initiation into this unique and charismatic blend of folk and rock. As a songwriter, Kristofferson took it one step further—folk rock could be a confessional, autobiographical form that could strike harmonious and universal notes when combined with his own original intonation, rhythm, and phrasing. Kristofferson did not feel intimidated by Dylan, but *inspired;* here was someone stretching the boundaries, mixing the genres, and it felt alright.

There was great energy and excitement in the Village in the early

'60s. When Paul Stookey talks about the loose community there of aspiring musicians, songwriters, vagabonds, and dreamers, the reader can feel how the electric and cozy atmosphere invigorated all the artists and how they influenced and supported each other whether consciously competing for audience acclaim at the Gaslight Club on MacDougal Street or listening to jazz at the packed Kettle of Fish Tavern next door. At coffeehouses like Café Wha? the audience passed the basket around and the musicians were paid with tips.

The folk music scene in the early 1960s and the rock revolution it spawned contrast greatly with the manufactured rock scene of today, dominated by mega corporations owned by foreign conglomerates. Today music videos and overblown, theatrical performances have made image and spectacle more important than talent. They have also created an artificial distance between the musician and his or her audience. Unfortunately, the more that the music scene focuses on business and theatrics rather than making music, the farther it seems to get from the originality and magic of live performances. The delicate intimacy of folk and the joyful spirit of good rock 'n' roll seem lost in many of today's superficial and overblown performances.

It wasn't always like that. In the early '60s, all you needed was a guitar, an imagination, and ambition. Dylan had those—and more—in spades. In 1961 folk was a form enjoyed by intellectuals and bohemians, rock 'n' roll was synonymous with Elvis and Little Richard, and a 20-year-old Bob Dylan felt that anything was possible. Indeed it was. In 1966, by the age of 25 Dylan had released *The Freewheelin' Bob Dylan*, written "Like a Rolling Stone," "Blowin' in the Wind," and "The Times They Are A-Changin','" and was recording *Blonde on Blonde*.

Younger people I talk with look at the '60s with a slight twinge of envy: All that community, "make love not war," what was that like? Speaking for one who was there, it was a euphoric time to be young in America, and the generations that came of age in the '60s and '70s had a feeling of belonging to something larger than themselves. Folk music gave birth to protest songs, a process which Pete Seeger traces in his book on the songs of the civil-rights movement, *Everybody Says Freedom* (co-authored with Bob Reiser, Norton, 1989). The music had an incredibly moving, spiritual power. When Martin Luther King, Jr. gave his "I Have a Dream" speech at the March on Washington in 1963, Dylan and Joan Baez sang together in front of a quarter of a million people, and Peter, Paul, and Mary sang "Blowin' in the Wind."

During the '60s, whether fighting for racial equality or protesting the Vietnam War, music was the glue that held the community togeth-er: Our common language. It was not just the dynamic power that emanated from Dylan's band playing "Like a Rolling Stone" or "Maggie's Farm," or the explosive passion that smoldered from Hendrix as he wailed "Purple Haze." It was also the words that unified people, the words that connected people, and Dylan was the master.

> *Come mothers and fathers*
> *throughout the land*
> *And don't criticize*
> *what you don't understand*
> *Your sons and your daughters*
> *are beyond your command*
> *Your old road is*
> *Rapidly agin'*

—"The Times They Are A-Changin'"
B. Dylan Copyright 1963. Renewed 1991 by Special Rider Music
All rights reserved. International copyright secured. Reprinted by permission.

From the simplicity and universal feeling of "Blowin' in the Wind" and "The Times They are A-Changin'" to the hymn-like reverence of "With God on Our Side," Dylan crafted songs that became poetic anthems of the civil rights and peace movements. As Joan Baez said, "Nothing could have spoken better for our generation than 'The Times They Are A-Changin'.'" Yet he did not rest there. Later, with savage imagery in songs like "Desolation Row" or "It's Alright Ma (I'm Only Bleeding)" he rode like an outlaw where others had not tread:

> *Darkness at the break of noon*
> *Shadows even the silver spoon*
> *The handmade blade, the child's balloon*
> *Eclipses both the sun and moon*
> *To understand you know too soon*
> *There is no sense in trying*

—"It's Alright Ma (I'm Only Bleeding)"
B. Dylan. Copyright 1965 by Warner Bros. Inc. Copyright renewed 1993
by Special Rider Music.
All rights reserved. International copyright secured. Reprinted by permission.

Dylan combined the influences of the Beat poets Gregory Corso, Lawrence Ferlinghetti, and Allen Ginsberg with his own rhythmic, driving lyricism and painted vivid portraits of the streets, of confusion, despair, irony, and love. Other songs would contain softer, more musical, poetic rhymes: "*I once loved a woman/ A child I am told/ I gave her my heart/ But she wanted my soul.*" ("Don't Think Twice, It's All Right"). Yet as Baez said, it was his "disjointed, magnificent, and magical words" that would set him apart from songwriters of yore.

> *To dance beneath the diamond sky*
> *With one hand waving free*
> *Silhouetted by the sea, circled by the circus sands*
> *With all memory and hate driven deep beneath the waves*
> *Let me forget about today until tomorrow*
>
> —"Mr. Tambourine Man"
> B. Dylan Copyright 1964 by Warner Bros. Inc. Copyright renewed 1992
> by Special Rider Music
> All rights reserved. International copyright secured. Reprinted by permission.

Through the power of his lyrics, Dylan redefined folk rock. By expanding the genre's boundaries he cleared a path for others to follow. Many artists have covered Dylan songs, yet certain musicians have distinguished themselves with their handling of the material. When Bruce Springsteen was heralded as "the future of rock 'n' roll" by Jon Landau in 1974, he was also compared to Dylan, a great compliment. The powerful images and political import of songs by Pearl Jam and U2 also owe a debt to Dylan. Both bands also covered many Dylan songs, from Pearl Jam's "Masters of War" to U2's "All Along the Watchtower." It's exciting to hear Bono talk about his gratitude for Dylan's inspiration and the spirit he tries to capture when he performs Dylan songs like "Hurricane" and "Maggie's Farm." When Springsteen inducted Dylan into the Rock and Roll Hall of Fame in 1988, he told the audience at the black-tie dinner at the Waldorf Astoria in New York that he wouldn't be where he was if it were not for Dylan's inspiration. "There isn't a soul in this room who doesn't owe you their thanks," Springsteen said to the honoree in front of the music-industry crowd.

Dylan was the first to blend rock with great literary influences. By synthesizing his musical roots—Little Richard, Chuck Berry, Hank Williams, Robert Johnson—with the poetic influences—Allen Ginsberg, Kerouac, Woody Guthrie, Blake, and Rimbaud—he elevated rock to a new form. Consider the impact of "Desolation Row," "Visions of Johanna," and "Sad-Eyed Lady of the Lowlands." In writing such songs, Dylan expanded folk and rock boundaries to new, rich, and original levels of musicality. He also introduced to rock music the hard-bitten realism and social conscience prevalent in folk, moving the rock genre from the lilting love songs of the 1960s to a more socially relevant, aware music that captured the times, from "The Lonesome Death of Hattie Carroll" to "Subterranean Homesick Blues" and "It's Alright Ma (I'm Only Bleeding)."

And what did he look like in the early days? We have seen the photos, now we hear from his friends. Joan Baez introduced Donovan to Dylan in 1964. Donovan described him thus: "Dressed all in black, he wore a pair of Anello & Davide boots worthy of any gypsy. He was quite small and slight of frame, a very pretty young man with bad teeth and curiously solid hands. His slim features were widened at the jawline with powerful muscles. Definitely the thinking girl's dreamboat."

When Dylan came on the music scene, he was paying tribute to Woody Guthrie and his simple, plain-spoken "songs for the folk," populist songs celebrating our country like "This Land is Your Land" or the workers' anthem "Pastures of Plenty." The thread that connected Dylan to Woody Guthrie, Leadbelly, Dave Van Ronk, and Seeger was woven more elaborately by Dylan's fertile imagination, and he continued that strain through the romance of "Boots of Spanish Leather" and on to the mesmerizing "A Hard Rain's a Gonna Fall" and many other songs.

That influence continues today. Somewhere, in some small or large town, there is a young musician starting out who will also write beautiful poetry and melodies and by so doing, perhaps change contemporary music as we know it.

But as it happened in our time, it was Dylan who forged the changes. In 1961, at a time when pop music charts were dominated by songs by Bobby Vee, Frank Sinatra, and other crooners, popular music was sharply divided. There were the commercial ditties on the radio appealing to teenagers like "Itsy Bitsy Teeny Weeny Yellow Polka Dot Bikini," and in the folk clubs, a funkier, unadorned guitar and banjo music played by originals like Seeger and Ramblin' Jack Elliott.

Into the New York folk scene walked a 20-year-old naïve, idealistic, and ambitious Bob Dylan, known then as Bobby Zimmerman, fresh from Hibbing, Minnesota. As he wrote in *Chronicles*, "I was there to find singers, the ones I'd heard on record—Dave Van Ronk, Peggy Seeger, Ed McCurdy, Brownie McGhee, Sonny Terry, Josh White, The New Lost City Ramblers, Reverend Gary Davis, and a bunch of others—most of all to find Woody Guthrie."

GREENWICH VILLAGE AND BEYOND
1961–1965

NOEL "PAUL" STOOKEY
OF PETER, PAUL, AND MARY

Retna, Inc

Noel "Paul" Stookey, Mary Travers, and Peter Yarrow.

*N*oel "Paul" Stookey came to New York in 1959, after attending Michigan State University. A music aficionado, by 1961 he was spending all his time at the clubs in the Village. The native of Dorsey, Maryland had performed in high school R&B bands and brought his guitar along to New York to play "as a hobby" but never anticipated what would follow.

The early '60s were a hopeful time in America, a time when postwar posterity still prevailed. In 1961 John F. Kennedy was President, the space program launched a chimp into space, and middle-class Americans drove boat-sized Chrysler Imperials and Pontiac Safaris. Ads in Life magazine at the time showed stay-at-home moms dressed in aprons feeding their families Chef Boyardee canned ravioli. Yet Greenwich Village, where Stookey settled, was a world of its own with its beatniks, bookstores, poets, and artists. Whether watching folk singers perform in Washington Square on Sundays or hanging out in cafés, Stookey felt at home. The Village embraced him with its warmth, offbeat creativity, and promise.

In the following interview, Stookey talks about his earliest impressions of the 20-year-old Bob Dylan né Bobby Zimmerman, who had just arrived in New York and begun performing at The Gaslight Café where Stookey was the emcee. Stookey traces their friendship through Dylan's own skyrocketing career and the hectic, successful years of Peter, Paul, and Mary's ascension into the upper reaches of the folk world. His reflections take us across a time span of 40 years, highlighting many seminal moments in the folk-rock continuum.

The drive from Boston to the campus of the Mount Hermon prep school, where Stookey and his wife live, offers a 150-mile journey into contrasting facets of the landscape of western Massachusetts. It is a cool and sunny February day. The drive out of the Boston area on Route 2 extends from the affluent Boston suburbs of Concord and Acton to the farming towns of Princeton and Westminster on through Gardner, "the furniture capital of New England," and west to small working-class towns like Templeton and Erving. The route passes by miles of snow-covered, empty farmland; later the road is bordered by bare birch and maple trees that cover acres of land. Two hours west of Boston, Route 2 snakes its way past icy ravines that pour blue icicles down their rocky crevices alongside a river that rushes with sparkling exuberance. In the tiny factory town of Erving, blue-jeaned and bearded workers come into sight. They are emerging from their faded and dusty cars and heading into the Erving waste-treatment plant this cool and crisp winter morning. Erving's small commercial area features the predictable Wendy's, McDonald's, and the occasional gas station; a thrift shop on a corner has several wooden rocking chairs out front, their seats filled with snow. A ramshackle white house bends towards the highway where an old abandoned pick-up truck sits listlessly in a narrow driveway.

Route 2 eventually merges into 91 North. The highway speeds north where the exit for the Northfield-Mount Hermon prep school quickly comes into view. I turn off on Route 10 towards Northfield.

Further along toward Mount Hermon, there are verdant forests reaching above luxurious snowy hills. The atmosphere is permeated with the peace, security, and self-satisfaction of a smart New England prep-school town. Northfield-Mount Hermon was founded in 1879 and is now a merged school; the girls' school, Northfield, was united with its brother institution, Mount Hermon, in the early 1970s. The entrance to the campus cannot be missed; it is announced by a large carved wooden sign on a hill off Route 10. Entering the wooded campus drive gives the feeling of entering Sherwood Forest. Might Robin Hood and his band of Merry Men be far behind?

Not sure of the exact road to Stookey's home, I stop the car to ask a bearded man in a flannel shirt and jeans who has parked by the road. He is drawing sap from the maple trees in the forest with his two daughters. He points straight ahead to a fork in the road that curves through the woods to the school campus. Since I am early for my interview, I drive slowly through the expansive campus and park on a hilltop to admire the view of rolling, snow-covered hills dotted with evergreens, stretching as far as the eye can see. Stately, brick buildings are scattered around the large campus; students wearing fleece vests and down parkas scurry between buildings, several carrying violin or cello cases. Ahead of me is the ancient grey stone church, the Mount Hermon chapel, where Elizabeth Bannard Stookey, Noel's wife of 42 years, conducts Sunday services. Elizabeth received her degree from Harvard Divinity School in 1997 and has been school chaplain since that time. On most Sunday mornings Stookey joins his wife's service, playing folk songs to children whose parents may have attended many of his famous trio's concerts in the 1960s.

When I arrive at the large yellow frame Victorian house called Oak Knoll Cottage, Betty Stookey greets me warmly. An attractive brunette, she wears a navy wool sweater, turtleneck, and corduroy pants. She chats with me while her husband is getting ready, and lets me know that soon the two school campuses will be combined into one campus at Mount Hermon. The institution will be experiencing many layoffs as a result of the consolidation and after the academic year, the Stookeys will be moving on. Betty is looking into a number of new job opportunities. Her attitude is upbeat and optimistic, and she clearly shows great admiration for the students of Mount Hermon; not just the youngsters of the elite but also the creative and brilliant scholarship students she has come to know. She mentions that the Stookeys are also building a house in Maine. Soon her 6'3" bearded husband joins us with a cup of coffee in one hand and a guitar in the other. With the snowy landscape as our backdrop in the couple's comfortable living room, Noel "Paul" Stookey begins to tell his story.

In 1961 the 24-year-old Stookey was emceeing at The Gaslight Café on MacDougal Street in the Village when he first met Bob Dylan, a 20-year-old Minnesota native who had just arrived in New York. "Bobby's first appearance was not particularly notable," said the relaxed Stookey, leaning back on his sofa and sipping coffee. Behind him a wide window looked out to a snowy and serene country landscape. "I had heard the songs before. Bobby did songs by Guthrie, tunes Dave Van Ronk had introduced me to, and songs sung by Len Chandler and Luke Askew, who later went to Hollywood to become a movie actor. I only vaguely remember hearing Bobby sing."

A long-haired cat climbs onto a nearby ottoman. Stookey pets his cat as he speaks. Stookey recalls that Dylan went away from the Gaslight for a while, and when he returned, Stookey asked the young wanderer where he had been.

"New Jersey," Dylan replied.

"So you're on the road... you're a folkie," Stookey had said. "That was the extent of the conversation. Bobby gets on stage, and I don't remember what else he played... but he sang a 'Talkin' Blues' that told about working in a chess club in New Jersey. He was singing and talk-ing," Stookey said. Stookey had heard the concept before. Dylan's new song was based on a traditional song called "Talkin' Trapper Blues," which tells the story of a man working with other trappers at a Maine store. When it came time to be paid, the worker was paid in pelts; the store would accept them as trade.

"This was a very authentic song," Stookey said, his blue eyes sparkling. "At that time there was a huge thirst for authenticity in the Village. The story was very welcomed."

Dylan adapted that concept to his own song about performing at the chess club. "So Bobby starts singing at this chess club, and at the end of the engagement, the owner gives him a chess set. He says, 'What am I gonna do with this?' The guy says you can spend it just like money. So he goes to the bar and orders a drink, and the bartender takes a King and gives him two rooks and a bishop," Stookey recounted.

"I cracked up when I saw what was happening. I'm realizing it 40 years later sitting here with you. He understood folk music's *capacity* and its storytelling power. It wasn't formulaic. He saw how folk was able to inform timeless messages." That night, Stookey quickly became con-vinced of the 20-year-old's brilliance. "His talent was so palpable, you could feel it. Either that day or a couple of days later I told Albert Grossman that he had to sign Bobby," Stookey recalled.

At the time, thanks to the ingenuity of his new manager Albert Grossman, Stookey was also in rehearsals with Peter Yarrow and Mary Travers for the trio that would become the hottest in folk music: Peter, Paul, and Mary.

It was pure luck that connected Stookey to this fledgling folk trio. The year before, club owner and folk manager Albert Grossman—an astute 30-year-old businessman and devotee of the folk scene—had seen Peter Yarrow perform at a Village club and began booking him in folk clubs around the country. Given the popularity of the Kingston Trio and the Limelighters in the late 1950s, Grossman believed that a folk trio with a woman singer could be successful. He had seen The Weavers, who included a powerful female singer named Ronnie Gilbert, score major hits in the early '50s with harmonized pop arrangements of traditional and contemporary folk songs. Grossman wanted to create a new folk trio, two men and a woman, and Yarrow was the first musician he selected for the group.

In 1961, with Grossman's encouragement, Yarrow went looking for a comedian and performer to join him in the act and found Stookey working as a comic at the Gaslight. Yarrow said, "He was brilliant and I thought he'd be a great person to work with." Everyone concurred that Noel was a perfect addition to the trio. Yarrow then searched for a woman to join them, and he and Grossman spotted a photo of the blonde, lithe Mary Travers at Izzy Young's Folklore Center on MacDougal Street. Travers had been recording folk music since high school and was something of a Village fixture although she had a fear of performing. She had even sung folk songs earlier with Stookey at the Gaslight on occasion. Grossman persuaded her to try out in the trio. Grossman also suggested that Noel change his stage name to Paul for the musical sound of the trio's name. When the three fresh, energetic folksingers began rehearsing together, it worked.

When he was not rehearsing with his trio, Stookey worked at the Gaslight; it offered him a wonderful perspective of the Village music scene. "Folk music in the early '60s was such a burgeoning category that there were a lot of great pretenders," Stookey recalled. "There were people who wore Spanish boots, tight-fitting pants, and played one merengue on the guitar. You only had to know four or five tunes and you could do a set at any of the coffeehouses. So I saw a lot of people come through." At the time Stookey was rooming with singer/songwriter Tom Paxton, who was in the Army reserves, at 629 East 5th Street.

As he looked back on his early days, Stookey described his job at the Village's Gaslight Café as "a jack-of-all-trades." He ran lights, introduced acts, and took people to tables. His three performing roles were to be the emcee, to perform as a stand-up comic, and to sing ballads. "I did the ballads with a classic feel." He picked up his guitar and played

Bach's Fugue in G Minor to which he sang the jazz ballad, "You'd Be So Nice to Come Home To." This was perfect Village. It conjured up the funky Gaslight in a lovely way. Others recalled what a great comic Stookey was. He was known for doing a convincing imitation of an old-time flush toilet; around the Village he was known as "the Toilet Man."

As Stookey watched Dylan perform at the Gaslight, he realized the young musician could do anything with information; he could write songs on any topic. A few days after he had heard Dylan's song on the chess game, Stookey gave the young musician an article he'd read on June 19, 1961 in The *New York Herald Tribune*. It was about a boat cruise up the Hudson River to Bear Mountain that had gone awry due to the fact that counterfeit tickets had been sold.

"A lot of people refused to believe they had been sold counterfeit tickets, and by the time they put 1,200 people on a boat for 800, the boat sank," said Stookey. "Bobby came back *the next night* and had written "Talkin' Bear Mountain Picnic Massacre Blues."

Despite Stookey's raves about Dylan, Grossman did not sign Dylan right away. "Albert had his hands full with us," Stookey said of Peter, Paul, and Mary. "We all remember the comment he made, 'If nothing happens, *you're* gonna happen. '" Grossman's faith in the folk trio was unshakable and did much to encourage and sustain the naïve and hopeful musicians who were all in their 20s at the time.

In *Chronicles, Volume One* Dylan writes about playing card games at the Gaslight with Stookey, Paul Clayton, and others. "We were all waiting to go on to perform in the holding room for the stage," nodded Stookey, recalling the poker games. "Whoever was on the bill was back there: Len Chandler, Dave Van Ronk, Dylan, Tom Paxton, myself, Luke Faust. Not that we played for much money. Now that I think of it there was one person who kept winning," he chuckled. "I think it was Luke Askew, Jake Brandt, or Wavy Gravy. Does Dylan talk about Wavy Gravy in his book?" Stookey admitted he had not read *Chronicles* or any other Dylan biographies in which he is mentioned.

Stookey remembered one person being very important to Dylan at this time: Dave Van Ronk, whom he describes as "an irascible character with a heart of gold." The highly regarded folksinger, whose large frame and beard belied his 25 years, took the 20-year-old Dylan under his wing and let him sleep on his sofa at the 15th Street apartment he shared with his wife, Terri. One gets the sense that the intense and insecure Dylan could relax around Van Ronk. "Absolutely," confirmed Stookey.

"Part of the connection with Bobby was that Van Ronk was a historian and Bobby was very well-read. Bobby read Balzac, Ginsberg, the poets. Van Ronk had this amazing retentive memory—as well as a most kind regard, what's the word, a *reverence*—for the past. And Bobby had discovered that so many things are timeless." Stookey remembered that Van Ronk taught Dylan an old blues song: "Baby Let Me Follow You Down," which was adapted by Van Ronk and Eric Von Schmidt.

By late 1961, within nine months of his arrival in Greenwich Village, Dylan had earned a rave review in the *New York Times* from Robert Shelton and was signed by John Hammond, Sr. to a Columbia recording contract. On his first album, he included the blues tune Van Ronk had taught him and "House of the Rising Sun." After Dylan landed the recording contract, Grossman signed him to a management and publishing contract.

Despite having encouraged Grossman to sign Dylan, Stookey only observed their relationship from a distance. "Peter [Yarrow] was closer to Albert, so he was privy to a lot of first happenings. Things would happen in Albert's office. I never hung out with Albert. I had my own life, and by 1963 Betty and I were married," he said.

Stookey and Yarrow were also extremely busy with the growing success of Peter, Paul, and Mary. In 1962, when Warner Bros. Records released the trio's debut album, *Billboard* magazine noted, "It became an instant classic. The album was in the Top 10 for ten months. It remained in the Top 20 for two years, and did not drop off the Hot 100 album chart until three-and-a-half years after its release." The trio had a quick succession of hits with "Lemon Tree," "If I Had a Hammer," and "Puff, the Magic Dragon." Stookey was 26, becoming rich and famous, yet he dared not imagine what the future held. "Mary [Travers] has reminded me that my natural reserve forbade me to assume that I was going to have a career from folk music, " Stookey mused. "At the time I'd say, 'yes, this would be fun to do for three or four years, then I'll get into graphic art and animation.' When I realized that a successful career in one area can open doors to another, I thought, 'this is not so bad.'" He leaned his head back and laughed. Later in his career Stookey did an animated cartoon for Warner Bros. He also has maintained a great interest in and affinity for computer graphics and web design.

The camaraderie in the Village meant a lot to Stookey. It was an intimate place where artists were supportive and encouraging of each other. "I called it Greenwich Village University. I was so lucky–luckier than what shows. As an entertainer in the late '50s and early '60s, folk informed me ethically. Had I gone the lamé jacket/Vegas route, who knows!" he grinned.

He has always possessed a great respect for folk music's heritage. "The messages and stories were so important," he said of the material he was singing with Peter, Paul, and Mary. "The fact that the songs came from people who had endured hard times and were sustained by commonality was significant. As an only child, folk music became my family." Peter, Paul, and Mary's later participation in civil-rights marches in the South was a logical progression of folk's commitment to freedom. Participating in and singing at marches, "became practicing folk's ethos," he noted.

Stookey believed that the music of Peter, Paul, and Mary and Bob Dylan filled a void in early '60s American culture. "The times in which we began to sing were very hungry for authenticity," he said. "People wanted to hear music that put them in touch with their lives and reminded them of that which is real. Some people could sing comfortably in a folk idiom or a Celtic dialect, but we never sang anything that we couldn't believe in or feel. Maybe that's why people called PP&M too slick. We were doing what Bobby did with the chess song. We saw folk music as a vehicle for expressing the contemporary." Indeed, Peter Paul and Mary became so popular that some folk purists felt they had "sold out" by becoming too commercial. Referring to his trio, he said, "Our own audience says to us today, 'We grew up with your music.' My response is, 'We did, too.' We weren't that far ahead of the curve." As for folk music's potential, he observed, "We were all discovering it at the same time."

Even as Peter, Paul, and Mary's success grew and the trio performed bigger and more lucrative gigs, Stookey continued to keep up with Dylan's progression as a songwriter and witnessed how he was changing folk music itself. "After the Gaslight and other Village venues, the next time I saw Bobby was the Town Hall concert [April 12, 1963] in New York, which was amazing. The music was so impressive. Part of the discovery of authenticity was that Town Hall concert watching Bob Dylan. He came onstage with a guitar that had so obviously just been restrung that the head looked like Jimi Hendrix's... strings all over the place," Stookey laughed as he remembered. "And he wasn't dressed up in a suit!" Stookey and Yarrow always performed in suits when onstage with their trio. "It was the real thing. I had known of his talent, what was obvious was what he was adding to his repertoire... the new songs were his *own* music." Dylan performed his love song, "Tomorrow Is a Long Time," and his antiwar song, "With God on Our Side," among his newly penned material.

About this time Grossman gave Peter, Paul, and Mary an acetate of two Dylan songs: "Blowin' in the Wind" and "Don't Think Twice, It's All Right." "Peter and I were on the road in L.A., trying to figure out the chord changes in 'Don't Think Twice,'" Stookey recalled. "Albert said, 'Why don't you ask Bob?' So we went to his hotel room in Hollywood and he showed us," Stookey said. And how did Dylan respond to the trio's recordings of his songs? "He loved them," Stookey nodded. So did the American public. In its first eight days of release in 1963, Peter, Paul, and Mary's "Blowin' in the Wind" sold 320,000 copies, making it the fastest-selling single in Warner Bros. Records' five-year history. It remains the most successful single recording of a Dylan song on the Hot 100. The song also "helped to center the group's focus internally and its public image in terms of the connection between folk and advocacy," Stookey observed.

Looking back, Stookey acknowledged the importance of Albert Grossman's role to Peter, Paul, and Mary. "He was instrumental. We would not have been a trio if it were not for Albert. When he took us on he was also handling Odetta, Bob Gibson, and Ian and Sylvia," Stookey pointed out. "Invaluable is not too strong a word for Albert," he added. Grossman had contacts, experience, and what Stookey calls "a certainty about his taste" that allowed him to bargain the better deal for his artists. Inevitably Grossman would say to a promoter: 'Okay this is the fee,' and the promoter would say, 'I can't pay that much.' So Grossman would agree to 80% of the ticket sales. "And through his contacts—the graphic designer Milt Glazer, and other means—20,000 people would show up for a concert. He did amazingly well, and his artists did very well. How did he know that?" Stookey asked rhetorically.

In the mid-'60s Stookey wrote a song called "Talkin' Candy Bar Blues" and the end of it did not work. "Albert asked me if he could show it to Bobby to see what he could come up with. So Bobby wrote an ending that had wheat germ and health food in it. Now this was 10 years before the health-food craze. I didn't like it, so the verse never made it. But that was the only thing Albert brokered between us after he gave us 'Blowin' in the Wind,'" he observed.

Later Dylan and other artists managed by Grossman would have trouble with the manager's hardball tactics. (Dylan sued to get out of the publishing contract that Grossman had signed him to in 1962.) Yet

Peter, Paul, and Mary never had problems with him. "There were no hard feelings between us and Albert. That never happened for artistic reasons," Stookey affirmed. "Part of Albert's success was that he never told you to do anything you would regret. He did tell you not to do some things you may have gotten away with, so he erred on the side of being conservative." Indeed, Grossman's astute taste in creating Peter, Paul, and Mary confirmed that the American audience-at-large was ready to embrace folk music. The trio was instrumental in popularizing folk with millions who had not tuned into it before.

Because of their involvement in the civil rights movement, in August 1963 Peter, Paul, and Mary were invited to perform at the March on Washington. "Everybody in the folk idiom was connected to the civil rights struggle," said Stookey. "The musicians who were there were *all* believers in the dream. Joan [Baez] sang there, too. What I remember is being surrounded by a large amount of people and realizing there were some people in America who didn't know this was important. That was what I remember. Mary said she never felt hope as being so palpable."

At the Lincoln Memorial, Peter, Paul, and Mary sang "If I Had a Hammer" by Pete Seeger and Lee Hays and, later, "Blowin' in the Wind." Dylan sang with Joan Baez. Stookey was not aware of the love affair between the two. "I didn't think of their having any kind of relationship until it was over. It wasn't evident to me at the time," he shrugged.

Throughout the '60s, as Peter, Paul, and Mary were navigating their successful careers and as Dylan's star ascended, Stookey lost touch with Bob. "We tried to reconnect again in late '60s. I can't remember if I called him or he called me, " said Stookey. "They were shooting a film up at Woodstock. Betty and I were still in our house in the Village on Bedford Street so it must have been about 1968. I was in one of Bobby's crazy films, *Eat the Document,* and ended up on the cutting room floor." (Stookey had bought his house at 70 Bedford Street in 1962 for $38,000. Clifford Odets lived two doors away; the bohemian poet Edna St. Vincent Millay had once lived in a tiny 20-foot wide house across the street from the Stookeys'. The singer/songwriter parked his Jaguar XKE in the alley next to their house. The sports car was a wedding gift from Peter, Mary, Albert Grossman, and another friend. During the Stookeys' stay at 70 Bedford Street, their first daughter, Elizabeth, was born.)

Stookey is quick to apologize for one gaffe on his trio's recording of a Dylan song. "I think he grew disenchanted with the trio's handling as music began to shift into rock and a more aggressive posture. He had a valid point. We were getting sloppy: Dissipated energies, too much time on the road. For instance, we recorded 'Too Much of Nothing" [a Dylan song] in 1968.

"Usually we're scrupulous about relationships, with promoters, writers, artists. We would apply that same nitpicking to music. We discussed deep and profound aspects of every song we did. Then in our recording of 'Too Much of Nothing' we say 'Say hello to Marion...' That is my aunt's name! We blew Dylan's rhyme scheme of Vivian," Stookey admitted. "Dylan never said anything. We never copped to it. But as a songwriter myself, I can imagine that you write a chorus with alliteration and poetic quality, and it all hangs on the name Vivian, then you hear Marion and say 'what's that?'"

The chorus of the song is:

> *Say hello to Valerie*
> *Say hello to Vivian*
> *Send them all my salary*
> *On the waters of oblivion*

By 1969, exhausted from endless touring, Stookey initiated the breakup of Peter, Paul, and Mary. "This was actually connected to Bob also. After Bob had his motorcycle accident and The Beatles were very big, a friend and I, Dave Dixon—a famous DJ from Detroit area—wanted to go see Bobby, in about 1967. We felt that The Beatles' music had significance in the way that folk music had a deeper meaning. It was speaking of a bigger purpose than entertainment. It had the ethics of folk music and was now expanding the human psyche," Stookey observed.

"So I called Bob up in Woodstock. He was with Sara still. He was recovering from the accident, and I was oblivious to his condition. I said, 'Hey I want to come up and talk to you.' He said, 'Okay, come up.' He was really gracious. What I was trying to say was that The Beatles were talking about Love, and I asked 'what's the difference between love with a 'small l' and love with a 'big L?' What do you think the Beatles are trying to say? You've been writing a long time, where are you headed now?'

"And Bob said, 'Based on your questions, Noel, I think you're going to like my next album.'" It was *John Wesley Harding*. The album, with its allegorical songs like "I Dreamed I Saw St. Augustine," "All Along the Watchtower," and "The Ballad of Frankie Lee and Judas Priest," was rich with Biblical metaphors. Stookey pointed out, "*John Wesley Harding* was a step into the more spiritual nature of Dylan, not that it wasn't evident in 'My Back Pages.'" Bobby also said, 'You should read the Bible, Noel.'"

Stookey was amazed that his philosophical question to his friend elicited such a specific recommendation, one that would have great resonance in his own life. "He could have said, 'You should read Balzac.' I took it to heart. Though it did not immediately lead to my Christian conversion, it was a step in the right direction. I started reading the Bible and gave it up almost immediately," he admitted. "The Old Testament was too thick, with all those 'begats' and 'begottens.' I didn't have the brain of Bobby, to be able to extricate essential truths from dense information. Then someone told me to read the New Testament. One year later, I did."

Stookey had spent so much time working and away from his family that by 1969 he was burnt out. That year, the schedule for Peter, Paul, and Mary included 260 dates and travel to several foreign countries. Unlike Stookey, Peter Yarrow and Mary Travers wanted to keep going "but they made the best of it," Stookey affirmed. By the time Peter, Paul, and Mary broke up in 1970, "I wanted a change of lifestyle," Stookey said. "I just had to be someplace quiet to figure it all out, like Dylan was doing in Woodstock with his cabin in the woods." In the following years, each member of the trio carved out a solo career. Although Stookey did not initially want a solo career, he surfaced as the most visible with the popularity of "'The Wedding Song (There Is Love)," which he wrote after his Christian conversion.

The song became a huge hit when it was released in 1971. That same year Stookey created a foundation to receive and distribute its royalties to charity. He chose the name Public Domain Foundation to signify that all revenues from "Wedding Song" were, in effect, public funds to be channeled to public good. One of the purposes of the foundation today is to encourage musicians to create and perform music of social and political significance. Stookey felt compelled to create the foundation because he felt the song came to him as a composer to be "given away."

Stookey considered himself fortunate to have taken time off in the 1970s before the road claimed him as a victim, as it has claimed so many musicians. "The balance provided to me was part of the folk-music ethic," he reflected. "In 1974, I moved my family to Blue Hill, Maine, Betty and I raised children [the couple has three grown daughters], and I became a gentleman farmer." In 1978, Peter, Paul, and Mary regrouped, rested and refreshed.

In 1984 the trio was on the bill of a Bill Graham production with Dylan and Madonna in New Jersey. "Bob had broken up with Sara by then and did not look well. We were the *assumed* accompanists to Bob on 'Blowin in the Wind', but he ended up singing the song with two of the Stones: Keith Richards and Ron Wood. I think he felt the gesture of inclusion and the message would mean more to Ron than with old-time friends like us," Stookey mused.

He added, "The dilemma that has chased Bobby through years is, as amazingly prolific and communicative as he is through his material, he can't talk. One-on-one he borders on autism. And he's so intelligent, creative, poetic. I'm not sure his brain is in the now." Dylan confessed as much in his song "Don't Fall Apart On Me Tonight" on the album *Infidels*. "*I ain't too good at conversation/ So you might not know exactly how I feel.*"

One of the stories about Dylan is that the audience booed when he switched to electric guitar from acoustic in 1965 at the hallowed citadel of folk, the Newport Folk Festival. Stookey had an opinion about this. He became animated and jumped forward on the sofa. "Oh! One thing you can solve—or I will before I die. I was there at Newport in 1965 when he went electric. Nobody booed until he walked *off* stage. They didn't want him to leave after two songs. He didn't say, 'Excuse me, I'm going to get my acoustic guitar.' I look at it as part of his mystique and probably what drives him: His incapacity to express himself in one way manifests itself in another. But I was standing there, and the audience was excited about Dylan going electric," Stookey emphasized.

Contributing to the myth that the audience booed was the fact that Pete Seeger, one of the organizers of the festival, was upset. "Absolutely," Stookey confirmed. Reports stated that Seeger felt that by going electric, Dylan had defected from folk music. Seeger offers his own opinion on the controversy in Chapter Three.

Despite the passage of 40 years, Stookey still feels a kinship with Dylan. He recalled being backstage at a Stevie Wonder TV special in 1986 in honor of Martin Luther King, Jr., which included Dylan and Peter, Paul, and Mary. "We were all in the rehearsal room and Bob asked me, 'Are you still into this Jesus thing?' I said, 'Yes, best thing that ever happened to me.' And I could tell he was sincere in his curiosity," Stookey smiled, a special affirming warmth in his blue eyes.

Finally, Stookey shared an anecdote from his band-mate Peter Yarrow. Yarrow was watching his son play soccer on a field in L.A., where Dylan was also watching one of his sons play, around the time of the Stevie Wonder special in 1986. "Bobby passed Peter and whacked him on the tush," Stookey said. "Now Bobby was never one for any of this guy stuff. He was not a back-slapping type; that's too comfortable. And I thought to myself when I heard that, 'Good, he's happy! He's *relaxing*.'" As Stookey finished his story, he stood up, stretched his tall frame, and breathed deeply, looking out the window of his old yellow house. From his hilltop home, the vast New England countryside covered with snow stretched far below.

Albert Grossman died of a heart attack in 1986 on a plane trip to London. He was 59. Peter Yarrow, 67, lives in Connecticut. Now 69, Noel "Paul" Stookey performs solo dates in clubs around New England and New York State. Until the spring of 2005, Stookey and Yarrow continued to perform with Peter, Paul and Mary, who in recent years also have made successful "pledge" shows to help PBS with fundraising. The trio had more than 40 concerts scheduled for 2005 that were cancelled because the health of Mary Travers, 69, had taken a turn for the worse. Mary is fighting leukemia. She lives with her husband in Greenwich, Connecticut. In 2006 her health improved, however, and a fall tour was planned. The Peter, Paul, and Mary Web site has updates (www.peterpaulandmary.com).

LIAM CLANCY

Tommy Makem, Pat Clancy, Tom Clancy, and Liam Clancy

*P*erhaps *no musician in this book has had as long and enduring a friendship with Dylan as Liam Clancy. After hearing
the Clancy Brothers sing their Irish drinking songs at the
White Horse Tavern in the Village in 1961, Dylan used to follow
Clancy around and try to imitate him in song. Dylan said to Clancy,
"You don't get it, man—but you're my hero!" Here Liam Clancy, the
irrepressible Irish troubadour whose music has played a major role in
popularizing Irish folk music, fondly remembers the days in the
Village when he first met Dylan. I had already read Liam's wonderful memoir,* The Mountain of Women, *and I was excited to meet
this natural-born storyteller and passionate entertainer.*

*Liam was born in Carrick-on-Suir in County Tipperary in 1935,
the eleventh out of as many children. His memoir describes memories
of childhood, "bounding over hills, streams, and the occasional
mountain, getting lost, and eventually found, and making mischief
in the way of a typical Irish boy." His innocent and bucolic life
changed one day when he was 19 and a woman who was collecting*

17

and recording regional Irish folk music came to his door. She had heard that Liam's mother, Mammie Clancy, knew some of the arcane songs. This woman was heiress Diane Guggenheim, who went by the name of Hamilton to disguise her wealth. She would come to play an important role in Liam's life. Diane invited Liam to accompany her on her travels through the British Isles and the American Appalachians in search of folk music. After falling in love with Liam, she brought him to Greenwich Village, where on his first night in America he was thrown into a party with some of the most creative and exciting performing artists of his generation, among them folksingers Josh White, Logan English, and Paul Clayton, and folk aficionado and radio host Oscar Brand. As his book describes the adventure, Liam was in New York to become an actor. He also played and sang with his brothers Paddy and Tom and fellow countryman Tommy Makem in Village pubs like the White Horse Tavern.

I was expecting I might have to go to Ireland to interview Clancy at his home and recording studio in Ring County, Waterford, but after sending him a letter I received a phone call one day from some- one with a thick Irish accent, "This is Liam Clancy." He told me he was planning to vacation on Cape Cod in a few weeks. "Why don't you come down to the Cape with your tape recorder?"

"I'd love to!"

On a warm August afternoon, with a gentle sea breeze blowing in from the nearby Nantucket Sound, we sat under trees on the lawn of the inn where Clancy and Kim, his wife of more than 30 years, were stay- ing. Wearing his trademark white sailor's cap along with a beige shirt and slacks, Clancy picked up his story, recalling 1956.

"Although I came to America to act, I soon got involved with my brothers and Tommy Makem in singing. One of the folksingers' gather- ing places was Izzy Young's Folklore Center. Izzy had started a club and then Tom Porco took over. At first it was called The Fifth Peg, then Porco renamed it Gerde's Folk City," said Clancy. The Clancy Brothers were invited to perform at this folk showcase.

A lover of Yeats and Joyce—drawn to the world of poetry, ideas, music, and writing—Clancy was earning $45 a week as an actor when he first arrived in New York. He subsisted on hamburgers and beer at the White Horse Tavern in the Village. When he was offered a singing gig at The Fifth Peg, he jumped at it. "The pay at The Fifth Peg was $125 a week, and I was able to pay off my bar tab at the White Horse

Tavern," he grinned. The Clancy Brothers and Tommy Makem also began recording on the Tradition Records label, which they co-founded with Diane Guggenheim. One night in 1961 at Gerde's Folk City, Clancy met a shy young guy recently arrived from Minnesota. "He grabbed everyone's attention. We would ask, 'Is it a girl or a boy?' He was skinny and slight."

It was inevitable that Dylan would migrate from his cold, isolated hometown of Hibbing, Minnesota to New York. He had already been influenced by Elvis Presley, Pound, Camus, T.S. Eliot, and e.e. cummings, individuals who were "mostly expatriate Americans off in Paris and Tangiers," he said in the *Biograph* liner notes. His influences included, "Burroughs, *Nova Express*, John Rechy, Gary Snyder, Ferlinghetti, *Pictures from the Gone World*, the newer poets and folk music, jazz, Monk, Coltrane, Sonny and Brownie, Big Bill Broonzy, and Charlie Christian," he added. Dylan said, "It all left the rest of everything in the dust… I knew I had to get to New York. I'd been dreaming about that for a long time."

At Gerde's, Clancy came to know the aspiring folksinger who called himself Bob Dylan. Clancy remembered events rather simply and said that after he met Dylan, "We all had the same problem; we couldn't tune a guitar. Many people wouldn't have come together if they had known how to tune a guitar.

"Bobby would whip around from one subject to another, fidgeting all the time. The only thing I can compare him to is blotting paper," said Clancy of the animated, active newcomer. "He soaked up everything. He had this immense curiosity, and he was ready to suck up everything that came within his range… In fact someone sent me a tape recently called *Bob Dylan Roots,* and on it Dylan is doing an imitation of an Irish accent," said Clancy. "Then he says, 'I want to sing a song Liam Clancy sang at the White Horse Tavern.'" But when Dylan performed "he was insecure, giggling, very amateurish," Clancy recalled.

The Clancy Brothers and Tommy Makem were performing at many fundraising events and benefits for Woody Guthrie. They also participated in hootenannies where the group of 15 included Pete Seeger, Brownie McGhee, Sonny Terry, and Josh White. They were all swapping songs and learning new originals. Clancy remembered Seeger vividly. "The Kingston Trio had popularized folk, but the Weavers and Pete… had such stage presence," he said. "Pete was bound to the cause [of social justice]. I would see him at gatherings. I felt he was talking through me to humanity. He was sending me a message. One time he told me to learn a Scottish song called 'Freedom Come All Ye,' and it was a Communist anthem. Yes, Pete was preaching."

Although a newcomer to the Village, Dylan soon became a protégé and friend of not only Seeger and Woody Guthrie but of Cisco Houston and Ramblin' Jack Elliott. He also quickly made friends with Dave Van Ronk, Fred Neil, Paul Clayton, Mark Spoelstra, and Peter LaFarge, in addition to the Clancy Brothers. The Clancy Brothers soon signed a management contract with Marty Ehrlichman, Josh White's manager. (A few years later Ehrlichman discovered Barbra Streisand and still manages her today.) After renting them a rehearsal hall where they could practice for days, Ehrlichman and Rosenfeld opened doors for The Clancy Brothers and Tommy Makem. Soon they grew in confidence and performed at popular clubs like The Village Vanguard and The Village Gate on a regular basis.

"A combination of Josh White and our background in theater helped us learn how to handle the stage, how to infuse it with a sense of illumination, the way O'Neill built a play to a climax. It is so tough. That was how we went about arranging our shows," Clancy recalled. They also continued to play Gerde's Folk City and The White Horse. Dylan used to follow the Clancy Brothers around "like a puppy dog," Clancy said. "And in a way, we have never lost that relationship," he said of the young Dylan's hero worship. Liam remembered that the Clancy Brothers helped Dylan get a break shortly after he had arrived in New York, too. "John Hammond of Columbia Records was producing an album of Carolyn Hester, and he phoned my brother Paddy at Tradition Records to see if he could recommend a good harmonica player. Paddy suggested the new guy in town, Bob Dylan." Eventually Dylan signed a contract with Columbia and was produced by Hammond, who had also produced Billie Holliday and Count Basie and promoted Benny Goodman.

To this day, Dylan treats Liam reverently, as one of his teachers. Dylan was fascinated with Liam because he was authentic. Clancy emphasized, "He so much wanted that kind of authenticity. He would say, 'I want to be like Liam, or like Mississippi John Hurt.' Here was a 19-year-old kid who was Jewish, from Minnesota, wanting to sing like an old black man." According to Clancy, others wanted that same authenticity. "Dave Van Ronk, wanted it, too. Though his name doesn't sound it, he had Irish roots because his mother was Irish. He drank triple Irish whiskey. I think the conflict that came into Dylan's life was that he wanted to be Elvis, a rock 'n' roll star, he wanted to be Lightnin' Hopkins, he wanted to be Woody Guthrie... He had the voice—a voice of race—and could be like these singers and a pop stars. It was a dilemma trying to be all those things."

Clancy added, "Dylan eventually ended up becoming an icon because of his protest songs. But as he said in his book *Chronicles*, that haunted him. When he became successful, he felt trapped. As a poet, in those early days the words were tumbling out of him. After a session at the White Horse, he would get a hold of me and say, 'You've gotta listen to these verses that I wrote,' and he would take these baby steps." Clancy recalled that Woody Guthrie, too, used to write 20 songs a day. "A lot of them went in the garbage, then there would be a memorable one like 'This Land Is Your Land.'"

Clancy taught Dylan traditional Irish folk songs. Clancy said, "He loved 'Eileen Ardon.' We would sing that together. He used to imitate me." In the loose, creative, and exciting Village scene, he and Dylan used to swap songs and occasionally share girlfriends, too. "Dylan had this image of the lost waif, and all the girls wanted to mother him," Clancy said. "We used to go to Carla and Suze Rotolo's house for dinner because their mother was a great Italian cook. There was nothing between Carla and me, but Suze and Dylan were serious. Kathy Perry and I were then serious, and when I was traveling she started seeing Bobby." It was years later that Clancy asked Dylan about it, and Dylan said, "She was lonesome for you, man. I just offered her comfort. She missed you, man, and you weren't there. I was there, man." Clancy added, "Kathy wanted to get married but I was still tied to Tina." Tina was his serious girlfriend who bore him a child before he was ready to marry and settle down. "Kathy was distressed. I used to get letters in Ireland saying, 'I went out with Bobby last night...' Everybody shared girlfriends. It was a tight community. We were all discovering so much. ...We felt like newborns and everything was exciting."

In the Martin Scorsese film, *No Direction Home*, Dylan spoke warmly about his early admiration for Liam Clancy. "Liam was profound," Dylan said. "Besides all his rebel songs, he had his acting career, and he had these incredible sayings. I remember him saying," and Dylan imitated Liam's thick Irish accent, "Remember, Bob: No fear, no envy, no meanness." Dylan recalled, "I said to him, 'Hmm, right.' What I heard in those rebel songs of the Clancy Brothers [was that] they were Napoleonic in scope. The brothers were musketeer-type characters, and on another level they did romantic ballads that would slay you in your tracks. The sweetness of Tommy Makem and Liam..." he trailed off. Dylan then added with insight, "All the great performers that I had seen that I wanted to be like, they had one thing in common: In their eyes. Their eyes said, 'I know something you don't know.' I wanted to be that kind of performer," Dylan affirmed.

The Clancy Brothers' careers took off after their managers booked them into the uptown club The Blue Angel. Though some diehards in the Village thought they were "selling out," all their friends from Gerde's came to their shows. Shortly thereafter, they made an appearance on the *Ed Sullivan Show,* which launched the group into stardom. As it happened, a scheduled act for Sullivan did not show, so the Clancy Brothers were asked to perform beyond their scheduled time allotment in what ended up as a record-breaking 16-minute performance. The quartet recorded numerous albums for Columbia Records and enjoyed great success during the 1960s.

Dylan was moving fast, too. In his book, Clancy remembered one night at the bar in Folk City when Dylan said to him, "'Hey, Lem! Man, my records are sellin' man! I'm goin' ta be as big as the Clancy Brothers, man!' He laughed his little-kid-caught-in-the-act laugh." Clancy said in an interview that he felt that Robert Shelton, the music critic of the *New York Times,* played a major role in Dylan's success. "Shelton, more than anyone, was responsible for Bob Dylan," Clancy said. "He pushed and pushed and pushed. He thought Bobby Dylan was a tremendous poet. He had made a very folkie record with John Hammond at a time that the industry wasn't doing anything. Shelton just kept pushing. It was a little later that the whole thing caught fire. Shelton used to bring Bobby to our concerts and tell him, 'Now this is how you have to put a show together!'"

It was standard in folk circles to swap songs and borrow melodies. Clancy recalled that Dylan borrowed the melody of "Patriot Game" for "With God on Our Side." Dominic Behan, the writer of "Patriot Game" was furious. But, Clancy noted, "Behan was a scrapper. He had taken a popular song by Jo Stafford, 'The Nightingale,' popular in the '40s and '50s and wrote 'Patriot Game.' Then Dylan borrowed that melody and wrote 'With God On Our Side.' It went on all the time. That's folk music. The song was originally an American tune, so it's come full circle." It was also standard in the folk genre to tell complete stories. When he was interviewed on video for the Dylan's 30th Anniversary Concert held at Madison Square Garden, Clancy remembered a time when Dylan stopped him on the streets of the Village wanting to play a song he had just written. "The song went on for about 12 verses," Clancy chuckled. He told the young songwriter, "You have a fantastic imagery and talent, now if you could just make it a *bit shorter.*" Judy Collins was also charmed by Dylan's Woody Guthrie persona when she saw him at Gerde's Folk City in 1962. Since then, she has covered dozens of his tunes and stole a compositional technique: "[Dylan] has a trick of taking an ancient song and setting a new melody to it," she said. He makes you feel as though you already know the song. And he'll use a very simple melody to carry the weight of complicated lyrics."

My interview with Liam Clancy moved from the quiet seaside lawn to a Cape restaurant where we feasted on lobster, shrimp, linguine, and other Cape delicacies like calamari, for which Clancy noted, "You must sauté it for only two or three minutes if you cook it." Clancy spoke about the years from 1961 to 1965, when Dylan emerged from anonymity to being the most important folksinger in the scene. Clancy and his wife Kim were at the 1965 Newport Folk Festival; he was filming for Murray Lerner, who was making a film about the festival and thought the controversy over Dylan's going electric was silly. As Kim listened, Clancy recalled, "After going electric, Dylan performed his second set and came out with his acoustic guitar. He looked like this stoned, Chaplin-esque figure. He sang 'Mr. Tambourine Man'... When I heard him sing, *'Your ancient empty streets/ too dead for dreaming'* it was so personal for me. I knew it was Sullivan Street on a Sunday." (Clancy and Dylan both lived on Sullivan Street in the Village. Sundays were very lonely; the clubs were closed, and there was no place to get together after the Washington Square hootenannies.) "I started crying. I also knew I was seeing the emergence of a major artist." Clancy was taken aback by his emotions. "It was just before my thirtieth birthday, and I thought I was over the hill. I went to Murray Lerner's place on Martha's Vineyard, where I was learning to sail, and I felt so out of the loop!" Songs like "Mr. Tambourine Man" and "Gates of Eden" demonstrated Dylan's affinity for the French poets Rimbaud and Baudelaire that his girlfriend Suze Rotolo had turned him on to, as well as his affinity for the beats: Kerouac, Ginsberg, Corso, and Ferlinghetti.

Although he is an emotional and intense Irishman, he was not as deeply affected by Dylan's success as others in the Village. "Singer/songwriter Phil Ochs couldn't take Dylan's success and committed suicide," Clancy said. "Peter LaFarge committed suicide by slitting his wrist in Kathy Perry's shower." Many musicians were jealous of Dylan. "I traveled South with Paul Clayton, an aspiring songwriter. He wrote 'This Old Town,' and with one hit, it went to his head. He was intensely jealous of Dylan's success." In the Scorsese film, Dave Van Ronk was shown speaking about the reaction of other Village musicians when Dylan signed with Columbia, "When Bobby signed with Columbia that was big news on the street. Everybody couldn't admit that they were that hungry. They turned it into a moral issue. They had to. Otherwise they were going to take long looks at themselves and might not like what they saw." In Clancy's book he noted that Paul Clayton (referred to as Pablo in Dylan biographies) was so devastated that, they say, he committed suicide by pulling an electric heater into the bathtub. Fortunately, whatever feelings of inadequacy Clancy was feeling on the Vineyard soon passed. Of Dylan's quick ascent, he said, "I was sorry to lose a friend in one way but excited to see his star rising."

Perhaps the secret to Clancy's enduring friendship with Dylan is that they "were never competitors." Clancy speaks admiringly of working alongside Dylan. "He has remained so loyal in his affections. He broke with his own tradition of not giving interviews and gave a lengthy interview for a film that was made on the Clancy Brothers," Liam said.

Clancy and his wife befriended another Village singer/songwriter, Richard Fariña, and his wife Mimi, Joan Baez's sister. In late 1965 the two couples went to the Woodstock area home of Albert Grossman, who had been managing Dylan for several years. Clancy said, "It was a beautiful house, but haunted—very strange. Bob had been living there. Remember his album cover of *Bringing It All Back Home?* He was sitting there with a cat, and there was a kind of frame around the tableau. As soon as I walked into Grossman's house, I realized that this is where the picture was shot. The cat was there, and [there were] rolls of colored cellophane that the photographer had used to get the tunnel effect. Fariña told us that all of Dylan's stuff was locked in a room downstairs that had been nailed shut because Al Grossman had so many visitors. Dylan was very protective of his stuff. There might have been manuscripts in there that he wouldn't want anyone to get their hands on. "We spent a couple of lovely evenings up there in Woodstock, coming home in the evening and lighting a big fire."

On one such occasion, "Fariña started telling us about a book he was writing." His book *Been Down So Long It Looks Like Up to Me* is a beat novel filled with sex and drugs with scenes set on a college campus, in Las Vegas, at a nuclear site, and in Cuba. Clancy adds ironically, "When I read the book, I could find no similarity whatsoever in what he was telling."

Clancy recalled the sobering spring day in 1966 when Fariña's book came out. "The day the book was published, it got a whole page in the literary section of the *New York Times*, and I came into the Lion's Head with this newspaper under my arm. My brother Pat was there, with Tom, and Tommy Makem was up at the top of the bar. I went over to him and said, 'Jesus Christ, did you see this? Did you see Fariña's write-up?' He had this very somber look on his face, and he said, 'Fariña was killed last night.'" Fariña died in a motorcycle accident on April 30, 1966. "We were all very young, and this was the first time a contemporary had died. At the time, I thought we were all immortal."

For 15 years, Harold Leventhal, who managed Pete Seeger and handled Woody Guthrie's estate after Guthrie's death, produced the Clancy Brothers in concert at Carnegie Hall on a biannual basis. In the early 1970s, Liam left The Clancy Brothers to pursue a solo career. A few years later, he teamed up with his old pal Tommy Makem and the two recorded several hits and toured together until the late 1980s.

In one interview Clancy recalled a time, in the early 1980s, when he was coming through La Guardia Airport with his guitars. "I felt this body behind me, and I got this great, hairy kiss on the cheek. Now when that happens in New York, you're going to turn around and belt whoever it is. I turned around and it's Bob Dylan, who said, 'Hey, Liam, hey man, how's Paddy? How's Tom? Where's Tommy? I'll come down to the Pavilion to see you, we're gonna have to talk. Where's Shelton?' Dylan and I stood talking for a little while, and suddenly the whole thing flooded back to me—what it was like at that time, the early days. Dylan said, 'I love you guys, and I love Shelton for bringing me to your first concert at Town Hall. You know what I remember about that concert, Liam? You sang a commercial about Donnelly's sausages!'"

Unlike this serendipitous meeting at La Guardia Airport, Clancy's path did not cross often with Dylan's in the late 1980s. Liam Clancy continued performing, and as many young performers in the Celtic music scene like Enya, U2, and The Corrs became well-known, they acknowledged their debt to the Clancy Brothers. In 1990 Liam rejoined his brothers and nephew Robbie O'Connell, though he still performed some shows with his Fairweather Band as well as with the Phil Coulter Orchestra. From 1997 to 1999, Liam toured with his son Donal Clancy and Robbie O'Connell. The group, known as Clancy, O'Connell & Clancy, delighted audiences across North America and Europe and released two highly praised albums.

In 1992 the Clancy Brothers were invited to perform at Madison Square Garden at the 30th Anniversary Dylan concert. The video shows them in great form, performing a high-spirited version of "When the Ship Comes In." Today looking back, Clancy is critical of his performance. "Madison Square Garden is a cavern," the singer said. "It's hard to keep your pitch. The performers who did stay on pitch, like John Mellencamp, wore an earphone so they could hear themselves sing. They were used to playing places that big." Nevertheless, the night was a memorable one. Clancy recalled that there was a party after the concert. "Some of the people felt they wanted it at the Waldorf Astoria, but Dylan chose Tommy Makem's Pavilion. Tommy had trouble getting into his own pub because he forgot his ID! At the party, Dylan said, 'Where's Willie?' He used to call me that, as my brothers did, too. And we talked all night. We were drinking pints of Guinness. As the night wore on, I said, 'Let's get a guitar, and we started singing Irish drinking songs like 'Roddy McSorley.' I forgot a verse so Dylan took the guitar, said, 'Let me show you,' and sang the verse. I looked up as we were singing and this group of guys were singing in a row with their arms around each other. There was George Harrison, Tom Petty, Dylan, and me. It was great night!"

About seven or eight years ago, Dylan was performing in Dublin at a concert, and a national radio program asked Clancy to review the concert. As it happened, Clancy, his wife Kim and son Eben were staying at the same hotel where Dylan was staying, and Clancy was invited to the post-concert party. When Clancy arrived Dylan had not yet shown up, and there were many people waiting around for him. Clancy sat at the bar with Bono. Soon Dylan showed up wearing a hooded sweatshirt with the top covering his head and sunglasses. Clancy recalled, "Dylan said to me, 'I thought you were in the audience last night, and I was so disappointed that you weren't. I played 'Eileen Ardon,' and I was amazed that the young people didn't know it." Clancy said that Dylan sat next to him at the bar and talked for hours, with Bono on Clancy's other side, listening in. Occasionally Bono would pipe in, "All the people you're talking about, they're all dead!" Dylan talked about the house he bought in Barcelona, and told Clancy he wanted to buy a home in Ireland.

Looking back on his career, Clancy acknowledged that the taste of fame he had did not whet his appetite for more. "After we did the *Ed Sullivan Show*, there were huge demands on us. Every TV show and radio station wanted us to appear. We met everyone in the business." Clancy saw Richard Nixon come out of the back of a recording studio one night "wearing so much make-up and furious at some man. I've never seen such an angry man!" Clancy admitted that he and his brothers turned down offers to have a TV series in Hollywood, and "we did not want to become super-famous. The taste we got of it—people treat you like you're not human." Despite having sold millions of records worldwide, Clancy appeared to be a very grounded man with an appreciation for balance in life, and an impish, picaresque wit. After all, when he first told his father that he wanted to be an actor, his father said to him, "Aren't there enough people in the world acting the goat without you joining them?"

Nothing has dissuaded him from feeling blessed for having such a fortunate career filled with adventure and good times. "Entertaining is the best job in the world," Clancy said after the sumptuous seafood dinner. "People come to my concert after work, and for a few hours I take them out of their mundane world through my music."

He ruminated on his life's work. "It's a gift, being an entertainer—you're giving enjoyment. I tried to retire a year ago but it didn't last. I wanted to continue to perform. And applause is like a drug." Thus Clancy can appreciate his friend Dylan's need to continue touring. Clancy mused, "A singer named Joe Heaney was from Connemara. He grew up in the Gaelic tradition. He said there were three categories of performers. The first is a person who wants to be a celebrity and be part of popular culture, who wants the paparazzi to follow him. Then after he has been ill-treated by them, he will complain about the press. The second wants to achieve excellence at what he's doing. The third, and this is Joe Heaney, is the voice of his tribe, and when he sings, he almost evaporates as a person."

Clancy put down the spoon with which he was savoring vanilla ice cream. He looked at me and said thoughtfully, "I felt that in Dylan you had all three."

PETE SEEGER

Retna, Inc.

*B*anjo player and singer/songwriter Pete Seeger helped start the first urban folk group, The Almanac Singers, with Lee Hays and others. In the 1950s he went on to co-found the singing group called The Weavers, who enjoyed a hit when they recorded a version of Leadbelly's "Goodnight Irene." It was the most popular song of 1950. Before he moved to New York in 1961, Dylan heard many of Seeger's songs on the Folkways records he listened to at the home of his Minneapolis friend Mike Baker. During his long life, Seeger has helped to write, adapt, or otherwise spread an incredible array of songs, such as "Where Have All the Flowers Gone," "Turn, Turn. Turn," "If I Had a Hammer," "We Shall Overcome," and "Guantanamera" by Cuban poet José Martí. A few years ago the hip-hop artist Wyclef Jean had a huge hit with "Guantanamera," which demonstrates the enduring quality of Seeger's music. But Seeger has never heard it. "I don't have time to listen to records," he admitted.

Seeger was born into an old New England family in 1919. His mother taught violin at The Institute of Musical Art, now Juilliard.

His father Charles was a musicologist. Pete learned from him how to approach music from a historical and social perspective. Charles believed that music could help to shape society. Charles was also interested in mixing music and activism. American historians have written about how, in the early twentieth century, intellectuals "discovered" American folk music and tried to give the music a wider audience. In addition to Charles Seeger, these intellectuals and folklorists included John and Alan Lomax. John Lomax got President Theodore Roosevelt to write a foreword to his book Cowboy Songs *(1910), and his book* American Ballads and Folk Songs *(1934) did much to preserve a vanishing musical tradition. He was the father of musicologist, record producer, and network radio host/writer Alan Lomax. Together they did the greatest field survey of American roots music ever, which led to the development of the Library of Congress' Archive of the American Folksong.*

Pete's parents divorced when he was about 10 years old. In 1932 Charles remarried modern composer Ruth Crawford. The couple's four children included Mike and Peggy Seeger, who also became prominent folksingers. When Pete was at Avon Old Farms boarding school in Connecticut, he bought his first tenor banjo for $25. In 1936 Pete went to the Asheville Mountain Song and Dance Festival in North Carolina with his father. Pete became an instant convert to the old five-string banjo. About 18 years later, in Greenwich Village, Mike formed the old-time string band, The New Lost City Ramblers with friends. Peggy became a singer and married Ewan McColl; together they recorded many traditional ballads.

Pete began Harvard in 1936 as member of the class of 1940 along with John F. Kennedy, but dropped out in 1938. He headed for New York in 1938 and worked at the Archives of American Folk Music, where Alan Lomax encouraged Pete in all aspects of folk music. He soon began performing on banjo, guitar, and vocals with a clear, bell-like soprano. Seeger first met Woody Guthrie in 1940. A year later the tall, angular, and good-looking Seeger formed the politically oriented Almanac Singers with Lee Hays and Millard Lampell. They were later joined by Bess Lomax, Woody Guthrie, Sis Cunningham, Sonny Terry, and Brownie McGhee. They sang at labor meetings and gatherings of migrant workers, performing both traditional folk songs and pro-union and anti-fascist songs that they had composed. Seeger learned basic musicianship from Guthrie and Leadbelly and brought to his earliest performances a sense of mission.

In 1946, when Bob Dylan was five years old, Pete Seeger was organizing People's Songs, a singing labor organization in which Pete and his colleagues would publish a newsletter of union songs and form a national network, singing on picket lines and at demonstrations. He was soon followed by the FBI in the late '40s for singing "subversive" folk songs. When People's Songs filed for bankruptcy in 1949, that was the last office job for this musician/activist. Not long after, Seeger helped to found Sing Out! magazine, *the Bible of the folk revival. Also in 1949, the producer/manager/concert promoter Harold Leventhal met Seeger. Later he became his manager, and managed him up until the producer's death in the fall of 2005.*

With his early '50s folk group, The Weavers, Seeger performed a lively version of "If I Had a Hammer," which Lee and Pete wrote. This was well before Peter, Paul, and Mary rewrote it into a 1963 hit. The song now has a life of its own. The popularity of The Weavers cut across all boundaries of race and class. American poet Carl Sandburg praised them, saying, "The Weavers are out of the grassroots of America. When I hear American singing, The Weavers are there." But in the early '50s, at the height of their popularity, Seeger and his friends were viewed as a public menace by J.Edgar Hoover and the FBI. Problems with the FBI, blacklisting, and questions from the House Committee on Un-American Activities sent Seeger onto the college circuit.

Seeger was called before the House Committee on Un-American Activities (HUAC) in 1955, where his refusal to answer questions or invoke the Fifth Amendment eventually led to a contempt of Congress conviction. In 1961 he was sentenced to one year in prison, but the sentence was reversed by the appeals court in 1962. Seeger only spent four hours in jail.

Seeger always felt that folk music and songs with political content went hand in hand. As he told a reporter, "We had an idea that working people were going to be the saviors of the world, and we should learn more about working people's music. And the most honest working people's music was the old country songs, even when they weren't strictly working people's. I mean 'Greensleeves' is obviously not a working person's song. It was a pop song of the sixteenth century."

He was deeply influenced by his friend and fellow musician, Woody Guthrie, who taught him "the genius of simplicity." Seeger said in an interview, "He didn't try and get fancy, he didn't try to show how clever he was. He had done a lot of thinking and he read voraciously." Seeger had never written songs before he met Woody. "Then I got the idea that you could write songs. I first tried putting new words to old tunes, which is what [Woody Guthrie] did, and found that I was better at putting new tunes to old words." This is what Seeger did with "Turn, Turn, Turn" which is based on a passage of Ecclesiastes from the Bible that includes "To every thing there is a season..." Roger McGuinn first arranged "Turn, Turn, Turn" for Judy Collins and then had a hit with the song with his group, The Byrds, in 1965.

In the early 1960s, Seeger played a key role in the second folk revival. His version of "We Shall Overcome" became the unofficial anthem of the civil rights movement, and the marches and protests in which he had been participating for 20 years spread like wildfire across the South and galvanized Americans.

Since the 1940s, Seeger has recorded about 100 albums either alone or with others. He has authored or co-authored more than 27 books with titles as intriguing as Carry It On: The Story of America's Working People in Story and Song *and* Where Have All the Flowers Gone. *The latter is the definitive book by and about Pete Seeger for those who love his music. With this rich history as a background, Seeger spoke at the log home he built with his own hands on a mountainside near the Hudson River in New York. He lives there with his wife, Toshi, whom he met in 1939 at a square dance in New York. They married in 1943. In 1969, Seeger helped to launch the 100-foot-long traditional cargo sloop Clearwater, which started a Hudson River cleanup campaign that he has championed for several decades. Related to these efforts, General Electric was hauled into court for contaminating the river with PCBs.*

Upon first meeting the young, scruffy, 20-year-old Dylan in 1961, Seeger said, "I was bowled over by his talent. He wrote great songs. He came into Greenwich Village in about 1961, and it was like Shakespeare coming into London."

Seeger arranged for the young songwriter to meet former Almanac Singers colleague Sis Cunningham. They were launching the folk music magazine *Broadside*, which was, Seeger said, "mimeographed, with a cir-culation of about 500." Seeger introduced Bob Dylan to Sis Cunningham, saying, "Here's a wonderful songwriter."

Seeger recalled, "Both Bob and Phil Ochs sang songs for us. I felt like I was in the same room with two of the best songwriters in the world." Seeger said, "I think Bob sang 'Who Killed Davey Moore?' at that get-together." Soon after, the debut issue of *Broadside* included Dylan's song "Talkin' John Birch Paranoid Blues," a satire on the right-wing John Birch Society.

Seeger staged the annual *Sing Out!* hootenanny in 1962 at Carnegie Hall. A young and precocious Dylan was included on the program. "I was the emcee," Seeger said. "We had a supper before, and because there were so many people on the program, I told everyone they each had 10 minutes so they could sing two or three songs. Then Bob smiled his sly smile and said, 'I've got one song that is 10 minutes long.'" Seeger also recalled that the young newcomer did not ask him for advice. "He was into the music. He had a wry sense of humor. But he didn't talk too much."

Some biographers have said that Seeger had a role in attracting Dylan to Columbia. "I don't think I did," said Seeger. "His reputation had spread around the Village. John Hammond had gotten permission from Columbia to record other musicians besides jazz musicians and he took me on and he took Dylan on." To this day, Dylan records on Columbia Records, now part of Sony Music Entertainment.

But Seeger does remember one interesting conversation with Dylan from the early days. "Bob did tell me one thing. I recommended he get a job singing at colleges, that the students would like his music. Bob said, 'Yes, I heard you at the University of Wisconsin.' I remember the show in 1958," Seeger continued. "It was not a big audience—maybe 300. I asked him, 'You were there when the American Legion picket line was there?' Bob said 'Yes.' The poor American Legion, they were just carrying out orders of the John Birch Society. What they didn't realize was they were just giving me free publicity," Seeger noted with irony.

Since the folk music movement had emerged from the Left, Seeger was accustomed to participating in non-violent protests and other civil disturbances and being the target of such. The American Legion frequently protested his concerts, viewing them as left-wing propaganda. Seeger himself participated in marches sponsored by anti-nuclear groups and civil rights groups, and began singing in black churches in the South during the height of the civil rights movement. Seeger's singing moved more people to action than many speeches could, according to biographer David Dunaway.

In 1963, Harold Leventhal arranged a trip for musicians to visit Mississippi when the Student Non-Violent Coordinating Committee (SNCC) was organizing rallies in the South to register African-Americans to vote. There was to be a rally in Greenwood, Mississippi. Among those scheduled to perform were The Freedom Singers,

Theodore Bikel, Seeger, and Dylan. Said Seeger, "I was surprised Bob went. We were both invited by Theodore Bikel. They didn't invite any women. There was a black speaker with a fierce grin. We went to Greenwood, MS. Two filmmakers wanted to interview me. They made a film called *The Streets of Greenwood*, probably seen by a few thousand people. Greenwood was a very racist town. Interestingly enough, we performed on the edge of a big, big field that was a cotton patch with an improvised stage. There were a few hundred people there. Now," he laughed heartily, "there is an annual Delta Blues Festival there that attracts thousands."

Seeger continued, "I think Bob played 'Only a Pawn in Their Game,' and it started them thinking that just one person could make a difference. [It was a time] when they were bound up in that murderous Jim Crow game." Dylan's song is about the killing of Medgar Evers, a Mississippi field secretary for the NAACP. Evers had been shot dead in Jackson, Mississippi a month earlier. (Byron De La Beckwith, a member of the Ku Klux Klan, was indicted for the crime and later was acquitted twice by all-white juries. In 1994, Beckwith was brought to trial again based on new evidence from statements he made to others. In February 1994, Beckwith was finally convicted and died in prison.) At the end of the Greenwood concert, as it was growing dark, Bikel, Dylan, and Seeger joined hands with the Freedom Singers and sang "We Shall Overcome" in front of the black audience of farmworkers. After being extremely moved by the event, Dylan made a contribution to SNCC.

Seeger went South three or four times as part of his activism in the civil rights movement. During one of his visits, he recalled, "I was performing in a small town in front of a couple hundred, singing in a church, when I was asked to give the news that the bodies of the three young slain civil rights workers had just been found. There was no applause…just silence. Lips moved as though in prayer."

The last time Seeger spoke to Dylan was about 20 years ago. He recalled, "I was singing at a small occasion in the Topanga Canyon area of Los Angeles for Will Geer, the actor, who was a lifelong gardener. When Will performed at the Stratford, Connecticut Shakespeare Festival, he would plant vegetables and flowers that appeared in Shakespeare's plays. When he came to see me here at my home in Beacon, he spent an hour hoeing our garden!" Seeger burst into laughter.

On this particular occasion at Topanga Canyon, Seeger was performing for two or three hundred people. "Arlo [Woody Guthrie's son] was there. He said, 'Hey, Bob's here. Would you like to see him?' Bob had driven up in his car. He wasn't staying as part of the audience. We had a friendly, cordial visit. I remember that I asked, 'Are you over your motorcycle accident?' He was almost killed from that." Dylan had recorded what was Seeger's favorite Dylan album after the accident. "There's one record he made that I listened to over and over again. I have a wintertime skating rink that I built near my house. I have an outdoor loudspeaker, and over and over again I played *John Wesley Harding.*'"

When asked if the twists and turns in Dylan's career have surprised Seeger, the elder statesman of folk said, " Nope–I've seen it happen with other musicians. Bob is determined to be independent." That might offer an explanation for the controversy that ensued when Dylan went electric at the 1965 Newport Folk Festival.

Seeger is happy to set the record straight. "I wasn't mad at him for turning electric. I *was* furious at the sound system because it was very distorted. I ran over to the man working the sound and said, 'Fix it so we can understand the words,' and he shouted back, 'No, this is the way they want it.' Since Bob was on stage, perhaps he couldn't hear how distorted it was."

Of all Dylan songs, Seeger probably performed "A Hard Rain's Gonna Fall" the most often. Dylan wrote the song during the time of the Cuban missile crisis in 1962, and it was performed by many Village musicians including Seeger that fall. The song's powerful lyrics, which forecast an ominous future, resonated with antiwar activists:

> *I'll walk to the depths of the deepest black forest,*
> *Where the people are many and their hands are all empty,*
> *Where the home in the valley meets the dark dirty prison,*
> *Where the executioner's face is always well hidden,*
> *Where hunger is ugly, where souls are forgotten...*
>
> *Then I'll stand on the ocean until I start sinkin',*
> *But I'll know my song well before I start singin',*
> *And it's a hard, it's a hard, it's a hard, it's a hard,*
> *It's a hard rain's a-gonna fall.*

—"A Hard Rain's Gonna Fall"
B. Dylan © 1963 by Warner Bros. Inc.

Seeger, a lifelong pacifist, believes that in the song Dylan is "absolutely right... it's a very poetic way of approaching the problem. Louis Menand wrote a *New Yorker* article about Edmund Wilson, which ended by saying, 'He realized the world was not going to last long.'" Seeger continued thoughtfully, "All my life I have felt we had a 50-50 chance of survival before someone might set off an atomic bomb. I feel more optimistic now than I have in 60 years. In the '50s and '60s, I felt a sense of doom. I feel more optimistic now because we are seeing America at its best: Literally millions of Americans are involved in committees to improve their communities, whether it is New Orleans hurricane relief efforts or some other grass-roots community work," he affirmed. "Right here in my hometown we have a Clearwater Club. Citizens have gotten involved in saving the town waterfront. They've built a beautiful waterfront park, and now they're talking about building a floating swimming pool," he said proudly. "All of these little efforts make this country better. The establishment has so much power, they control the media and can do anything they want... but what can they do when 10 million citizens work to help their own communities?" No doubt this Beacon, New York, Clearwater Club owes its origins to Seeger's environmental efforts with his sloop, the *Clearwater.*

Returning to the subject of Dylan, Seeger spoke affably and generously about the prolific songwriter's contributions over the years. In interviews Dylan has decried any notion that he set out to write outright political songs. "The songs are there," Dylan said in *Sing Out!* magazine in 1962. "They exist all by themselves, just waiting for someone to write them down. I just put them down on paper. If I didn't do it, someone else would." Seeger is careful when he is asked to sum up Dylan's contribution to folk music: "I wouldn't bother using the words folk music. Musicologists might say in the late twentieth century that folk music became electric music. Folk music originally meant music by the peasants, redefined by John Lomax who dug up old cowboy songs," Seeger explained. "Then young people said, 'Hey, I want to sing some of those songs.' Putting his thoughts into historical context, Seeger added, "So here's Dylan, picking up an old idea—a four-line verse then a two-line refrain and making up a song that means something. As Plato said—I'm not sure I have the quote right: 'It's dangerous to allow the wrong kind of music in the republic.'

"Throughout the ages," he continued, "the king, emperor, or ruling class gets very worried when people sing songs that make them think. As Herbert Hoover said to Rudy Vallee, 'If you can sing a song to make people forget the Depression, I'll give you a medal.' So he would sing cheerful songs... there was one Bing Crosby sang," and Seeger launched into a lilting '30s tune: "Wrap your troubles in dreams, and dream your troubles away." In the Martin Scorsese film, *No Direction Home*, Seeger had added, "To think that entertainers always have to be happy is a kind of shallow thing. In fact I remember one of Bob's quotes, 'Happy? Anybody can be happy. What's the purpose of that?'" So both Seeger and Dylan were drawn to songs with content, not whimsical ditties but serious, beautiful songs that truly had something to say. Seeger also said with admiration, "It's a wonder that Bob has survived all the fame and fortune."

Referring to a 2005 Dylan concert he had recently attended, Seeger commented that he could not make out the words Dylan sang. "I went to hear Bob at a local baseball stadium about three months ago. There were 4,000 people there. I could hear every word Willie Nelson sang but my old ears could only hear one or two words in Bob's songs. People were cheering and all. There must have been 1,000 standing up." Despite his reaction to this recent concert, Seeger does not embrace the attitude of naysayers who claim Dylan should not be touring if he's not doing his old songs.

Seeger laughed and shrugged it off. "I'm singing old songs still. I teach the audience the refrain. They sing some things all the way through like 'This Land is Your Land,'" he said enthusiastically. Acknowledging the power and poetry of folk music, Seeger once said, "I look upon myself and other songwriters as links in a long chain. All of us, we're links in a chain. And if we do our job right, there will be many, many links to come." When Seeger was inducted into the Rock and Roll Hall of Fame in 1996 by Arlo Guthrie and Harry Belafonte, their tribute to him stated:

> In Seeger's capable hands, from the Forties to the present day, a concert isn't regarded as a one-way proceeding but a group sing-along. Indeed, Seeger's gently assertive insistence that his audience sing out can be read as a larger metaphor for the necessary involvement of citizens to insure the healthy functioning of democracy in America. Seeger has recorded and performed tirelessly throughout his career, honoring the folksingers' timeless commitment to spread the word and involve the audience. "My ability lies in being able to get a crowd to sing along with me," he said in a 1971 interview. "When I get

up on a stage, I look on my job as trying to tell a story. I use songs to illustrate my story and dialogue between songs to carry the story forward."

In this way, despite the passage of years, Seeger is still the same buoyant folksinger who led The Weavers on their enthusiastic tours and concerts in the 1950s, charming audiences from Maine to Minnesota, where one of Woody Guthrie's songs like "This Land Is Your Land" was as likely to light up the crowd as a pro-union ballad. The special respect Dylan had for Woody Guthrie is something that was always easy for Seeger to understand. Dylan has said that when he began singing folk and got to Woody Guthrie, "it opened up a whole new world at the time. I was still only 19 or 20. I was pretty fanatical about what I wanted to do, so after learning about 200 of Woody's songs, I went to see him and I waited for the right moment to visit him in a hospital in Morristown, New Jersey. I took a bus from New York, sat with him, and sang his songs. I kept visiting him a lot and got on friendly terms with him."

As a member of The Weavers, Seeger did much to popularize Woody's songs and pay tribute to the great folksinger's legacy. "Of course, Bob made up his great 'Song to Woody' that I heard him play at the Town Hall in 1963," Seeger noted. "My manager, Harold Leventhal, produced the concert. I visited Woody in New Jersey when he was ill." Guthrie suffered from Huntington's disease. "Woody would get out of the hospital on Sunday and get together with five to ten people at the nearby apartment of friends [Bob and Sidsel Gleason]," Seeger continued. "He couldn't speak but he listened to us. Woody was an extraordinary intellectual with a great appetite for reading. When he was a child, a woman from the library fed him books, and as a teenager in Texas he continued to read all the time. So by the time he got to New York, he had read more than most college students read. When he got on the air, he was speaking and singing in the language of working people." And that was a language that Dylan copied when he began his life as a performer, speaking like Woody Guthrie with his Okie twang.

In the Scorsese film Seeger added, "The moment I became acquainted with old songs, I realized that people have always been changing them. Think of it as an age-old process. It's been going on for thousands of years. People take old songs, change them and adapt them for new people. It happens in every other field, lawyers change old laws to fit new citizens. So I'm one in this long chain and so are millions of other musicians." Seeger adapted both "We Shall Overcome" and "Guantanamera." Dylan also reworked a handful of old folk songs when he began writing in the early 1960s.

Seeger watched his friend Woody Guthrie fit right into that. "He was always making up verses. Folk music is about real people, real events. The idea is that you make up a song about something real–don't expect that it'll make any money. Maybe it will only be heard by a few dozen people, but who knows? I looked upon us all as Woody's children," he said warmly.

Concluding our interview, Seeger said, "I remember one time Woody asked my sister-in-law if he could borrow a book by Rabelais that she had. He read it in about one day and in the following weeks he was using literary devices from Rabelais, stringing together 10 adjectives at once. So I could understand and appreciate Bob's natural affinity for Woody."

When Pete Seeger was awarded the Presidential Medal of the Arts—the nation's highest artistic honor—at the Kennedy Center in December 1994, President Bill Clinton hailed him as "an inconvenient artist who dared to sing things as he saw them... He was attacked for his belief, and he was banned from television—now that's a badge of honor."

JOAN BAEZ

Retna, Inc.

*I*n *his autobiography,* Chronicles, *Dylan recalls his first year in New York, when he was just breaking into the folk scene. He writes, "The 'Queen of Folksingers,' that would have to be Joan Baez. Joan was born the same year as me and our futures would be linked but at this time to even think about it would be preposterous. She had one record out on the Vanguard label called* Joan Baez *and I'd seen her on TV. She'd been on a folk-music program broadcast nationwide on CBS out of New York. There were other performers on the show including Cisco Houston, Josh White, Lightnin' Hopkins. Joan sang some ballads on her own and then sat side by side with Lightnin' and sang a few things with him. I couldn't stop looking at her, didn't want to blink. She was wicked looking—shiny black hair that hung down over the curve of her slender hips, drooping lashes, partly raised, no Raggedy Ann doll. The sight of her made me high. All that and then there was her voice. A voice that drove out bad spirits. It was like she'd come down from another planet.*

"She sold a lot of records and it was easy to understand why,"

Dylan continued. "The women singers in folk music were performers, like Peggy Seeger, Jean Ritchie, and Barbara Dane, and they didn't translate well to a modern crowd. Joan was nothing like any of them. There was no one like her. It would be a few years before Judy Collins or Joni Mitchell would come on the scene. I liked the older women singers—Aunt Molly Jackson and Jeanie Robinson—but they didn't have the piercing quality Joan had. I'd been listening to a few of the female blues singers a lot, like Memphis Minnie and Ma Rainey, and Joan was in some kind of way more like them. There was nothing girlish about them and there was nothing girlish about Joan, either. Both Scot and Mex, she looked like a religious icon, like somebody you'd sacrifice yourself for and she sang in a voice straight to God— also was an exceptionally good instrumentalist.

"The Vanguard record was no phony baloney," wrote Dylan. "It was almost frightening—an impeccable repertoire of songs, all hard-core traditional. She seemed very mature, seductive, intense. Magical. Nothing she did didn't work. That she was the same age as me almost made me feel useless. However illogical it might have seemed, some-thing told me that she was my counterpart—that she was the one that my voice would find perfect harmony with. At the time, there was nothing but distance and worlds and big divides between her and me. I was still stuck in the boondocks. Yet some strange feeling told me that we would inevitably meet up. I didn't know much about Joan Baez. I had no idea that she'd always been a true loner, kind of like me, but she'd been bounced around a lot and lived in places from Baghdad to San Jose. She had experienced a whole lot more of the world than I did. Even so, to think that she was probably more like me than me would have seemed a little excessive."

He added, "There was no clue from her records that she was inter-ested in social change or any of that. I considered her lucky, lucky to get involved in the right kind of folk music early on, get up to her eye-balls in it—learn how to play and sing it in an expert way, beyond criticism, beyond category. There was no one in her class. She was far off and unattainable—Cleopatra living in an Italian palace. When she sang, she made your teeth drop."

The ensuing romance Baez had with Dylan was a huge one in her life, as she admits in her autobiography. She was young, 22, impression-able, on top of the world as the most popular folksinger in the country when she met him and they fell in love. She had begun her career at 18, singing in Harvard Square coffeehouses in Cambridge, Massachusetts, where her father taught at MIT. Her father was a research physicist and his career had taken the family to college towns like Ithaca, New York and Palo Alto, California and to exotic locations like Baghdad. Her gigs in coffeehouses led to hiring a manager, Manny Greenhill, and getting a record deal with Vanguard in 1959. In 1960, she played college concerts and then, as she describes it, watched in amazement as her first album, *Joan Baez*, soared to Number Three on the Top 100 best-selling albums in the country in the winter of 1960. When she went on the road after the album's release, she was a star.

Joan, who began singing in high school, has told the story of her relationship with Dylan in her lovely memoir, *And a Voice to Sing With*. She writes that she first saw Bob Dylan in 1961 at Gerde's Folk City in Greenwich Village. "He was not overly impressive. He looked like an urban hillbilly, with hair short around the ears and curly on top. Bouncing from foot to foot as he played, he seemed dwarfed by the guitar. His jacket was a rusty leather and two sizes too small—his mouth was a killer: soft, sensuous, childish, nervous, and reticent. He spat out the words to his own songs. They were original and refreshing, if blunt and jagged. He was absurd, new, and grubby beyond words," she writes. When his set was over, Dylan was ushered to Joan's table. In David Hajdu's book *Positively 4th Street* about the period, he quoted Joan saying of Dylan, "He had that silly cap on, and he seemed like such a little boy. But he was a joy to experience. He was captivating. He made me smile." At the finale of the evening's show, Joan got up to perform.

But Dylan, according to Hajdu, had told another friend there that he had a song he wanted Joan to hear. Hajdu describes a scene where, at 2 a.m., Dylan followed Joan and her sister, Mimi, out of the club and on the sidewalk asked if he could play a song for Joan. When she said, "Of course," she took her Gibson out of the case for him, since he had left the club so quickly that he didn't take his guitar. Dylan propped Joan's guitar up on his leg and played her his newly penned "Song to Woody." Although he had wanted Joan to hear this song, Dylan decided to record it himself. It would be many months before the two crossed paths again.

At the time that she broke into singing in Harvard Square coffeehouses, Joan lived with her family in Belmont, Massachusetts. When her father decided to take a new job in Europe with UNESCO in the summer of 1961, Joan decided to strike out on her own. She left Cambridge and moved to California. She rented a house in the Carmel Highlands on the picturesque Big Sur peninsula. As Hajdu noted, she had a hit album and her performances at concert halls and university theaters around the country invariably sold out. "Everything was happening too fast," Hajdu quotes her as saying. "I was like, 'I don't want to think about the music business. I'm going to escape it all—and I'm going out west to live the pure life.' I associated California with some kind of purity. The West Coast for me was like that, something pure. I didn't really have any intention of stopping my music. I was touring the country, but I was not at home as much as I wanted, and I needed to retrench and stop and think about what I was doing and why I was doing it."

Joan loved the peace and serenity she found in Carmel. The next time she saw Dylan was in April 1963 in Cambridge. Dylan played "With God on Our Side" for her, and then, "I took him seriously," Joan told Hajdu, "I was bowled over. I never thought anything so powerful could come out of that little toad. It was devastating. 'With God on Our Side' is a very mature song. It's a beautiful song. When I heard that, it changed the way I thought of Bob. I realized he was more mature than I had thought. He even looked a little better." She saw him again at the Monterey Folk Festival the next month, and by that time had learned the song. Dylan's performance wasn't going well, but soon Joan walked out on the stage, and she joined Dylan to sing "With God on Our Side." They left the crowd cheering. The two became closer at the Monterey Folk Festival, Hajdu reports, and after the festival Joan invited Dylan to visit her house in Carmel Highlands. She drove him there in her Jaguar XKE.

As she got to know Dylan, Joan would write in her autobiography, she found "His humor was dry, private, and splendid. Sometimes he would start to chuckle. A little at a time, his lips would move from a genuine smile to a pucker. Then, instantly, he would tighten them backing, until a tiny convulsion of laughter would bring them back to the smile, and sometimes, a full grin followed by laughter." Their early months of romance together were idyllic. "There were times to come when we would sing together, laugh and horse around, get crazy, talk, go to movies, ride motorcycles, sleep," she writes. As Dylan got ready to leave Carmel, Joan invited him to join her on a tour of the Northeast that she had coming up. He readily agreed.

About nine weeks after Joan joined Dylan on stage in Monterey, they performed together at the 1963 Newport Folk Festival, opening and closing the festival together. This was after the release of his second album, *The Freewheelin' Bob Dylan*. Joan was now championing the cause of Bob Dylan. She felt he had such important things to say and she wanted the world to know him. She was the star of folk music, regularly performing to audiences of 10,000, and had appeared on the cover of *Time* in November 1962. She was introducing an unusual singer/songwriter whose fame would soon eclipse her own.

On Sunday, Joan closed the final concert of the festival. She wore a simple knee-length white dress that clung to her body, Hajdu writes, and she sounded as stunningly unadorned as she looked. He continues, "At the conclusion of a set peppered with the Bob Dylan songs that she had been learning, including a pointed 'Don't Think Twice, It's All Right,' she thanked the audience effusively. "Tonight is one of the most beautiful nights I've ever seen," Joan said with a broad smile. "I'm all up here with it. I feel sort of like exploding." She bounded offstage and came right back with Bob Dylan in tow. Together they sang 'With God On Our Side' again." Dylan and Joan Baez were "the King and Queen of the festival," remembered singer-songwriter Tom Paxton. Biographers noted that this period caused special angst for Suze Rotolo, Dylan's girlfriend from the Village, who appears on the cover of *Freewheelin'*. She had heard the rumors swirling around the folk-music community about a romance between Dylan and Baez, and it hurt.

A variety of photographers captured scenes from Newport 1963, Paul Williams observed, and in them we see Dylan singing into a microphone with "joyous power." A famous photo by Jim Marshall shows Dylan linking hands with Baez, Pete Seeger, Theodore Bikel, the Freedom Singers, and Peter, Paul and Mary, on the festival stage, singing "We Shall Overcome."

If Joan played a major role in promoting Dylan at a critical time in his young career, Dylan also helped her. Dylan's powerful and unique songs helped Joan evolve from a singer of traditional ballads and obscure folk music to one of the key voices of the civil-rights and anti-war movements. Her stirring versions of "With God on Our Side," "Blowin' in the Wind," "Don't Think Twice, It's All Right," "Farewell Angelina," "A Hard Rain's a Gonna Fall," and "Love Is Just a Four-Letter Word," among others established her as an important voice of protest, fighting injustice.

In August 1963, Joan set out on tour and invited Dylan to sing in her concerts. She was following the example set by Bob Gibson four years before. "I was getting audiences of up to 10,000 at that point, and dragging my little vagabond out onto the stage was a grand experiment and a gamble which I knew he and I would eventually win," Joan writes in her book. At first her audience was not pleased by the appearance of this unknown singer. Dylan's appearances on stage were often met cool-ly by a distracted audience more eager to hear the beautiful, dark-haired soprano. But Joan admonished the audiences "to listen to the words, because this young man was a genius. They listened… I've never expe-rienced charisma like that which Bob displayed in his reverse-showman-ship performances. There was a strong out-of-place forlornness about his appearance on stage." Dylan and Baez did 10 concerts in the north-east in the month of August. She would sing some of his songs in the first half of her show, and then bring him on in the second half; they'd sing together, and he'd do some songs alone. When Dylan wasn't on tour with Joan, he was at Columbia Studios in New York recording his third album, *The Times They Are A-Changin'*.

On August 28, 1963, Dylan sang with Joan at the Lincoln Memorial in front of 250,000 people at the March on Washington, the same event where Martin Luther King, Jr. gave his "I Have a Dream" speech. This appearance helped to foster the image that Dylan was a leader of polit-ical change, which was not entirely accurate. As affecting and searing as his "political" songs were, compositions like "Masters of War" and "The Lonesome Death of Hattie Carroll" were in the tradition of folk songs that celebrated the downtrodden. Dylan himself did not want to be viewed as a political spokesman; he certainly did not embrace social and political activism the way Joan did then and has throughout her life.

Still, Baez was passionate about Dylan's songs. In her view, "Nothing could have spoken better for our generation than "The Times They Are A-Changin'." The civil rights movement was in full bloom, and the war which would tear this nation asunder, divide, wound, and irreparably scar millions upon millions of people was moving toward us like a mighty storm," she says in her autobiography. " When that war began, I, along with thousands of others, would go to battle against it. We would lose Bob to other things, but before the first official bullet was fired, he had filled our arsenals with his songs: 'Hard Rain,' 'Masters of War,' 'The Times They Are A-Changin',' 'With God on Our Side,' and finally, 'Blowin' in the Wind.'"

After touring together, Dylan and Baez spent time together in Woodstock, New York, at the home of Dylan's manager Albert Grossman. According to Howard Sounes, when they were in New York

City, they stayed at the Earle Hotel on Washington Square. During this time, Sounes says, Joan attempted to transform Dylan, buying him a jacket, white shirt, and lavender-colored cuff links. Joan then left Woodstock and returned to her home in Carmel Valley. Dylan came out to California and spent time with her at her house: She bought him a piano so he could write songs there. According to Sounes, each morning he went straight to the typewriter near a window overlooking the mountains. He worked at the typewriter throughout the day, drinking black coffee all morning, said Joan's friend Nancy Carlen, then "rot-gut" red wine the rest of the day. During his visit to Carmel, Baez recounts in her book how they talked playfully about their futures, and he "mumbled something about marriage… It had not been a proposal; it had been a noncommittal continuation of our fun and games which might very well have led to a noncommittal joining of our lives in a noncommittal marriage."

In her book, she continues, "I loved the fame, attention, and association with Bob, but soon our real differences surfaced and began to dominate our relationship. Once I asked him how he came to write, 'Masters of War.' His reply was that he knew it would sell; I didn't buy his answer then and I don't now. I think his active commitment to social change was limited to songwriting. To my knowledge, he never went on a march. He certainly never did any civil disobedience, at least that I knew about. I've always felt that he just didn't want the responsibility. Once he commented to me about the kids in the audience calling out for 'Masters of War': 'They think I'm something I ain't.' And then he joked about it and told me to take care of them and 'all that stuff.' I told him I'd do my best." She beautifully evoked their differences in this scene: "We were outside somewhere; I was yanking up blades of grass, troubled that our paths were splitting and going in very different directions. I asked him what made us different, and he said it was simple, that I thought I could change things, and he knew that no one could. I was upset by his remark. Perhaps he would end up Rock and Roll King to my Peace Queen."

She later learned that in 1964, while she was away from Dylan, he had called up Sara Lownds, to whom the Grossmans had introduced him. At the time, however, Joan was oblivious to the fact that there was a Sara, and after one visit to see Dylan in Woodstock, "I left happily with memories, songs, some disillusionment, and a blue nightgown I'd found in a closet in Albert's house, which [Dylan] said I could keep." Joan admitted that 12 years later, when she and Sara finally met and became friends, the two women compared notes about the time when "the Original Vagabond was two-timing us." The nightgown was Sara's.

Dylan invited Baez on his tour of England in the spring of 1965, which would be captured in D.A. Pennebaker's documentary, *Don't Look Back*. Joan was thrilled, and naturally expected to join him onstage, as he had joined her during her tours. But that was not to be. From the moment they landed at London's Heathrow Airport, Dylan was besieged by the press and fans. "It never calmed down," Baez writes. She was miserable during the tour, and admits, " For the first time in my short and monumentally successful career someone had stolen all my thunder from under my nose. I simply hung around and got sick." Joan gave her own concert in London. It was a sold-out success, but she claimed she was too sick to enjoy it. "That sold-out concert was the first of many to come, but I couldn't know that at the time," she writes, recalling her despair. " I'd forgotten that I had a career, a huge following, a voice of my own. It never occurred to me that many English and European fans had followed me for five years already and didn't care about the 'original vagabond,' the unwashed phenomenon, at all."

In her book, she concludes her chapter on Dylan with a memory that illustrates how far apart they had become. Although Joan had not been asked to his room, she went out to buy him a present [a dark blue shirt] and took it to his room. "I went unannounced and uninvited to knock at his door," Baez writes. "It was answered by Sara, whom I'd never seen before and who had been flown in to look after Bob. Everyone had carefully avoided telling me she was there. She took the package from me with a patient and quizzical look on her face, blinked her massive black eyes, thanked me softly, and shut the door."

Bob Dylan married Sara Lownds several months later on November 22, 1965 in a secret ceremony under an oak tree outside a judge's office on Long Island. The only guests were Albert Grossman and a maid of honor for Sara. Dylan adopted Sara's daughter, Maria, from her first marriage. Between 1966 to 1969, the couple had four children together: Jesse, Samuel, Anna, and Jakob. They divorced in 1977.

The passage of time inevitably changed Dylan and Baez's relationship again. In 1975, Baez wrote the beautiful song "Diamonds and Rust" inspired by him. In the mid-'70s, he invited her to tour with the Rolling Thunder Revue, and she appeared in the ill-fated *Renaldo and*

Clara with Dylan's soon-to-be ex- wife Sara. Joan had no expectations for the film, and thought the project was a silly one. Concert promoter Bill Graham arranged a European tour in 1984 for Dylan, Carlos Santana, and Baez, but the experience was not a happy one for Baez. Once again, as 20 years earlier, she had expected to perform with Dylan but, except for two short songs together, he did not invite her onstage at most of the concerts. Discouraged, she left the tour abruptly.

Perhaps their relationship can be best summed up by Baez's interview in the 2005 Martin Scorsese film *No Direction Home*, where Joan admitted, "Bobby is one of the most complex human beings I have ever met. At one point I thought I could figure him out, but," she shook her head hopelessly, "no." She ended her interview in the film performing a searing, moving version of Dylan's song, "Love is Just a Four-Letter Word." Her eyes seemed to reflect the pain of a long and complicated love affair. In art, as in life, music expresses the feelings for which words do not suffice.

BOBBY VEE

Retna, Inc.

*O*ne of the most the endearing stories in Dylan's autobiography, Chronicles, *is his anecdote about performing with Bobby Vee in the summer of 1959. Vee, the handsome, clean-cut pop star of the late '50s and '60s had hits with "Take Good Care of My Baby," Devil or Angel," and "Rubber Ball." In the 1960s, 14 of Vee's singles hit the Top 40. A native of Fargo, North Dakota, Vee was reared on the rockabilly sounds of Elvis and Gene Vincent. His first regional hit in 1959, was "Suzie Baby," recorded for Amos Heilicher's Minneapolis-based Soma label when he was a mere 15. In 1959 18-year-old Bob Dylan—then known in his hometown of Hibbing, Minnesota as Bobby Zimmerman—performed with Vee's band. It was Dylan's first performance with a "professional" group—that is, a band that had released a record. As Dylan recalled in* Chronicles:

> His band was called the Shadows and I had hitch-hiked out (to Fargo) and talked my way into joining the group as a piano player on some of his local gigs, one in

the basement of a church. I played a few shows with him but he really didn't need a piano player and besides, it was hard finding a piano that was in tune in the halls that he played.

Bobby Vee and me had a lot in common, even though our paths would take such different directions. We had the same musical history and came from the same places at the same point in time. He had gotten out of the Midwest, too, and had made it to Hollywood....

Then Dylan jumped ahead to seeing Vee in 1961 in New York:

I wanted to see him again, so I took the D train out to the Brooklyn Paramount Theater on Flatbush Avenue where he was appearing with the Shirelles, Danny and the Juniors, Jackie Wilson, Ben E. King, Maxine Brown, and some others. He was on top of the heap now... I told him I was playing in folk clubs, but it was impossible to give him any indication of what it was all about... I wouldn't see Bobby Vee again for another 30 years, and though things would be a lot different, I'd always thought of him as a brother."

Now back home in the Midwest after spending years in California, Bobby Vee is a family man living in St. Cloud, Minnesota. He records and performs regularly throughout the year for audiences who love his early '60s rock 'n' roll and the other standards in his repertoire. Talk to Bobby Vee, and you get the sense of a musician who has enjoyed every minute of his life as an entertainer and does not have an over-inflated sense of himself. He does not try to over-complicate his life or his music. The sincerity and sweetness of songs like "Take Good Care of My Baby" seem to be very much a reflection of the singer himself. "Take Good Care of My Baby" was written by the husband-wife team of Gerry Goffin and Carole King. (King later wrote and recorded the album "Tapestry," one of the best-selling albums of 1971.)

Vee vividly remembered when Dylan briefly joined his band in 1959. He said, "After we cut 'Suzie Baby,' which was about five months about [Buddy] Holly's death, we started working in the [North Dakota] area. The record looked like it was doing well, and we had a vision of success in the group. And we worked June, July, August, somewhere around there and we thought to ourselves that maybe we should add a piano to the band. It was just a rhythm section at that time, and in doing that we would probably have the ultimate rock 'n' roll band," Vee said.

"We thought about how cool it would be to have a piano in the band like Little Richard. Not any old piano player but someone who could put it down like Jerry Lee. But hey, the '50s was about Fender guitars—not pianos!" Vee said. "We couldn't find a rock 'n' roll piano player anywhere. Then one day my brother Bill came home and said he was talking with a guy at Sam's Recordland who claimed he played the piano and had just come off of a tour with Conway Twitty.

"So Bill made arrangements to audition him at the KFGO studio. They plunked around a bit on the station's piano and played 'Whole Lotta Shakin'' in the key of *C*. Bill said he was a funny little wiry kind of guy and he rocked pretty good," Vee recalled.

"Wow! This must be the guy! He told Bill his name was 'Elston Gunnn' (with three n's). Kind of weird but we thought, let's try him out. By now, we were making enough money to buy him a matching shirt and with that he was in The Shadows. His first dance with us was in Gwinner, North Dakota. All I remember is a old crusty piano that hadn't been tuned ... ever! In the middle of 'Lotta Lovin'' I heard the piano from hell go silent. The next thing I heard was the Gene Vincent handclaps, bap bap... bap. BAP, BAP... BAP and heavy breathing next to my ear, and I looked over to find Elston Gunnn dancing next to me as he broke into a background vocal part. Obviously, he had also come to the conclusion that the piano wasn't working out," Vee said.

"The next night was more of the same," Vee continued, "He was good-spirited about the fact that none of us had the money to secure a piano for him and there were no hard feelings on the part of anyone as he made his exit for the University of Minnesota."

Vee added, "Bill was right. He sure had the spirit, and he rocked out in the key of C. We felt bad that it didn't work out. We decided not to use the piano. We paid him $15 a night. Hey, he would have been great on the Floyd Cramer tunes. That's basically the Bob Zimmerman story as it relates to The Shadows. Bob aka. Elston aka. Bob Dylan. It's been easy to chuckle and to minimize the story in view of Elston's amazing success. It was even suggested at one point that he had been fired. Not true. The truth is simple... it just didn't work out. What I remember most is his energy and spirit. Confident, direct and playful, A rock 'n' roll contender even then."

Dylan's boyhood friend Dick Kangas recalled that Dylan got mileage out of his playing with Vee. "He told his friends he was with Bobby Vee," Kangas said. "He liked that recognition: He was with Bobby Vee."

Vee also once told a reporter that, about a year later, The Shadows were playing outside New York City. One of the guys in the band saw their former bandmate: Bob a.k.a. Elston in the audience—this was before he was popular—and he said, "I saw Bob Zimmerman in about the second row." And we all said, "No kidding? I wonder how he got so far east." Because he was just a spacey little guy, y'know, just worming his way around. And then about a year after that I was in Greenwich Village and I saw an album—his first album cover. And I realized that was him."

Now, more than 40 years later, Vee talked about his reaction when he read Dylan's anecdote that mentions their past history in *Chronicles*. "I was totally surprised and blindsided by it." Did he hear about it because a friend called him? "Everybody called me!" Vee laughed.

How did Vee feel about Dylan describing their relationship as that of "brothers?" "Those are Bob's words and very accurate," said Vee. "I had that feeling of affection, a brotherly feeling. And Bob was fun: He was funny, scruffy, all those things you expect from a teenager. I think that part of it was that we were a bunch of young guys dreaming the dream. It was the joy of being 16, 17, and the possibilities of rock 'n' roll. When I lose track of myself, as we all do, I go back to that time. It was the most honest time. It tells me the most about our passion for the music. It reminds me that we were all once comrades-in-arms. It was fun." Turning back the clock to 1959 recalls a picture-perfect Norman Rockwell era. The tensions of the Cold War seemed far away from placid, comfortable Midwestern towns like Fargo, North Dakota and Hibbing, Minnesota. Eisenhower was in the White House, *To Kill a Mockingbird* by Harper Lee was on the bestseller list. Topping the charts were Bobby Darin's "Mack the Knife," Ray Charles' "What'd I Say," the Crests' "16 Candles," and Dion and the Belmonts' "A Teenager in Love." It was an era as uncomplicated as the music. Teenage girls wore bobby sox, tight sweaters, and ponytails. Clean-cut boys donned button-down shirts and khakis and gathered at drive-in diners like the one immortalized in George Lucas' *American Graffiti*. It was also the year that shapely American girls hit the beaches in a new form of attire: the bikini. In an interview, Vee described what it was like growing up in Fargo in the 1950s, "It was America, USA. Fargo was a small town. It was a city in a stretch of land that was mainly country. It was where all the farmers came to sell their wares. We had a Class C baseball team there. I used to go to all the baseball games. My job was delivering the *Fargo Forum.* I played saxophone in the high school band. It was just rural America. It certainly was not a place you would go to get into show business. So I was pretty fortunate," and noting the irony, he laughed.

One of the most dramatic moments of Vee's teenage years was February 3, 1959, when he heard that an airplane crash had claimed the lives of three of rock's most promising young stars: Buddy Holly, the Big Bopper, and Ritchie Valens. His story is just as vivid and heartwrenching as that of Don McLean, who described "the day the music died" in his 1968 hit "American Pie."

"I was in my sophomore year at Fargo High School and home on my lunch break when my brother Sid told me about a news flash he had just heard on the radio about Buddy Holly, Ritchie Valens, and the Big Bopper being killed in a plane crash in Iowa," Vee recalled. "I was sure he had heard wrong."

The tragedy seemed all the more personal to Vee because the bands were due to play in Moorhead, North Dakota that night along with the Crickets, Dion and the Belmonts, and Frankie Sardo. "I had my ticket," recalled a disbelieving Vee. "Holly and the Crickets were my favorite band. I had every record of their young career. 'Buddy Holly, the Big Bopper, and Ritchie Valens, scheduled to appear at the Moorhead Armory this evening, were found...' went the KFGO radio report over and over again. I was in shock."

The event also had an effect on the singer's career. The promoter of the Moorhead concert station announced on the radio station that the remaining acts would appear as scheduled and asked for local acts to help fill in. So Vee and his band were asked to play that evening. Subsequently, it became the biggest gig of their career to date, and "we were off into a rock 'n' roll twilight zone," Vee recalled. They got an agent as a result of this concert, who booked the bands in dates around the Midwest, and their popularity steadily grew.

Bobby Vee's 1960 hits "Devil or Angel" and "Rubber Ball" were followed by "Take Good Care of My Baby," which Vee recorded in 1961 and became his biggest hit. It stayed Number One for three weeks. Vee remembered, "There were only a couple times when I heard a song and knew it'd be a hit, and that one I knew right away." Vee backed his songs with a full, strings-laden sound that enhanced their romantic nature.

At the same time that Vee was developing a reputation as a handsome teen idol, the newcomer Bob Dylan was in Greenwich Village singing his "Song to Woody," his bare, sparse tribute to Woody Guthrie, and falling under the spell of politically aware folk luminaries like Pete Seeger and Dave Van Ronk.

In *Chronicles,* Dylan says he felt a rapport with Vee because they both were from the Midwest and then made it to Hollywood. Yet Vee said that he never had a grand plan to make it in the "big time." "At the time my dream didn't extend that far. I didn't think about it," he confessed. He was a teenager with a great voice, a smooth style, and a good band, who got a break the night he filled in for Buddy Holly. "All of a sudden it just started happening, and I was doing concerts and making records," Vee said. In 1961, Vee moved to Los Angeles, where he led the life of a busy and successful pop star who had numerous appearances on TV shows and in beach-blanket movies. He kept company with entertainers like Ray Charles, the Rolling Stones, and Dick Clark. He also toured around the world.

During his career, Vee has placed 38 songs on the Billboard Top 100 and has recorded six Gold singles. Out of the more than 25 albums he has recorded, two went Gold. In recent years, he has joined many oldies package tours with singers like Brian Hyland ("Itsy Bitsy Teeny Weeny Yellow Polka Dot Bikini"), Fabian, and Dion, and the Chiffons. He still does about 100 shows a year, including casino dates. In 1981, Vee and his wife of more than 40 years, Karen, moved back to the St. Cloud, Minnesota area after spending 20 years in L.A. During their years in California, they had kept a lake cabin in Minnesota and always tried to ensure that their four children were brought up with Midwestern values. His three sons, Jeff, Tom, and Robb Velline, perform in his band. His sons also help him run his recording studio, Rockhouse Productions, in a historic bank building in the small farm town of St. Joseph, just west of St. Cloud, Minnesota. Vee's daughter, Jennifer, is a graphic designer in Minneapolis who helps out when the studio needs artwork.

Vee embodies a solid Midwestern stability, and doesn't mind being called an oldies act. "He's such a laid-back, modest, Fargo kind of guy, he never had the ego/career problems that a lot of other singers had to come to terms with," said his son, Jeff.

Vee also felt a sense of pride at the former "Elston Gunnn's" success. "Throughout his career Bob was cutting such great records and has always written such great songs. My son Jeff is really the Bob Dylan expert in our family," he said enthusiastically. "We played 'Every Grain of Sand' (from *Slow Train Coming*) at my father's funeral. We played 'Forever Young' (from *Planet Waves*) at our in-laws' anniversary. His music has such broad strokes and such intimacy."

In addition to getting a kick out of being mentioned in Dylan's auto-biography, Vee loved the quirky, original book. "I think that Bob wrote his book like he writes his songs; if he doesn't go to places he can't write about it. He's very vulnerable and the book is almost stream of con-sciousness. He doesn't deny his feelings." Vee had been reading *Blink* by Malcolm Gladwell, a book about the importance of spontaneity and first impressions. "When you think of slicing images, intuition, and responding to the first thought that comes to you, Bob has that very natural way of creating." Vee compared him to the great Buddy Holly, adding "What Buddy Holly did was not that different from what Dylan does and where Dylan goes. It allows him not to edit himself and to take chances." Vee had a point. In *Chronicles* Dylan himself said he had long relied on instinct and intuition in writing songs.

Since he has lived in Minnesota for a long time, Vee and his band sometimes perform in Dylan's hometown of Hibbing. He is well aware of how the townspeople feel about what Abe and Beatty Zimmerman's son has made of himself. "Everyone in Hibbing feels a certain sense of pride about Bob," Vee concluded, "more than you would know."

The last time that Vee saw his old friend Bob Dylan was when the singer/songwriter returned to Fargo to perform in 1990. "I bought tick-ets to his concert," Vee recalled. "And I wrote him a letter and gave it to one of the sound guys, whom I happened to know, and asked him, 'If you see Bob, please give this to him.' He did, and during the concert they paged me. My wife and I went into this dark backstage area that I knew well because I had played at this venue in Fargo. We made our way to his dressing room, and we had the nicest chat.

"It was just a simple, plain, clear conversation," Vee recalled. "We talked about our mutual friend Jeff Lynne from ELO. Bob asked about my brother Bill, and we talked about old times. We knew that Del Shannon had played his last show here. It was just a conversation about the simplest things, but it had to do with friendship and feelings.

"He was wonderful, pleasant, and that was it," Vee said simply.

MARIA MULDAUR

Corbis Corporation

*I*n 1974 Maria Muldaur's "Midnight at the Oasis" brought the blues and jazz singer fame in the rock and R&B worlds. Since the time of that hit, she has recorded more than 30 albums and continues to perform almost 200 shows a year. The San Francisco Chronicle has written of her style, "Muldaur approaches her material with a jeweler's precision, cutting each tune scrupulously into a fine gem. She can sing circles around the young thrushes who dominate today's pop charts."

Muldaur grew up in Greenwich Village where she became steeped in Appalachian music, gospel, rock, blues, oldtimey music, and R&B. Over dinner in the Village, with characteristic deadpan humor and energetic loving recall, Muldaur spoke about growing up here and getting caught up in its music scene when she was about 16. Her music has been described as sensuous and passionate. So too is the woman: Piles of curly brown hair cascaded down her shoulders, and she wore an elegant silver cross on a chain around her neck and a flowing skirt. As a teenager, Muldaur went to Washington Square

Park on Sundays to enjoy hootenannies, where people were playing banjos and fiddles and singing everything from protest songs to Appalachian music to bluegrass to blues. "At the beginning of my senior year, I was 17, and I had one last altercation with my parents and ran away from home. I was already living in the Village, so I didn't run very far," she told me. She threw herself into music, never quite planning to make a career of it. She met fellow musician Bob Dylan in 1961, when he had first arrived in the Village, and their friendship has lasted over 40 years.

Muldaur recounted the early days in the Village, her experiences in Woodstock and its musical community in the '70s, and her move—in the mid-'70s—to L.A. where she firmly established her music career.

When Muldaur ran away from home in 1960, she actually ran to the building at 30 Jones Street where she was staying during her current visit to New York. She took a job as a mother's helper for one of the families in the building. It gave her free room and board while she finished high school. At the time, the Village was a mecca for people "to be running away to" as Muldaur put it. "I was going to the Black Fat Pussycat and Figaro. I was part of the beatnik scene. I'd go to poetry readings with Allen Ginsberg, Gregory Corso, Wavy Gravy, Ted Jones." She also had a buddy named Jeremy Stein who went to the High School of Music and Art and later became a famous jazz flautist. He turned Muldaur on to jazz. "We'd go hear Thelonious Monk for a $2 cover charge. We would lie about our age and hear Gerry Mulligan at the Village Vanguard. When rock 'n' roll got diluted with teen ditties, I turned away from it and realized there was a cornucopia of interesting music just waiting to be explored and listened to," she said.

Though her job gave her room and board, it did not pay a cent. On Saturdays, to make lunch and subway money, she would clean houses of various bachelors she knew. Coming home one day, she spotted the Allen Block Sandal Shop at Jones and Fourth. Their custom-made sandals were made to fit perfectly to a drawing of one's foot. Muldaur recalled, "I fell in love with a pair of roman sandals that laced up your leg. They were $11—which in those days was so out of my price range," she confessed. "So he worked it out that I would pay $1 a week until it was paid off." Every Saturday afternoon after cleaning houses she would stop by Allen's sandal shop to pay $1.

She dropped in about the time Block would shut down his store and host an old-time Appalachian music jam. "People piled into this small store: John Cohen, Mike Seeger, people who went on to become the New Lost City Ramblers. (I'd had the biggest crush on John Cohen. I just told him that recently.) That was the first time I had heard old-timey fiddle music. I'd pay my $1 to Allen and stay all afternoon. The guys were playing banjos, fiddles, and autoharps. Now his daughter Rory Block, who was 12 at the time, is an incredible blues artist. That was my first exposure to the old-timey Appalachian music that is the precursor to bluegrass."

The family Muldaur worked for also inadvertently deepened the teenager's musical knowledge. "The mother worked for the *New York Times* and the father was an editor at *Sports Illustrated.* Every night they'd have cocktails and go out to some soirée and then leave me with the two girls," said Muldaur. " I'd put the girls to bed and notice they had walls of every record imaginable: Every possible kind of record. Lots of LPs, lots of 78s, all original Bessie Smith 78s, original Louis Armstrong, Duke Ellington, Fletcher Henderson records." With the parents out every night, Muldaur had a lot of time to explore this sophisticated music library. "I saw 'Empty Bed Blues' by Bessie Smith, Part I and Part II and thought, 'That sounds interesting.' To hear this incredibly intense, soulful voice coming over this scratchy record was a pivotal moment for me. So that was my first exposure to the real blues—especially early blues, which has remained a love of mine for my whole life," she said. Quickly the petite Muldaur—who wore a long braid down her back—started learning old blues songs and began singing "Empty Bed Blues" at parties.

In the Village, people were forming bands, jamming, and loosely getting together. "By the time I was out of high school I was on the scene 24/7," she said. A group of people formed the Friends of Old Timey Music and were starting to discover people who were at the time mythical figures: People like Mississippi John Hurt, Skip James, and Son House. They would bring these rural Southern musicians to New York to perform concerts. They brought up Appalachian fiddler Doc Watson and his family and Clarence Ashley, whom the Village folk aficionados had heard on Folkways anthologies. Muldaur fell in love with Doc Watson's sweet and simple fiddle playing. Watson soon invited Muldaur to visit him in North Carolina, where he and his father-in-law, Gaither Carlton, taught her to play the fiddle.

"I began living with a really sweet guy named Walter Gundy, a banjo player, in a little $35-a-month apartment in Little Italy on Spring Street," Muldaur said. "We'd go down to North Carolina in our VW bus and stay with Doc Watson or his father-in-law Gaither. I went down two or three times and learned to play the fiddle from Gaither Carlton, staying in their funky mountain home. For a gal who had only grown up in New York and gone to the country in New Jersey every summer, this was like going back in time to a distant universe, and I loved it, going to their mountain home high in the Blue Ridge Mountains." She also added a wealth of Appalachian songs to her growing repertoire.

In 1961, Muldaur formed a musical alliance in the Village with Annie Bird, an autoharp musician from Virginia. Together they performed Carter Family duets at the little basket houses where they were paid from the cash that the audience threw into the basket when it was passed. Muldaur met Bob Dylan, recently arrived from Minnesota, when she was playing the basket-house scene. "He was very nice and he was fun to hang out with. There started to be a buzz about him pretty early on."

As Dylan said in the film *No Direction Home:* "I was ready for New York. I started playing immediately, and I realized I had come to the right place because there were so many places to play." Guitarist Bruce Langhorne said, "I remember him. He had a little hat like a watchcap and was playing Woody Guthrie songs. There's a quality of determination and will that some people have. When they're doing something, they're really doing it and you know you have to pay attention to it."

At the time, different musical factions were starting to emerge in the Village. There were those who were into bluegrass, or old-timey, or blues. "Then there was the 'protest song movement,' which didn't interest me," Muldaur said, "because musically it was less than appealing." Dylan himself admitted, "Folk music was a strict and rigid establishment. If you sang Southern Mountain Blues, you didn't sing Southern Mountain Ballads and you didn't sing City Blues. If you sang Texas cowboy songs, you didn't play English ballads. If you sang folk songs from the '30s, you didn't do bluegrass tunes or Appalachian ballads. ... Everybody had their particular thing that they did. I didn't much ever pay attention to that. If I liked a song, I would just learn it and sing it the only way I could play it."

When Muldaur first met Dylan, she didn't pay too much attention to him. "I'd see him around. He was in on some jams. He was interested in some traditional music. I remember when he wrote and played 'Talkin' Bear Mountain Picnic Blues.' I'd see him at Gerde's almost every Monday night. Everyone was saying, 'Isn't that clever, isn't that great.' I thought he was a nice guy, but I was not getting the buzz at all," she confessed. "I'd enjoy sitting and having a glass of wine with him. I was not in awe of him. At the bar near us there would be characters like Cisco Houston, Peter LaFarge, Josh Logan: 'The old guard leftist, Woody Guthrie types,'" she recalled. Muldaur had not yet witnessed the daring individualism and style that shortly afterwards made Dylan folk music's darling, but she soon would.

One day Muldaur was rehearsing with Annie Bird at The Third Side, a club owned by Annie's boyfriend Charlie Washburn. "We were practicing our little Carter Family songs, and we hear this rapping on the window, and there is Bob peering in. He says, 'Man, am I glad you're here. I cut my finger. Have you got a Band-Aid? I've got a gig tonight.' He was all upset," she recalled.

"So we found him a Band-Aid in the back and sat him down and reassured him he was going to live. We made him a cup of coffee to help to calm him down. We were sitting on upended crates in the kitchen of The Third Side. I think he began to feel sheepish that he made such a fuss, because it wasn't so bad," she added.

Then Dylan said, "Thank you girls, wanna hear a song I wrote?" To be polite, the women said, "Sure." Dylan took his guitar out of its case and started singing the thoughtful and insightful "Only a Pawn in Their Game." Muldaur's eyes widened.

"At that point, my head split open and I became aware of a greater reality," Muldaur recalled. "All the other protest songs were very self-righteous polemics on the terrible rednecks of the South: They're wrong and we're right... strum, strum... they're so prejudiced... strum, strum... segregation is so horrible. This song had a much more cosmic and far-reaching overview. He pointed out that the people the movement were vilifying as enemy were really just pawns in a larger game, a game where corporate greed and the politicians were playing them against the blacks and keeping everyone down. Then, as now, those forces–the politicians and corporate greed heads they served–were manipulating the whites into positions they held. I loved the song. It was such a loving and forgiving overview... It was deep.

"So I absorbed the song and looked at him and thought, 'Oh, I get what everybody is talking about. I'm in the presence of a great mind who sees a lot and has the passion to express it in a way.' I heard him do 'Masters of War' at Gerde's not long after, and from that moment to this I was a huge fan," she said with conviction.

Critic Paul Williams has noted that what fed Dylan's writing process during this time was "Guthrie, folk, country, rock, gospel, anything or any piece of something that happened to stick in there." Williams wrote, "The richness of Dylan's language and music is partly a reflection of the richness of the music and language he's taken into himself and partly a function of his unselfconsciousness about using whatever comes to mind—and mostly a gift, a talent, handled with skill and grace, a mystery, a gift of tongues."

Muldaur's own career took an interesting turn soon after. When she had returned to New York from one of her trips to North Carolina, she went to Washington Square and ran into John Sebastian and Dave Grisman, who told her they were forming a jug band called the Even Dozen Jug Band. The jug-band music that so interested Sebastian, who later formed the Lovin' Spoonful, was an old form of American music then reemerging into the fringe of alternative culture. In the 1920s and 1930s, jug-band music had been the rural area's answer to the more polished New Orleans blues and jazz emanating from radio. Rural musicians were not able to afford some of the more expensive instruments, so they would improvise, creating their own bass sounds on jugs and washtubs. They substituted a washboard played with thimbles to recreate the percussion of a drum kit and simulated Dixieland sounds of trumpets and clarinets with kazoos and harmonicas. Mandolins, guitars, and banjos completed the jug-band sound.

Sebastian told Muldaur that blues diva Victoria Spivey had signed them on her record label. Spivey had told them, "You boys sound good but you need some sex appeal—get that little girl I've seen," referring to Muldaur. So Muldaur said, "Sure, where do I sign up?" The band members themselves were very young. "Some of them had their baby fat, they were being brought to rehearsal by their mothers, still in their Clearasil phase," she wryly noted. Spivey then took the charismatic young singer under her wing and played old blues records for her. Muldaur instantly fell in love with Memphis Minnie. "I heard her 'Tricks Ain't Walkin' and finally recorded it this year [on her *Sweet Lovin' Soul* CD]," she added.

At about the same time, Victoria Spivey let Dylan play harmonica on one her recordings in October, 1961. The album was *Victoria Spivey: Three Kings and a Queen, Volumes 1 and 2*. Critic Paul Williams wrote about the fact that for a white kid to play with black blues singers—at their invitation–was all but unheard of in 1961; for a white kid to play with this much soul is still remarkable. Williams said that Dylan had a genius for the blues, as these recordings revealed.

By forming his Even Dozen Jug Band, Sebastian thought he was onto a new trend. In the early 1960s, Jim Kweskin and his jug band had released an album on Vanguard. Dave Van Ronk also had a jug band. "People thought jug bands were gonna sweep the nation!" Muldaur cracked. "Eventually Jac Holzman of Elektra bought out our contract from Victoria." By this time, Muldaur was a happy-go-lucky 18-year-old, just living day-to-day and happy to be involved in music. She was oblivious to any competition in the Village, nor did she feel that the fact that a few careers were beginning changed anyone. "We each got $65 for recording the Elektra album." When Muldaur was in the jug band, the band's first two gigs were in the basement of a church and Carnegie Hall. "We did a 'Sing Out' hootenanny with Pete Seeger and two other jug bands. I think Dylan was there. A month later we played there again to open for Nina Simone and Herbie Mann, and then did a 'Hootenanny show' that was filmed at Fordham—for TV—with the New Christy Minstrels and the guy who sang 'Tie Me Kangaroo Down Sport.' It was fun, it was happening."

After those four big gigs, the jug band had a short life. "I fell in love with [blues vocalist and washboard player] Geoff Muldaur, who was with the other jug band—the Kweskin Jug Band—and ended up leaving poor Walter on Spring Street and moving up to Cambridge in 1963," she recalled. She later married Geoff Muldaur. "In those days, moving meant you get eight grocery cartons at the local grocer's and loaded your stuff in your VW bus and off you went. One of the members of the Jug Band eventually left and I was asked to join the band."

During her Cambridge days, Muldaur saw Dylan intermittently when he would cruise into town with his friend Victor Maimudes. "There's a wonderful photo of Bob and me. Bob is at the piano with Bob Neuwirth, Mimi Fariña, and Eric and Debbie Andersen. It was after hours at Club 47. Once of us was playing there and he showed up. I remember we were singing 'Money Honey,' and a friend of ours took this casual snap. He has this look on his face. He was beaming at me with this incredible smile," she said.

In 1964 Muldaur was on hand for one of Dylan's biggest performances of the year. The Kweskin Jug Band had a three-week stay at L.A.'s Troubadour. They also had a gig on the *Steve Allen Show*. So the Muldaurs got in their VW bus and drove across country with a sack of macrobiotic brown rice in the engine block. They stayed with various hippie friends along the way. "We were in Austin, Texas visiting friends when The Beatles were on *Ed Sullivan*," she remembered.

The Muldaurs got to L.A. and slept in their bus in front of a friend's house while the Kweskin Band began their three weeks at the Troubadour. "Every night there would be people like Roger Miller and Hoyt Axton on the scene and parties in the Hollywood Hills with a lot of pot-smoking, which we thought was the hippest, coolest thing. We were in with the 'in crowd' and very much in demand socially," she said. Then she heard that Dylan was coming to town to play the Santa Monica Civic Auditorium.

"Bob, Bobby Neuwirth, and Victor had come across country in their big old blue station wagon. Bob had written 'Chimes of Freedom' and was writing some of his best stuff then. It was a golden moment for him," she fondly recalled. The Jug Band was working the night of Dylan's Santa Monica concert on February 29, 1964 and could not attend, but Bob had Victor Maimudes pick up Muldaur and Jim Kweskin's wife to take them to the Santa Monica Civic Auditorium.

At this concert, Dylan's music was raw and exciting. He had stage presence, and through his songs conveyed his mysterious yet magnetic personality. He was a supreme storyteller. "I was blown away," Muldaur admitted. "I sat in the audience and realized he had reached another level, and it was mind-boggling. The place was sold out. Two songs before the end, someone came to get me and said, 'Bob wants me to take you backstage.' So I was backstage when the concert ended. He might have had a little stage fright. I imagine it was a big deal for him... 3,000 people, sold out. We're backstage and he's glad to see a face from home," she recalled. Dylan and his friends then planned to go to a party at Benny Shapiro's [a friend of Grossman's] house in the Hollywood Hills. But when Dylan, Muldaur, and the others tried to leave the backstage area, they found throngs of people pressing against the door.

"People were saying they were his uncle, cousin, long-lost best friend from high school: Teenagers, parents, every possible sort of people," she said. "There was some young runaway they had managed to pick up in the room," said Muldaur. "Finally with the help of security we formed a 'V' with Maimudes and Bobby in front and got through the crowd to our car. I remember the sensation, such a press against me I almost couldn't breathe. My ribs were pushed in. Certainly in our funky organic folk scene nothing vaguely like this occurred. We made it out, pushed our way out, and people were throwing themselves on the hood of the car."

Then Muldaur looked in the back of the station wagon and saw the tarp over the band's equipment moving. She said, "'Victor... there's two little teenage girls stowed away there.' They had to be gently and firmly ejected, and we made our way in a zig-zag way to the party—trying to lose people following us." Wolfman Jack was on the radio, and Mary Wells was belting out "My Guy." "We loved that great soul music and were singing songs all the way to the party," she said.

When they got to the party in the Hollywood Hills, they were in for another surprise. "In Cambridge someone might have a nice frame house that could hold a lot of people for a party, but we had never seen anything like this—a big house in the Hollywood Hills overlooking the city, with sliding glass doors, patio length of the front, white carpets and matching furniture. All these people looked decidedly different from our crowd, too," said Muldaur. "These were sophisticated women. I sat on a stool and watched. I had a front row seat to what was unfolding: A pretty swank scene. It was a phenomenon for Dylan to go from fellow musician I knew who was part of the scene, a down-to-earth guy, who had emerged out of the folk scene, not particularly immersed in the rock star milieu. Then I saw an informal line of people trying to talk to him. Women would sashay up to him in matching baby-blue cashmere outfits. Here I was in sandals and a denim mini-skirt. I could tell it was making him nervous," Muldaur observed. "He's a nervous and high-strung guy, finely tuned. When he gets nervous his leg starts to twitch. It had to have been a new experience for him and one that was making him a little edgy."

She realized she was witnessing a turning point in her friend's career. Being treated like a star overtook what could have been a happy, sanguine moment after a wonderful concert. "Up to that time, I'd see Bob at a party or jam, no big deal. That night I witnessed the beginning of what would become his enormous rock stardom. The Jug Band eventually showed up, and they were mixing with this Hollywood crowd. I saw women throwing themselves at him [Dylan], and he was just this scruffy guy," she said, shaking her head at the incongruity of it all. Yet, unknowingly, Muldaur was also present at the beginning of the groundswell that was starting to rock the culture: The Beatles' ebullient and energetic music was sweeping America; Dylan was developing his original aesthetic and becoming a charismatic and prolific musician. His words and music, along with the songs of The Beatles, played an important role in changing the cultural experiences of the young.

Muldaur also was present a year later at the 1965 Newport Folk Festival when Dylan went electric. While there are several versions of what happened at that historic festival, Muldaur added her reminiscences to the mix. "The day before we had been at a blues workshop and Paul Butterfield played. Alan Lomax [the musicologist] had a scuffle where he got up and said something derogatory. But Butterfield and his guys, these were same guys who had played with Muddy Waters. A lot of authentic blues acts were electric," she offered.

She observed, "Bob always knew how to catch a trend and ride the front of the wave. I happened to know that they had rehearsed electric. I had performed in the first half of the show, so before Bob's set I went out in the audience with my friend Betsy Siggins who ran Club 47. We said, 'Oh good, this is gonna be so cool.' Dylan and his band plugged in. There was no sound guy, there were no monitors, one-third of the audience freaked and booed, one-third cheered and the rest didn't know what to do. When we heard the boos we went, 'What?' We couldn't believe it." Of the purported booing, singer-actor Theodore Bikel said, "Dylan made a tactical mistake. He should have started with acoustic music, then gone into electric. He didn't bother to reach out. He didn't talk to the audience. A lesser person would have given up performing after such a reception."

After the concert, the Newport Festival organizers had a party for all the musicians at one of the grand historic Newport mansions. Dinner was served and the Chambers Brothers were the party music; ironically they played electric blues.

"After dinner there was so much tension. I was sitting with Dick and Mimi Fariña and they were tapping Latin rhythms with the cutlery, as though it was a rumble. Everyone was talking about the fact that these young players went electric and the old guard like George Wein and Theo Bikel and Pete Seeger were saying it was horrible and affecting the purity of folk music," Muldaur said. "In our section everyone was beating out these rhythms, like they were fomenting a slight musical revolution. The Chambers Brothers started to play, so I got up to dance and was dancing with Mimi. Dick said, 'Look at Bob.' He was in a corner smoking a cigarette. Dick encouraged me to go over and ask him to dance. Now I've never seen him dance. But I went over and said, 'Hey Bob, Dick said to ask you to dance. You don't feel like dancing, do you?'

"He looked up with this weird and withered look, and said hoarsely, 'I'd dance with you, Muldaur, but my hands are on fire.' I didn't understand, and yet I did. It was such a Dylan-enigmatic thing to say," she admitted.

Muldaur felt sympathetic towards him and shocked by the audience response to his new direction. "I felt that he'd be damned if he would let that stop him for the next wave of what he wanted to do musically. I think he had recorded 'Like a Rolling Stone' then. [He had.] He could see himself more as a rock star—he didn't see a reason to just play folk to placate the old guard. He loved Muddy Waters, he loved the Rolling Stones. From that point he hooked up with the Band. I think John Hammond turned him on to The Band."

Looking back, Muldaur felt that both the experiences at Santa Monica and at Newport were intense for Dylan. "This wonderful, insightful, beautiful, prophetic stuff was coming through him, at a time when all this other stuff was going on in the country: civil rights movement, Vietnam War. People were starting to apply more consciousness to what was going on, and here came this voice. I mean, how does it get better than 'Masters of War?'" she asked rhetorically.

She recalled that in *No Direction Home*, Dylan is quoted as saying he never wanted to be a prophet. Muldaur notes, "In the Bible, a lot of times God chooses some people to speak for people, to lead them. Even Moses said, 'Why me, Lord? Are you sure you don't want somebody else?' People projected so much of their hopes and feelings on Dylan, and he couldn't take on the mantle of what people wanted. I think it happened, and he didn't want to be a spokesman. But he was one, not even of his own choosing."

She added, "You will find quotes where he said, 'This was coming through me, I didn't even think I was writing this.' The projections people put on you—getting all these megawatts of information flowing through him—he was on fire musically, creatively, politically, spiritually, to even be open and available to that channel. It's almost like the wiring can 'get amped out.' It would make even the sturdiest soul nervous."

After Dylan's meteoric ascendance in the 1960s, Muldaur crossed paths with him next when she and her husband Geoff moved to Woodstock in 1970. Albert Grossman, Dylan's manager, was also the Kweskin Jug Band's manager. "I loved Albert," Muldaur said. "I'm still good friends with his widow, Sally. Albert got the Jug Band off Vanguard and onto Warner Reprise. We'd hang out in Albert's house in Woodstock. After Dylan had his motorcycle accident [in 1966], he was there chillin'. Dylan and his wife Sara were with their son Jesse. My daughter Jenny was one year older than Jesse. Once in a while they'd come over. Sara was gorgeous, serene, elegant, and very good for him."

With the money Warner gave the Jug Band, the Muldaurs bought a house with a couple of acres for $35,000. They called it "Hard Acres." "Warners paid all the members of the band monthly to sit around in Woodstock, develop music, and get ready to make a new album," she recalled. Garth Hudson, organist for The Band, lived next door to the

Muldaurs, and they could hear him practice Bach on his organ.

Dylan made a surprise appearance at their house one winter evening. "Our friends Betsy and Bob Siggins from Club 47 were in Woodstock from Cambridge, and a friend, Jim Rooney, a bluegrass singer, came over for dinner. Everyone was sitting around. We heard a knock on the door, and there's Bob wearing one of those little Russian fur hats with the flaps down," Muldaur said. "He just showed up, and it was like he wanted to touch base with his old friends who knew him before he was a big famous rock star. Sometimes when Dylan first arrived, there'd be this period of awkwardness. I learned to ride through it, just get through it, and then we could all relax. We went into a big studio we had next door and sang Hank Williams songs. I asked him to sing 'Corinna Corinna,' which I loved." [This blues standard appears on Dylan's second album, *The Freewheelin' Bob Dylan*.]

On another occasion, in the early 1970s, blues guitarist David Bromberg asked Muldaur and another woman to sing backup with him at a concert, so they went down to New York City from Woodstock on the bus. David took Muldaur aside and said, "I told Bob you were gonna be here. He might come by."

Muldaur said, "Sure enough, there comes Bob in a top hat... Everyone left the backstage and we just visited. He had just made 'Pat Garrett and Billy the Kid,' and he started singing 'Knockin' on Heaven's Door.' Every phase he's gone through—I've always loved all his songs. After 'Only a Pawn in the Game,' there's hardly a song I haven't loved."

Not long after, Muldaur's life took an unexpected turn. "My husband Geoff decided to join the Butterfield band Better Days and left me musically and personally to fend for myself and Jenny. I was really dismayed and hurt. I had no great aspirations to be a 'solo artist.' All I thought I could do was go to ask Albert for a waitressing job in one of the restaurants he owned. But God had another fate in store for me..." she recalled. On a visit to Brooks Brothers in New York to buy her soon-to-be-ex-husband a shirt as a going-away present, she ran into Warner Bros. executive Mo Ostin. Ostin decided to sign Muldaur as solo artist on Warner. It was the last thing she expected.

A few months later, she found herself in Los Angeles living in a bungalow previously owned by The Byrds when they were developing their band. Under Mo Ostin's direction, she recorded her first solo Warner Brothers album, which was produced by Lenny Waronker. She had top guns on the session: Guitarist Ry Cooder (*Buena Vista Social Club*), guitarist David Linley, and Dr. John, the New Orleans-style piano player who has been one of her longtime collaborators through the years. "My friend, the guitarist David Nichtern was sleeping on a mattress on my floor. I suggested as an afterthought this funny song he wrote called 'Midnight at the Oasis.'" At the time she also started doing little gigs at the clubs like Ash Grove with bassist Freebo, Nichtern, and Greg Prestopino.

"I was doing a gig at the Ash Grove once, and Bob and his cousin Louis Kemp showed up. [Kemp owns Louis Kemp Seafood.] There's Roger McGuinn or David Crosby… one of them… I think Bob had brought them all to see me. I hadn't seen him in a couple of years. Bob and Louis came in this big long Maserati, or some fancy sports car," she said. After the gig, the group of friends ended up going to Muldaur's bungalow. "I lit candles and served cheap red wine. We hung out; Bob had a guitar, and I had a guitar. We sang old songs and had a really nice time, then off he went with his cousin in the Maserati. They were quite pleased with themselves. Those were my encounters with him, very casual and random. Nothing planned."

When "Midnight at the Oasis" became a hit in 1974, Muldaur's debut album on Warner Brothers went Platinum in two years. In *Rolling Stone*, Jon Landau wrote a positive review of Muldaur's first album, "Like Ry Cooder, Maria Muldaur has found just the right balance between her commitment to the traditional material she favors and her ability to interpret it in a personal way." She recorded four other albums on Warner after that, including *Waitress in a Donut Shop*, which included her next hit single, a remake of the blues standard "I'm a Woman." That song has remained Muldaur's signature tune. Again, Landau praised her in *Rolling Stone:* "Muldaur is rock's first torch singer of the Seventies. Because she neither writes nor sings with the raw power of some women performers, she's had to develop an original musical personality. She's mastered aspects of gospel, blues, country, jazz, and rock singing, but imparts her own brand of cool to each. Maria has been called a fox, but she's much more. She sings about sex with an adult sense of joyfulness instead of a teenage leer. But she can sing about anything with maturity, self-awareness, and a touching sense of her own vulnerability."

In the process of recording 30 albums in the past 30 years, Muldaur has worked with many of the finest musicians in the folk, rock, and blues genres, including Paul Butterfield, Lowell George, Linda Ronstadt, Stevie Wonder, Junior Walker, James Booker, Benny Carter, J.J. Cale, Kenny Burrell, Hoagy Carmichael, and her beloved Doc Watson, to name a few. She has also maintained a longtime fondness for

New Orleans music and has dubbed the gumbo of straight-ahead blues, R&B, and Louisiana music, "bluesiana."

Years later, in 1979, Muldaur reconnected with Dylan after her young daughter's nearly fatal car crash. At the time, Muldaur was living in Marin County outside of San Francisco with John Conn, who played bass for 25 years in the Jerry Garcia Band (not The Grateful Dead).

Muldaur had continued to actively follow Dylan's progress. "When I had originally heard Mark Knopfler and Dire Straits, I thought Knopfler would be perfect to do an album with Dylan," Muldaur said. "Then I started hearing *Slow Train Coming* [Knopfler performed on this album] and heard the buzz that Bob was a born-again Christian. I had been born a Catholic but had been spiritually searching. I investigated every New Age mojo that came down the pike: I Ching, Zen Buddhism, macrobiotics, you name it." The radio stations were doing a preview of Dylan's new album. "I was driving around doing errands and listening in the car. I thought, '*Slow Train Coming* sounds musically better than the last 10 albums.' This was being presented in such a cool way, I love this. So I said to myself 'I'm gonna get this record.'"

About a week later Jenny, who was 13 at the time, was in a car accident and was rushed to the hospital. Muldaur sat outside her daughter's hospital room for many hours, through seven hours of surgery. "I was sitting there praying. When something like this happens, you don't start talking to Buddha or throwing your [I Ching] changes. I was praying to God. And I started hearing Dylan singing those songs."

Muldaur was so convinced she heard the album that she asked the nurses on the ward, "Are you playing the new Dylan record?" and they said no. "I now realize it's all on a spiritual plane. I guess those words got into my head and were manifesting themselves. They were witnessing to me a message, that no matter what worldly success and joy that you achieve, your life is nothing without a relationship to God. When I started praying, I realized my own life was fragile. I started to see my whole life flash before me, even though it was Jenny's life in the balance. I'd made such a progression since I was a young gal in the Village going to St. Joseph's Church. I saw how far afield I had come." She admitted that the Garcia Band used a lot of cocaine. "To smooth out the cocaine, there'd be red wine, I was smoking cigarettes... I was not enjoying it, but that was what was going on. I decided to give all that up. I promised God that if he spared Jenny's life, I would clean up my act," she admitted.

Seven hours later, doctors had microscopically put her daughter's shattered skull together. Three weeks later Jenny was back in school with "a very weird haircut," Muldaur said, remembering her vast relief and joy at her daughter's incredible recovery.

About a month later, Muldaur was in L.A. doing gigs. Her black producer invited her to a church service where she responded to an altar call and was converted. "From then on, things were palpably different," she confessed. "Everything looked clearer, like a dirty film had been lifted from my eyes." Three or four weeks later, Dylan was performing in San Francisco and Muldaur bought his album and a Bible.

She was looking forward to attending Dylan's concert to hear the music from *Slow Train Coming*. But when she read the concert reviews, she was disappointed to see that the critics had panned him, and the audience booed when he mentioned God. Muldaur decided to write Bob a long letter to tell him about Jenny's accident and how the record helped her reconnect to the source. "I told him, 'I was there the night they booed you for going electric, and they couldn't keep up with the pace at which you're changing, and that's what's going on now.' I said in my letter, 'This is your best album to date, and I want you to know the message reached one person and made an enormous difference in my life, and I thank you.'" She then dropped the letter off at rock promoter Bill Graham's office, and asked Bill to give it to Bob personally. [Graham was producing Dylan's San Francisco concerts.] One reason that critics did not react warmly to Dylan's concert was because *Slow Train Coming* was such a departure from the top albums of that year—1979—including The Clash's *London Calling*, Pink Floyd's *The Wall*, and Talking Heads' *Fear of Music*.

By the time she had driven home to Marin County, her answering service had received his call. "The service said, 'You're not gonna believe who called you—but Bob Dylan has called.'" When Muldaur talked to him, he said that the letter had come at a moment when he needed a little bit of encouragement. Dylan invited her to come to the concert as many times as she wanted and to bring as many friends as she wanted. Muldaur went to the show and loved it. "I was ushered backstage and told, 'Bob wants to see you.' He was very warm and asked, 'How's Jenny? Is she OK?'" Muldaur went back to the show several times and met the band's back-up singers, Regina McCrary, Mona Lisa Young, and Helena Springs.

Rumors flew at the time about Dylan's romances with several of his black back-up singers, but Muldaur will not comment. She did admit that Dylan seemed to be especially comfortable with black women, because they were not intimidated by him. "Each one of his back-up singers told me that when they got the call from him they hadn't a clue who he was," she said.

The following year, Dylan came through San Francisco again following the release of *Saved*. Again they were in San Francisco for one week and Muldaur had concert passes. She had put out a gospel album called *Gospel Nights* with the Chambers Brothers, which was an evening of American traditional gospel music, both Appalachian and black. "Bob loved that album. I had done a Staples Singer song called 'Nobody's Fault But Mine,' and he loved it. He invited me to come onstage, and he introduced me as a friend he met when he first came to the Village. I went out and sang. We played the song in concert completely different from the way we had rehearsed it, but that's okay. It took me aback, but Bob doesn't stay stuck in one place. I went with it. It was fun. It was an honor and a pleasure to play with the wonderful back-up singers [Regina Havis, Carolyn Dennis, and Clydie King] and a fabulous band." During these San Francisco shows at the Warfield Theater, Dylan had a number of guest performers: Carlos Santana joined the band for four songs during one show, Jerry Garcia of the Grateful Dead played guitar on four songs at another, and Roger McGuinn sang and played on "Mr. Tambourine Man" and "Knockin' on Heaven's Door."

Muldaur also invited Dylan and his band to her Marin home for Thanksgiving, since they were all going to be away from home during that holiday. "I prepared a full-blown 10-course Italian dinner, a stuffed turkey and all the trimmings. Bob was kinda restless. He spent time on the porch. Then he said, 'Mike Bloomfield lives in Mill Valley, doesn't he?' He wanted to try to get a hold of Mike. We called, and the line was busy. Bob said, 'I'd really love to see Mike.'" Dylan had strong ties to Bloomfield, and in 1965 called him "the best guitarist I know." A white Chicago blues guitarist, Bloomfield had played on the recording of "Like a Rolling Stone," and had played with Dylan when he went electric at Newport in July 1965. Critics said that it was Bloomfield's guitar style that bridged the blues influence with folk and rock on the classic *Highway 61 Revisited* album. Although Bloomfield had declined an offer to go on the road with Dylan, he played slide guitar in the Butterfield Blues Band until he left to give Elvin Jones "more space." He founded The Electric Flag, which did not hold together long, and recorded a classic '70s album, *Super Sessions,* with Al Kooper and Stephen Stills.

Maria knew that Mike had had a lot of drug and alcohol problems, but since Bob wanted to see him so much, they had the limo driver drive them up to his home. Muldaur recalled, "I went to the door, and there came Michael Bloomfield in his bathrobe and bedroom slippers. He said to me, 'What are you doing here?' I said, "I've got a surprise for you." He saw Bob, and they embraced, Mike was so happy to see him. He'd been watching *The Godfather* on TV."

They talked and had a nice visit. Bloomfield thanked Muldaur for persisting. The phone had been off the hook. Then he said, "Wait, Bob, I've got something for you. " He ran back and gave Bob his family Bible with a silver embossed cover. Bob said, "Are you sure you want to give me this?" It had Hebrew writing on one side and English on the other. Mike said, "I figured you should have it. I'll never read it but you will."

Muldaur said, "We got in the limo and Bob was looking at it, saying 'Man, this is deep. I can't believe he gave it to me.'"

Bloomfield later joined Dylan's band at the Warfield shows as a guest, playing lead guitar on "Like a Rolling Stone" and another song. Dylan invited Bloomfield to join the band, and Bloomfield had said to give him some time and he'd meet him on the road. That was not to be, however. Not long after that concert, on February 15, 1981 Michael Bloomfield was found dead in his car in San Francisco. The cause of death was ruled an accidental drug overdose. He was 38.

Looking back on Dylan's extensive repertoire, Muldaur noted that one of her favorite Dylan albums is *World Gone Wrong*, which was released in the mid-'90s "He was playing acoustic guitar, doing old American folk and blues. It's a beautiful album," Muldaur said, "Very spare, he's singing great and playing killer guitar. The music is very natural and seamless. He's not one to do a million takes. In the liner notes he says, 'Listen carefully to these songs, because they are not making songs like this anymore.' Basically the greatest writer of our generation is singing these classic, great blues and American folk tunes because they're not makin' tunes like this anymore."

When Muldaur saw Dylan at the W.C. Handy Blues Awards in Memphis in 1994 she briefly visited with him. "I was nominated and was playing, and he was there. I had gone to see Memphis Minnie's gravesite, my pilgrimage to these blues singers. That night I got the idea to record the CD *Richland Woman Blues*, inspired in part by his words in the liner notes of *World Gone Wrong*. Bob made me recognize that I wanted to pay homage to early blues singers." In her opinion, Dylan proved that a pared-down, spare presentation on voice and guitar could be extremely effective. Muldaur's resulting CD, *Richland Woman Blues* went on to be nominated for a Grammy and for two W.C. Handy Awards in 2001. It's an album that Dylan knows well, "He told me he loved it, " Muldaur smiled.

One of the secrets of her long-lasting friendship with Dylan is that "he knows I don't want anything from him," Muldaur declared. "I'm not an ex-girlfriend; I'm just a fellow musical traveler. We've drunk from the same musical fountains, and we love and respond to the same music. Every time I see him, he's nagging me to play the fiddle again. I always say, 'Next year.' It's very light," she said with girlish enthusiasm.

Thoughtfully, she concluded, "I feel blessed. I've heard a lot of old friends complain, 'Oh, he walked right passed me at this event,' and they get easily offended." The enigmatic musician who others have often described as reclusive, aloof, and solitary is not the Dylan that Muldaur knows and loves. "As far as I'm concerned, Bob has given me so much inspiration over the years, if he never wanted to talk to me again, I'd give him that space. He's already talked to me with a capital 'T' in such a profound way with his music... He's talkin' to me anyway, if he does or doesn't. I get a lot out of what he has to say."

JOHNNY RIVERS

Corbis Corporation

"*W*hen I finally did arrive in California, my songs and my reputation had preceded me. I had records out on Columbia and I'd be playing at the Santa Monica Civic Auditorium and meeting all the performers who had recorded my songs—artists like The Byrds, who'd recorded 'Mr. Tambourine Man,' Sonny and Cher, who'd done 'All I Really Want To Do,' The Turtles, who recorded 'It Ain't Me Babe,' Glen Campbell, who had released 'Don't Think Twice,' and Johnny Rivers, who had recorded 'Positively 4ᵗʰ Street,'" writes Dylan in* Chronicles.*

"Of all the versions of my recorded songs, the Johnny Rivers one was my favorite," he continues. "It was obvious that we were from the same side of town, had been read the same citations, came from the same musical family, and were cut from the same cloth. When I listened to Johnny's version of 'Positively 4ᵗʰ Street,' I liked his version better than mine. I listened to it over and over again. Most of the cover versions of my songs seemed to take them out into left field somewhere, but Rivers' version had the mandate down—the attitude* *and melodic sense to complete and surpass even the feeling that I had put into it. It shouldn't have surprised me, though. He had done the same thing with 'Maybellene' and 'Memphis,' two Chuck Berry songs. When I heard Johnny sing my song, it was obvious that life had the same external grip on him as it did on me."*

At first, Johnny Rivers had no idea he was mentioned in Dylan's autobiography. "A friend called me and said that Bob said some nice things about me in his book. It was very much of a surprise. I knew he liked my music," said Rivers in an interview at his Los Angeles production company, Soul City. "In 1964, when I was working at the Whisky-A-Go-Go, Bob would come in there. He had a couple of albums out, but they were underground, obscure and not the world I was in." In fact, at the time Rivers was recording R&B-flavored hit songs like "Memphis," the jivey, hootchie-kootchie "Maybellene," and "Mountain of Love," which made the Top 40. He had a soulful, original sound and played a simple, understated rhythm guitar.

"I knew the buzz about Dylan in New York," Rivers said. "With 'Positively 4th Street,' I liked it as a song, and it was on my album *Realization*. It was the last of 10 songs on the album. I also did 'Blowin' in the Wind' and 'Mr. Tambourine Man.' I thought 'Positively 4th Street' fit the theme on my album—it was a revelation, an honest piece, speaking from the soul." Rivers offered his opinion of Dylan's statement in his book, that "it was obvious that life had the same external grip on him as it did on me." "What I think Dylan is referring to is that a lot of our background is similar," he said. "We were both playing around our hometowns and knew that if we were to get anything going we had to travel. I grew up in the Bronx and moved to Baton Rouge; it was going to the right place at the right time."

Rivers continued, "Our roots are similar. Bob left Minnesota for New York and the folk scene. I formed a band that became successful. Bob had to get to New York to meet Woody Guthrie. I went to New York to find Alan Freed, and through him I got a recording contract. There are similarities in our music, too. I'm into R&B, soul, really strong Southern grip. What changed Bob's life was hearing Robert Johnson and the blues. I listened to the blues all the time in Baton Rouge. That's when I started writing a lot. That's why I felt I was at the right place at the right time."

Rivers was very much affected by Southern music. He was born John Henry Ramistella in 1942 in New York City. When he was about five, his father lost his job so his family moved to Baton Rouge, Louisiana. There, an uncle who worked at the Louisiana State University art department got Rivers' father work painting houses and antiquing furniture. "My dad and uncle used to get together and play these old Italian folk songs on mandolin and guitar," Rivers said. His father had a gut-string guitar, and Rivers' first good guitar was a Gibson J-45. He learned to play by observing his father as well as attentively watching other guitarists. He also listened to R&B on late-night radio megawatt stations like WLAC in Nashville. And R&B was a way of life in Baton Rouge. He recalled that at his junior high, "Fats Domino, Jimmy Reed, and guys like that used to play at our dances."

Rivers also remembered the first time he saw Elvis, before either of them became stars. He and a buddy went to their local high school to see a country concert starring Minnie Pearl and Little Jimmy Dickens. Opening the show with a two-song set was an unknown kid named Elvis Presley. "I got to see Elvis right around the time he had released his first record. He got up and performed at the auditorium of my old high school in Baton Rouge!" he laughed.

"Minnie Pearl brought him out," Rivers recalled. "She called him the Hillbilly Cat. They were setting up. He's trying to talk about his new record on Sun Records, and everybody around us started laughing at him. He was wearing a pink suit and white buck shoes, and my buddy and I went, 'Wow. This guy's really cool.' He had an incredible energy about him."

By junior high, Rivers was playing guitar and sitting in with local bands, including one led by Dick Holler, who later wrote "Abraham, Martin, and John." Rivers formed his own band, called The Spades, in 1956. "We played all Fats' tunes and Little Richard, Larry Williams, Bobby Bland," Rivers said. "We became the hot little band around Baton Rouge. Then Elvis Presley and Jerry Lee Lewis hit, so I took on a little touch of rockabilly."

In 1957, when he had just started writing songs, Rivers flew to New York during a school vacation and stayed with a relative. He wanted to meet [rock 'n' roll DJ] Alan Freed. He stood out in front of the radio station WINS at Columbus Circle on a freezing cold day. Freed came up with Jack Hooke, who was his manager. Rivers said, "My name's Johnny Ramistella. I'm from Baton Rouge, Louisiana. I have a band. I play and write, and I'd like you to hear my music." Freed gave the 15-year-old his card and said, "We have an office down at the Brill Building on Broadway. Why don't you come down tomorrow afternoon?" Rivers went to Freed's office and played four or five songs. He made quite an impression.

Hooke called George Goldner, owner of Gone and End records, whose office was also in the Brill Building. Otis Blackwell, the writer of "Don't Be Cruel" and "Great Balls of Fire" arranged River's debut single "Baby Come Back" backed with "Long, Long Walk." Freed is also responsible for the young man's new name. Rivers said, "I was sitting around with Jack and Alan, and they were getting ready to release the record. Alan [said], 'Your name…you need to come up with something a little more musical. We were talking about the Mississippi River where I grew up and somehow Rivers came out of that. That was the first time I used that name." "Baby Come Back" was released in March 1958. These New York contacts led to Rivers' recording a couple of other songs, but none were hits.

Rivers continued to play guitar and sing with his band in Nashville and Baton Rouge until 1960. At a club in Alabama he met Audrey Williams, Hank Williams' widow, who invited him to Nashville where he was introduced to Phil Everly and Roger Miller. Then back in Louisiana he met guitarist James Burton, who was home in Baton Rouge after working in California with Ricky Nelson. Rivers told Burton he had written a song that he thought was perfect for the teen idol. Burton took a tape of Rivers' "I'll Make Believe" back to California. Soon, Ricky Nelson decided to record it and it wound up on one of Nelson's biggest albums.

In 1961, Rivers decided to relocate to L.A. He was thinking of producing records and returned to the stage in 1963 almost by accident. Because Rivers was a musician and stayed up late, he wound up going to a little Italian restaurant, Bill Gazzari's club, late at night for good food. A jazz trio played there, too. One night the club owner told Rivers that his band was leaving and, knowing Rivers was a musician, invited him to come in and play for a few nights until he could find a replacement band. Rivers invited Eddie Rubin, a jazz drummer, and they played rock and R&B. What they intended to be a three- or four-day gig started to draw huge crowds. Gazzari didn't want Rivers to leave, so he offered him more money and Rivers hired a bassist, Joe Osborn.

Rivers also met two men at Gazzari's who would play major roles in his career: Lou Adler, who became his producer, and Elmer Valentine, who was opening an L.A. version of the Paris Whisky-A-Go-Go club on the Sunset Strip. Valentine offered Rivers a year's contract to appear at the new club.

Rivers opened at the Whisky on January 15, 1964, three days before

The Beatles' first single, "I Want To Hold Your Hand" was released in the U.S. He said, "The Whisky was a smash from opening night. I brought my following from Gazzari's." The Sunset Strip was hot, and the young, dark-haired, handsome Rivers and his red Gibson ES 335 guitar drew huge crowds night after night. Before long, he and his friend Lou Adler thought of cutting a live album with his tight, rockin' band. They recorded "Live at the Whisky-A-Go-Go" in two nights and took it to every record company in town, but no one wanted it.

Eventually, a Liberty Records executive convinced the company's president Al Bennett to release it on Imperial Records. In so doing, Bennett and Lou Adler formed Dunhill Records with two other producers. Dunhill Records eventually became home to the Mamas and the Papas, the Grass Roots, and Steppenwolf. By June of 1964, "Memphis," off of Rivers' first album on Imperial, was at the top of the charts and the album became a Top 10 record. His formula was vintage rock 'n' roll and R&B, played with energy and simplicity. "It was pretty exciting," Rivers said in an interview with *Vintage Guitar.* "I was just into the music. I loved playing, and I was actually working two jobs." Rivers worked at a club in downtown L.A. and at the Whisky-A-Go-Go. "All I was doing was playing all those funky blues tunes and rock 'n' roll songs I'd played with my band back in Baton Rouge in the '50s. No one was doing that in L.A. The Beach Boys were just getting started and it was that Jan and Dean, Beach Boys kind of surf music, real light kind of stuff. No one was playing get-down-funky blues or stuff like 'Memphis.'"

Over the next four years, Rivers released a steady stream of Top 10 hits: "Mountain of Love," Mose Allison's "Seventh Son," "Secret Agent Man," and "Baby I Need Your Lovin'." Rivers' basic recording band consisted of drummer Hal Blaine, bassist Joe Osborn, and keyboard player Larry Knechtel. They coalesced into a group that recorded some of L.A.'s classic pop hits. "Lou [Adler] used them on Mamas & Papas records and Barry McGuire's 'Eve of Destruction,'" Rivers said.

Rivers and Dylan crossed paths a number of times over the years. During 1965, Rivers had a hit with "Poor Side of Town." Dylan had just recorded "Like a Rolling Stone." "He was putting together an electric band," recalled Rivers. "He eventually hired our drummer Mickey Jones away from us to tour with him . Mickey did a documentary about their first tour. Bob was into taking care of his business then, as I was, too," said Rivers. "Then I didn't see Bob for awhile, then in the early '80s we did a show in L.A. at the Beverly Theater in Beverly Hills. Bob came to the show. He was dating Clydie King [she sang back-up with

Dylan in 1981 for the *Shot of Love* album], who sang for us. She said he was there."

He continued, "The last time I saw Bob was about seven or eight years ago in Milwaukee at Summerfest, where we were both playing. When one set finishes and the next one starts, they shift around the stages. Bob had finished his set and his bus pulled up. His road manager came out saying Bob would like to talk to me for awhile. We talked and then he said, 'Mind if I sit on the stage and watch?' We said, 'Not at all.' I remember it was hot and humid, and Bob had on this sweatshirt and sunglasses. If he was trying to go incognito it didn't work....he stood out. Everyone was sweating! He sat on a chair and watched. He had asked me to play 'Poor Side of Town,' so when I introduced the song I said, 'This one is for my friend, Bob.' Of course the audience had no idea who 'Bob' was. That's the last time I talked to him."

Rivers went to a 2005 concert of Dylan's that opened with Merle Haggard's band. "I was disappointed, " Rivers confessed. "I think most people just want to hear Dylan do what he did when he started. He doesn't need to have four guitars or to be as loud as the Dave Mathews Band. He doesn't have to compete. He should be what he is. He had the wrong type of microphone at the L.A. concert. As a record producer, I would have fixed that." Rivers thought about Dylan's stage persona in recent years. "Maybe he does it to shock people: Changing songs around, changing lyrics. ... Chuck Berry does that. A lot of people around Bob don't tell him what they think... What do you do when no one will tell you the truth?" he asked rhetorically.

He admitted that, as different as their careers might have been, Dylan has inspired him. "He's an inspiration for everyone in the industry. I like some of his new things—a song that was in a movie several years ago." Rivers was referring to "Things Have Changed" from *The Wonder Boys*. "As for his own tastes, when Johnny Rivers wants to kick back and relax he listens to jazz—Miles Davis or Kenny Burrell. "I love jazz and the blues," he added.

Rolling Stone has called Rivers "the quintessential music-business insider in the best sense." By the time he was 24, he had recorded eight albums in two years. In addition to recording and performing, he also decided to become a record producer. During the '60s and '70s, Rivers was instrumental in helping the careers of Glen Campbell, James Taylor, Fifth Dimension, Joe South, and Jackson Browne. Around 1966, Rivers had started his own production company, Soul City, as a label distributed by Liberty. Rivers had signed the unknown songwriter Jimmy

Webb to his publishing company, and Rivers had recorded his poignant song, "By the Time I Get to Phoenix." Rivers wanted to release it as a single, but felt it sounded too much like "Poor Side of Town." So he gave an advance copy of the album it was on, *Changes*, to Glen Campbell's producer Al DeLory. Copying Rivers note for note, Campbell wound up with a hit.

Around 1966 Rivers had discovered The Versatiles, a male and female R&B group he felt could be "the black Mamas & the Papas." When he met them, the five performers all dressed alike, in black mohair and black, patent-leather shoes. Rivers produced the group—renamed the Fifth Dimension—for Soul City. In 1967, they had a hit with "Go Where You Wanna Go," which was a remake of the Mamas & the Papas tune, and later that year their version of Jimmy Webb's "Up, Up, and Away" established them as pop stars. The song won two Grammys.

In 1970 Rivers almost beat James Taylor—the composer of "Fire and Rain"—to the punch with his cover of this soothing ballad. Someone brought him Taylor's first album; at the time Rivers had not heard of James Taylor, but he loved "Fire and Rain." Rivers put it out as a single and it started taking off. "Then," Rivers recalled, "Warner Bros.— Taylor's label—woke up and saw it hitting the charts and said, 'We've got something with this guy,' and they pulled out all the stops. The radio stations stopped playing my version and started playing James Taylor's."

Johnny Rivers sold more than 20 million records during the '60s and '70s and scored more than 20 hits. When it came to recording Top 40 songs, he had a golden touch, and his mainstream tunes are now rock classics. He is still involved in the music business, running his production company, and he has a unique perspective on survival in the industry. "The main reason I've been able to survive is that I've been true to my roots and style. I do what I do. I've stayed within certain limits. I've been true to myself, and I'm comfortable doing that. I'm playing to a different generation now. 'Secret Agent Man' was in the film *Austin Powers,* so I've got four generations of listeners." When Rivers was asked what he thinks accounts for Dylan's survival, he thoughtfully answered, "He's tenacious and serious about music. It is his life. He's like B.B. King and others who play until they drop. Frank Sinatra. That's all that gives them fulfillment. He's certainly not doing it for the money."

WOODSTOCK, NASHVILLE, AND BEYOND
1966–1976

KRIS KRISTOFFERSON

Retna, Inc

*K*ris Kristofferson was born into a military family in Brownsville, Texas in 1936. He became involved in the folk-music scene as a creative writing major at the small and liberal Pomona College in Southern California. His academic record won him a Rhodes Scholarship to Oxford University where he studied English literature at Merton College. While he was at Oxford, he cut a record in London, although it was never released. After two years at Oxford, Kris left and returned to the U.S., got married to Fran Beir, and went on active military duty. After jump school and helicopter flight school in Georgia, he extended his active duty from two years to four. He planned to teach English at West Point. His love of music, however, pulled him in another direction. When he was in Germany in the military, he had begun writing songs and formed a country band. In 1965, on leave from Germany, he visited Nashville and looked up a songwriter named Marijohn Wilkin, who was related to a friend of his. Marijohn liked the few songs Kris had written, and that brief visit to Music City excited him so much that he* *maneuvered for an early discharge from the Army. (This was possible because he had accumulated much reserve time while at Oxford.) Within weeks, Kris and his wife and daughter were in Nashville to stay. Shortly thereafter, however, Kristofferson's marriage fell apart. He later married fellow singer Rita Coolidge. They were married for seven years and made one of popular music's most attractive couples. They divorced in 1980.*

Kristofferson has been writing songs since the age of 11. As he told music critic John Morthland, "Everything I ever wrote was an attempt to follow in the footsteps of the best country songwriters I knew: Hank Williams, Johnny Cash, Willie Nelson, Roger Miller, Merle Haggard... and Bob Dylan." When Kristofferson got to Nashville in 1965, he was learning from Tom T. Hall, Mickey Newbury, and John Hartford ("Gentle on My Mind"). Kristofferson continued, "To me, country, as opposed to Tin Pan Alley, was white man's soul music. It was about real things like drinking, cheating, sex, things they didn't talk about in pop music." At a time when Nashville musicians wore crew cuts and spangled suits, Kristofferson had long hair, jeans, and a buckskin jacket. "All those stories about how new I was... was just something people had to say, because of the way they felt about country music, or maybe it was because I looked different," he told Morthland." But I really didn't think my songs were different from what Willie [Nelson] was writing."

In Nashville in 1965, when he was trying to break into songwriting and music business, Kristofferson was working in the Columbia recording studios as a janitor when Dylan came in to record Blonde on Blonde. *It was a prophetic moment for Kris. This is where he picks up his story.*

"It was my first week on the job as a janitor at the recording studios. I was the only songwriter in there," Kristofferson said. "The building was lined with police because Dylan was in there. They were such unusual sessions by Nashville standards. Usually, Nashville musicians would cut three songs in three hours. They are all alike.

"Bob came in and was working at the piano all night. His musicians were out playing ping-pong. He was out in the big Studio A at the piano working on stuff, writing, while the guys were waiting. After doing this for hours, in the morning they began recording *Blonde on Blonde*. I wouldn't have dared interrupt his creation." Kristofferson was already familiar with Dylan's music. "I had been listening to Dylan since I was in the Army in the early '60s. I had a little band over there in Germany. A guy brought us these Bob Dylan records and said this young guy was so good. I loved it. I loved his early folk and bluegrass stuff: Homage to Woody Guthrie and all. I was captivated.

"I began buying all his albums after that. To me, he was the measuring stick—the standard—by which everyone else was measured. Like Muhammad Ali! The guy affected all of us. I grew up in the days of the '50's Hit Parade. The songs were 'Look at the Doggie in the Window.' Then this force comes in—look at The Beatles and how they were influenced! It was a good, powerful influence, and he's still doing it."

As Kristofferson watched through a glass window, Dylan was recording the album that was widely considered by critics to be one of his masterpieces. *Blonde on Blonde* took Dylan a step farther from his folk roots, as the previous albums *Highway 61 Revisited* and *Bringing It All Back Home* had also done. In an interview with Ron Rosenbaum for *Playboy* in 1978, Dylan discussed that work, saying, "The closest I ever got to the sound I hear in my mind was on individual bands in the *Blonde on Blonde* album. It's that thin, that wild mercury sound. It's metallic and bright gold, with whatever that conjures up. That's my particular sound. I haven't been able to succeed in getting it all the time. Mostly, I've been driving at a combination of guitar, harmonica, and organ, but now I find myself going into territory that has more percussion in it and [pause] rhythms of the soul."

After watching Dylan record, Kristofferson was still in for more years of struggle. "When I turned 30, I was still working as a janitor," he confessed. But his work at Columbia allowed him to cross paths with many of Nashville's finest. Johnny Cash used to tell a story that Kristofferson landed a helicopter in his backyard and gave him some tapes of songs.

Kristofferson laughed when reminded of that story. "To be honest," he admitted, "John used to love to tell that story, and he did me so much good that I never disputed it. But the truth of it is that he had been listening to my stuff for four years. He used to tell me how good my songs were. I gave him tapes through his wife, June Carter. He was very encouraging. Then he made the recording of 'Sunday Morning Coming Down' and it became Song of the Year in 1970." Cash had a TV show that was very important in Nashville; Dylan overcame his dislike for live TV and did the show, as did Joni Mitchell, Linda Ronstadt, Buffy Sainte-Marie, and many others. Kristofferson recalled, "I hung out at the headquarters and just pitched songs to everybody."

He looked back to the late '60s: "The years of struggling before were tough. I certainly had doubts I would make it. I was a captain in the

Army and decided to quit. Within weeks I was without a job. My parents were horrified and my peers thought I was crazy. But I was committed and I credit Dylan a lot. I remember that when I was in the Army, based in western D.C., I had one of his albums with liner notes that said, 'Don't tell me Norman Mailer is more important than Hank Williams.' That floored me [that he appreciated Hank Williams].

"Dylan's relationship with Johnny Cash was so important to the popularity of country music," Kristofferson continued. "[Dylan] brought along his rock fans to country music and showed it respect. He gave real good country music credibility."

In 1969, country star Roger Miller recorded Kristofferson's unique song, "Me and Bobby McGee" and things started falling into place for the Texas-born singer/songwriter. Kristofferson had written the song when he was flying helicopters down in the Gulf of Mexico. He had a job down there for almost two years, working a week in the Gulf, living on an oil platform, then spending a week back in Nashville trying to peddle songs that he wrote out on the Gulf. "No wine, women, or song out there, so it was a good place to write," he said. Among the other country-music performers who were recording his songs then were Ray Stevens ("Sunday Mornin' Comin' Down"), Jerry Lee Lewis ("Once More with Feeling"), and Faron Young ("Your Time's Comin'").

Johnny Cash invited him to the Newport Folk Festival that same year. "That was really important to me," Kristofferson acknowledged. "I never would have performed. It was very scary. On the way to the stage John said, 'You're going to have to sing louder. At my house when you sing I can hardly hear you.' June [Carter] had to push me onstage. But that was John's endorsement of me onstage..." Kristofferson noted that Dylan gave Johnny tremendous respect, so Kris felt part of a chain—connected to Dylan through Cash. "Nobody knew me at the time. They were there to see Carl Perkins. Carl said I could introduce him as the 'late and great Carl Perkins,' Kristofferson laughed. "So I did!" That year he also signed a recording contract with Monument Records and his debut album for them was *Kristofferson*.

Another major development in his career occurred due to another good friend of Dylan's, musician and artist Bob Neuwirth. In the spring of 1970, Kristofferson played at The Bitter End in Greenwich Village, and Neuwirth liked his act so much that he brought his friends to see him. Neuwirth offered to introduce Kris to Janis Joplin, suggesting that they hop on a plane immediately and fly to the West Coast. When Neuwirth called Janis, she said she was ready to party. Neuwirth told her he had a buddy with him and she told him to bring him along.

When they arrived at the party in Larkspur (in Marin County, north of San Francisco), Kristofferson caught Joplin's eye right away. "She thought he was a honey," a friend said. Indeed, Janis fell for Kristofferson, who was lanky, with long, brown hair and handsome, movie-star looks. He was 34 years old and like her, a Texan. He was also starting to break into the music business. Kristofferson and Neuwirth stayed with Janis in Larkspur for a couple of weeks. During that time, all of them hopped through the Sausalito bars and consumed a lot of alcohol. Janis' friend James Gurley said, "Kristofferson wanted her to cut 'Me and Bobby McGee.' He was beginning to make waves with his own career."

Janis had a look at the song. Her friend Dave Richards, who was remodeling Janis' house, recalled, "I remember when [Kristofferson] introduced 'Me and Bobby McGee' to her. When I got there that day, she said, 'Listen to this song. This is a great song.' She was playing the guitar and sang 'Me and Bobby McGee.'" Janis eventually recorded the song on her album *Pearl,* although at the time Kristofferson was unaware it was happening. In the late summer of 1970 Janis died of a drug overdose. After her death Kristofferson broke down when he heard her version of "Me and Bobby McGee." The song became her only Number One single.

From 1970 to 1971, Kristofferson's compositions were in high demand. Among the artists recording his material were Ray Price ("For the Good Times"), Waylon Jennings ("The Taker"), Bobby Bare ("Come Sundown"), and Sammi Smith ("Help Me Make It Through the Night"). "For the Good Times" won Song of the Year from the Academy of Country Music in 1970, while Johnny Cash's version of the Kristofferson tune "Sunday Morning Coming Down" won the same award from the Academy's rival, the Country Music Association, in the same year.

After the success of Janis Joplin's recording of "Me and Bobby McGee" in 1971, Kristofferson said, "I felt I had stepped on a roller-coaster. I was out there on the road…constantly." He had made it as a songwriter, and with the success of his second album *The Silver Tongued Devil and I,* released in 1971, he established his career as a recording artist in his own right. Eventually, more than 50 singers recorded "Me and Bobby McGee," further confirming his talent and the fact that he had arrived.

Kristofferson also branched out into movies at this time. He made his acting debut in *The Last Movie,* directed by Dennis Hopper and in 1972 appeared in *Cisco Pike.* He followed that with an appearance in Paul Mazursky's *Blume in Love* and crossed paths with Bob Dylan again in 1972 in *Pat Garrett and Billy the Kid.*

Pat Garrett was based on a true story. William H. Bonney—aka Billy the Kid—was a hired gun who roamed New Mexico in the 1880s. Fellow outlaw Pat Garrett traveled with him until he was made a sheriff and ordered to hunt down his friend, whom he ultimately killed. In the Sam Peckinpah movie, Kristofferson played the Kid and James Coburn played Pat Garrett. Dylan played a supporting character, Alias, a friend of the Kid.

Kristofferson also had a part in Dylan's being hired for the role. "The producer [Gordon Carroll] wanted him. I'd seen Bob before when we hung out at Cash's house, doing the Johnny Cash TV show together. I knew he was interested in doing this, and he had screened another Peckinpah movie, 'The Wild Bunch.' When Bob had doubts I encouraged him: 'Yeah, do it,'" he said.

Kristofferson gave Dylan support and professional feedback during filming in Durango, Mexico. "I thought he was a wonderful actor," Kristofferson said enthusiastically. "He's like Charlie Chaplin, a very fresh artist. He makes choices that are very real. The movie was hard. We were doing a lot of hard horseback riding that was dangerous." There was a lot of drinking and crude behavior on the set, too. "Peckinpah was awful," said Kristofferson. The director drank too much and was constantly fighting with his studio, MGM. As author David Weddle reports in his biography of the director, *If They Move …Kill'Em,* Dylan and Kristofferson were in the screening room watching dailies when Peckinpah urinated all over the screen because the picture was out of focus. "I remember Bob turning and looking at me with the most perfect reaction, you know: 'What the hell have we gotten ourselves into,'" said Kristofferson.

Despite Peckinpah's drinking and unruliness, Kristofferson said, "I think Bob thought [Peckinpah] was an artist, and he respected him. He always felt that the producer put Bob in the movie for his name value. Sam was always battling the studio. I wanted Bob to play the part of the eyes through which you see the whole legend, but the whole film involved a lot of difficult circumstances."

For his part, Dylan recalled the experience as being "trapped deep in the heart of Mexico with some madman, ordering people around like a little king. You had to play the dummy all day. I used to think to myself,

'Well now, how would Dustin Hoffman play this?' That's why I wore glasses in that reading part. I saw him do it in *Papillon*. It was crazy, all these generals making you jump into hot ants, setting up turkey shoots and whatever, and drinking tequila 'til they passed out. Sam was a wonderful guy though. He was an outlaw, a real hombre, somebody from the old school, men like they don't make anymore. I could see why actors would do anything for him."

Kristofferson enjoyed spending the time with Dylan on the set, but confessed, "I have never been that comfortable around him. I have the greatest love and respect for him. But I have no idea what's going on in his head. He's a very nervous guy. Yes, around Cash he could relax more, but there were a lot of people around when we did the TV show." Kristofferson also acknowledged the fact that Dylan is shy in person but can be so beautifully expressive in his music. "It's ironic, and when you think about how hard he had to fight to get out there! I was thinking about myself, too. I'm not naturally inclined to get up in front of a lot of people and sing. It's very difficult. Sometimes I wonder, 'How did I end up here?' Yes, Dylan is an artist, and when he performs he goes into a zone. If you're serious and pay attention that's what you have to do."

As Dylan said in an interview with Ron Rosenbaum in 1978, "You have to have belief. You must have a purpose. You must believe that you can disappear through walls. Without that belief, you're not going to become a very good rock singer, or pop singer, or folk-rock singer…You must know why you're doing what you're doing." Rosenbaum also asked Dylan, "Do you think you have a purpose and a mission?" Dylan's reply was, "Obviously."

One of the greatest artistic outcomes of *Pat Garrett and Billy the Kid* was the music Dylan composed for the soundtrack. According to Howard Sounes' book *Down the Highway*, Dylan gathered an eclectic group of musicians in February 1973 for the recording: Booker T. Jones, Roger McGuinn, and another old friend from the Village days, Bruce Langhorne. Sounes recounted how they assembled in a studio in Burbank, California, in front of a giant screen on which a rough cut of the movie was projected. Bob scored the film in his own singular way. "I thought that Bobby didn't know anything about film scoring," Langhorne told Sounes. Langhorne, who had known Dylan since the early '60s in the Village, worked on film scores for a living at this stage in his career. He knew that it was customary to pay close attention to the cuts, matching tempo to action. But Dylan did none of this. "I realized afterwards that it really wasn't about them doing the best film score,"

Langhorne added. "It was about capturing the feeling of the film." Dylan succeeded in this. The incidental music he created was highly evocative of the Wild West, and of the two songs he wrote for the movie, one was the popular and long-lasting "Knockin' on Heaven's Door."

Despite having a great experience working with Dylan on *Pat Garrett and Billy the Kid,* Kristofferson understood some of Dylan's reticence with people. "He was a very private person and he liked being around artists," observed Kristofferson. "He would feel comfortable with people who did the same kind of work he did, musicians, who speak the same language. I always was afraid I'd embarrass him or myself. He is so perceptive. When you're around him, you're afraid you're gonna do something awful. He's a wonderful person."

Dylan did not appear in many films after *Pat Garrett and Billy the Kid,* with the exception of the film he produced, wrote, and directed, *Renaldo and Clara;* the film *Hearts of Fire;* and the Larry Charles' film *Masked and Anonymous.* Kristofferson, on the other hand, has had a busy career as an actor, starring in films like *A Star is Born* with Barbra Streisand, *Alice Doesn't Live Here Anymore* with Ellen Burstyn, and *Heaven's Gate* directed by Michael Cimino, in addition to writing scores for films made for television and TV shows. He also teamed up with Willie Nelson in 1984 for *Songwriter,* which earned him an Oscar nomination for Original Song Score.

Kristofferson possesses a humble, self-deprecating sense of humor, as witnessed by his famous quote from the '90s, "I think between us, Bill Clinton and I have settled any lingering myths about the brilliance of Rhodes scholars." Yet what shines through his personality is how much he loves what he does. Especially his career as a singer/songwriter. He is effusive in his enthusiasm. Several times he has said in public that since the success of "Me and Bobby McGee," he hasn't "worked a lick" and has had the privilege of performing with people he has revered, like Willie Nelson, Johnny Cash, and Waylon Jennings. "Just to have met them would have been an incredible thing, but to be their friend and their peer is wonderful," he has said. In 1985 the four country singers had a Number One hit with "Highwayman," from their album of the same name.

Rolling Stone has called Kristofferson "a poet... a songwriter's songwriter comparable to no one less than Bob Dylan or Townes Van Zandt. Unlike those two giants, however, Kristofferson deals not in obtuse, double-edge metaphors, but in hard truths laid down with the matter-of-fact directness of Hemingway: 'There's something in a Sunday/

Makes a body feel alone' ("Sunday Morning Coming Down"); 'I ain't saying I beat the devil, but I drank his beer for nothing/Then I stole his song.' ("To Beat the Devil"). Like Dylan and Van Zandt, Kristofferson's songs have often been best appreciated when delivered by better singers (Janis Joplin, Johnny Cash), but there's a ragged beauty to his own plainspoken renditions that somehow spells definitive."

Another highlight in Kristofferson's relationship with Dylan was being asked to serve as emcee for the 30th Anniversary Concert Celebration held in Madison Square Garden in the fall of 1992. There Kristofferson also performed "I'll Be Your Baby Tonight." The star roster of performers included Eric Clapton, George Harrison, Neil Young, John Cougar Mellencamp, Johnny Cash and June Carter, Liam Clancy, members of The Band, Tom Petty, and many others. "That concert was incredible," Kristofferson recalled con brio. "It was such a great atmosphere, so many people came out to show respect for Bob. It was a great thing. It started with Booker T and the MGs playing 'Gotta Serve Somebody' and went on from there. But poor Sinéad ... such a shock." Sinéad O'Connor was in the midst of a controversial period because of derogatory statements she had made on television about the Pope. When she appeared onstage, she was booed. "I had felt that the Garden was full of people who might be of the same spirit she was, but they weren't," reflected Kristofferson.

Today, Kristofferson lives in Maui with his wife, Lisa, and their five children. (He and Lisa married in 1983.) He doesn't cross paths with Dylan as often as he would like. "I just missed him in Scotland," Kristofferson offered. " I was there doing a movie and he was there getting a degree from a university. [In 2004 Dylan was awarded an honorary degree from the University of St. Andrews in Scotland.] There was an incredible photo of him in the papers. I was sorry I missed him. The last time I saw him, I worked with him, and opened for him at a concert in D.C, maybe in the late '90s."

Looking back, Kristofferson felt as though he missed opportunities to spend more time with Dylan. "One of the regrets I have is that I respected other people's privacy so much, now I wish I had invaded his privacy more." His reasons were respectful ones. "I didn't want to be intrusive backstage. It's the same with Bob's concerts with Willie, there is limited backstage activity. I understood Bob needed his space and privacy."

In September 2005, like millions of other people, Kristofferson tuned in to PBS to watch Martin Scorsese's documentary on Dylan, *No Direction Home.* "I loved it," Kristofferson said. "I loved his book, too.

He was so generous. It was great in the film to see the music in the context of the times. I watched it with my 14-year-old daughter and she said, 'Gee, Bob Dylan is great.' She's out listening to him now."

Many viewers were struck by 1966 footage of Dylan's tour of England with The Hawks (soon to become The Band), when they were booed for playing electric. "Incredible," Kristofferson said. "I was booed, too, when I played Isle of Wight, and it wasn't because I left folk for rock." How tough was it? Kristofferson just laughed.

Kristofferson concluded by commenting about his friend Dylan's personality and offered insights into his artistic genius. "I think he's amazingly sensitive to all kinds of outside experience, the same as any kind of artist who is really good at something. I feel fortunate to have been here while he was doing it. He is so shy, and everything pouring out of him is so absorbing. His songs take us to another level. He's absolutely a poet and one of the most important artists of our time."

To sum it up, he said, "Bob Dylan is probably the most important person in terms of my songwriting. He made songwriting into an art form and made it worthy of committing your soul to. Think of The Beatles before they had contact with Dylan. He was definitely the most important influence of all to me."

RONNIE HAWKINS
(WITH THE BAND)

Retna, Inc.

*R*onnie Hawkins is the rockabilly singer whose young, hard-driving band, The Hawks, played Toronto clubs with him in the early '60s and later backed Bob Dylan as The Band. It was in 1965 that Dylan heard The Hawks and asked them to go on the road with him as he moved from folk to rock. They changed their name to The Band and with Dylan developed their winning combination of rock, blues, country, and rockabilly. In the following years, The Band's lives and careers changed as they made music history, producing some of rock's best-loved albums, including Music From Big Pink *and* The Band. *Despite the great success that performing with Dylan brought them, The Band's music careers really began with Ronnie Hawkins. "We'd grown up with Ronnie Hawkins, playing that quicker tempo of tunes," said drummer Levon Helm. Hawkins has had insight into the lives of Dylan and The Band afforded to few others and has remained their loyal friend.*

"I've thought about you a thousand times!" was how Hawkins greeted me on the telephone when I called to schedule a visit with him. It was 1976 when we first met at The Last Waltz, The Band's farewell concert in San Francisco. The concert was filmed by Martin Scorsese and its eponymous documentary is one of the best rock films ever made. A reporter for People *magazine, I went to the Miyako Hotel the day before the concert. Many of the performers were staying there, and I met the friendly and funny Ronnie Hawkins in the hotel lobby, where he was chatting with Eric Clapton and Patti Harrison. He invited me to the dress rehearsal, where I met Van Morrison, Paul Butterfield, Albert Grossman, and others. Later there were casual get-togethers back at the hotel. The next night, after the concert—whose performing guests included Joni Mitchell, Dr. John, Neil Diamond, and Neil Young—Hawkins gave me backstage privileges and suggested we hop in a van that was taking musicians to the post-concert party at the Miyako. Hawkins and I jumped into the van after Bob Dylan. At the party we were among the first to arrive and sat at a round table with Eric Clapton, Dylan, and Ronee Blakely. Dylan nervously tapped his long, delicate fingers on the table, he was fidgeting and ready for drinks to be served. "The guilty undertaker sighs/ the lonesome organ grinder cries/ The silver saxophone says I should refuse you." Hawkins imitated Dylan as we chatted around the table. Hawkins' irreverent sense of humor helped lighten up everyone. "Hell, I have eaten so much sushi I feel like a 250 lb. thermometer!" he cracked about his stay in San Francisco's Japantown. Later, Neil Young came in with his arm around Joni Mitchell. He began jamming with Robbie Robertson and John Hammond, Jr. All the musicians who performed at The Last Waltz filled the party.*

During Hawkins' long, steady, and successful career as a rockabilly singer, he has collected a distinguished assortment of friends, including President Bill Clinton, Conway Twitty, Johnny Cash, Kris Kristofferson, John Lennon and Yoko Ono, and he has helped the careers of not only Robbie Robertson, Levon Helm, and all The Band, but guitarist Roy Buchanan, producer David Foster, actress Beverly D'Angelo, and many others. Their photographs adorn the walls of his spacious living room at his 200-acre lakefront farm outside Toronto, where Hawkins and his wife of 43 years, Wanda, have lived since the '60s. Seated on a comfortable sofa, surrounded by an ornate hand-painted piano and walls covered with awards from the music industry, Hawkins took a walk down memory lane and recapped highlights

of his career and friendship with Bob Dylan. He was at once honest,
brash, hilarious, and sentimental. The illnesses that he has fought in
the past few years have thinned his large frame, his brown beard is
now white, and he no longer possesses the Falstaffian girth of yester-
year. Yet the irreverent spirit is still present; he is the same ole Ronnie.
To wit: He was wearing a black T-shirt that read, "Same Old Shit,
Different Decade."

Hawkins was born in Arkansas in 1935. Music was his first love and
after college and the Army he put a band together called The Hawks in
his hometown of Fayetteville, Arkansas. He heard about a kid from
Marvell, Arkansas who sang and played guitar at several local county
and state fairs. His name was Levon Helm. Helm joined Ronnie
Hawkins' band on drums and they played regionally until Helm graduated from high school.

One of the places where they played was the Rockwood Club, which
Hawkins owned and operated in Fayetteville, Arkansas. The club
attracted the hot acts of the late '50s: Jerry Lee Lewis, Carl Perkins, Roy
Orbison, and a fellow named Harold Jenkins, who became famous as
Conway Twitty. Harold told Hawkins that Canada was a great place to
be a rock 'n' roll singer. Hawkins took his band to Canada around 1958,
touring and busting club records everywhere.

Hawkins played the work of Gene Vincent, Chuck Berry, Larry
Williams, and Fats Domino, and his fame grew. As Levon Helm recalled
in his book, *This Wheel's On Fire*, the Hawk was famous for his camel
walk, a funny dance step he learned from a black musician named Half
Pint, who shined shoes in Hawkins' father's barbershop. "It was like
Chuck Berry's duck walk; you looked like you were standing still, but
you were moving," Helm wrote. Hawkins and his band were playing a
rough, raucous, and provocatively rhythmic music.

Helm also said, "Ronnie Hawkins could really work a crowd on a
Friday night. I mean, he had 'em where he wanted 'em. He was big,
good-looking, funny, and had a good voice. He was an entertainer
rather than a musician. He had an instinct for crowd psychology and
could start a rumble across the room if he wanted to just by flicking his
wrist. It was this power he had over people. We'd hit that Bo Diddley
beat. Hawk would come to the front of the stage and do his kick, that
camel walk, and the thing would just take off." Hawkins had been a
champion diver as a teenager, so he could execute a front flip into a
split. Helm then continued, "He'd dance over and pretend to wind up

with Will Pop Jones, a big strong kid who hit those piano keys so hard they'd break. God, that rhythm was awesome! I didn't really know what I was doing on the drums, so I just kept time. People danced, so I figured everything was on target." After the show Hawkins gave Helm 15 bucks, "and I was in heaven," this drummer wrote.

"Stick with me," Hawkins advised Helm, "'cause this is just hamburger money. Soon we'll be fartin' through silk!"

In 1959 Morris Levy signed Hawkins to the New York label Roulette Records. This was his label until 1964. During that time the members of The Hawks were constantly changing, and eventually Ronnie brought in a young fan named Robbie Robertson, who started on bass guitar and went on to play rhythm guitar. Later Ronnie brought in Roy Buchanan to play lead guitar, and Robertson began studying Buchanan's guitar playing and became lead when Buchanan left the band. Richard Manuel then joined; Rick Danko and Garth Hudson, from London, Ontario followed soon after. The band now had two keyboards players: Manuel on piano and the classically trained Hudson on organ. Danko played bass guitar.

Hawkins made The Hawks practice for hours every day, and they played at clubs on Yonge Street in Toronto seven days a week. They played R&B-based rock 'n' roll heavily influenced by the sound of Chess Records in Chicago and Sun Records in Memphis. Helm said, "Ronnie Hawkins had molded us into the wildest, fiercest, speed-driven bar band in America." They played the music of Jerry Lee Lewis, Chuck Berry, and Bo Diddley, and "they knew they were good," said Hawkins. As Robbie Robertson recalled of those days, "It was a rowdy life. The places we played had tough audiences. They would throw things at you; they were rednecks. Fighting plays a big part in their life, you know—fighting and woman-stealing... We were all so young," Robertson continued. "We were 16, 17 years old at the time. We played in joints. That's what they were. Some of it was great, and some of it was scary, and some of it was horrible, and some of it was very valuable to us..." Yet Robertson feels the musicians took care of one another. "Instead of throwing a knapsack over your back and getting out on the highway to learn about life, we were able to do it together. We were protected by one another. We were secured by one another."

Hawkins also recalled, "When The Band was with me, they were getting offers from all kinds of people. They were happy. The world was their oyster then." Hawkins had rules for the band: No distracting girlfriends, no drinking on the job, and The Hawks eventually chafed under that type of control. They decided to go out on their own, and Ronnie put together another back-up band. The Hawks' lives were soon to change when opportunity reared its head.

In 1965, Dylan was ready for a change from folk and was about to shake up the music world. He wanted to put a rock 'n' roll band together to back him. Albert Grossman's receptionist, the Toronto-born Mary Martin knew the city's club scene, and she suggested he use members of a bar band that had been backing Ronnie Hawkins. "When they were playing a club down the street from me, the Friars Club, Dylan came in to watch a rehearsal. I didn't know that much about him," Hawkins said.

Getting back to his story, he said, "Dylan made The Hawks an offer," said Hawkins, "and the band told me how great he was. That was the time there were other acts breaking in Toronto: Ian and Sylvia, Neil Young. We had permanent gigs and Yonge Street was hot." According to interviews, Dylan was especially impressed by Robertson's guitar playing. Under the tutelage of Roy Buchanan and with all the steady work with The Hawks, Robertson had become a guitar virtuoso.

When The Hawks began playing with Dylan, Robertson has told interviewers that it was obvious that Bob had little experience playing with a band. Robertson said, "Dylan said he played with people like— he had a couple of names, strange names—Bobby Vee, but you could tell that he just didn't know very much about that." Yet Robertson said that Bob's lack of experience didn't hold either of them back; Bob approached each show "with quiet determination," even though he guessed correctly, according to Robertson, that the audience response would not be good because of the controversial electric part of the show. As biographer Robert Shelton noted, the booing that began at the Newport Folk Festival in July 1965 didn't stop there, but continued sporadically at Dylan's American concerts—with Robertson, et. al.— until October 1965. It continued during his world tour that spring.

When The Band went on their first tour to Europe with Dylan in 1966, their reception was mixed, as documentary footage in Martin Scorsese's film *No Direction Home* makes painfully clear. The folk stalwarts could not handle Dylan's conversion to rock 'n' roll, even though he still played half the concert with acoustic guitar. Helm quit halfway through the first tour of Europe and Australia because they were being booed. The sensitive Arkansas-born drummer couldn't take it, and took a break for about two years, working on an oil rigger in the Gulf of Mexico. Drummer Mickey Jones filled in for Helm, who rejoined the band after his break.

Robbie Robertson remembered, "That tour was a very strange process. You can hear the violence, and the dynamics in the music. We'd go from town to town, from country to country, and it was like a job. We set up, we played, they booed and threw things at us. Then we went to next town, played, they booed, threw things, and we left again. I remember thinking, 'This is a strange way to make a buck.'" Robertson also admitted that he gave Dylan credit for not getting rid of The Band. Robertson said, "He never once came to me and said, 'Robbie, this is not working.' The only reason tapes of those shows exist today is because we wanted to know, 'Are we crazy?' We'd go back to the hotel room, listen to a tape of the show and think, shit, that's not bad. Why is everybody so upset?" Jonathan Taplin, who produced *The Last Waltz* film with Martin Scorsese, was at the time the road manager for the tour. He remembers, "I had so much respect for the musicians, to go out and play night after night while being booed. Not to give up."

Dylan continued to break new ground, undeterred by criticism from the folk world. After the European tour The Band settled in Woodstock, N.Y. where Dylan had a home. When Hawkins visited his old friends at their houses in Woodstock, he saw how much Helm and Robertson respected Dylan. "Robbie told me Dylan has unbelievable lyrics," said Hawkins. He added that Dylan carried around one of those old-fashioned manual typewriters. "When Bob was with me, he liked to write everything down that I said. Levon told me: 'Bob is not a very good musician, but he writes as good as Shakespeare.'" Hawkins recalled in a deadpan way, "I said to him once, 'Nice melodies, Bob. Now I have to heckle you for your lyrics."

After his July 1966 motorcycle accident, Dylan cancelled concerts and found himself repeatedly having to justify his withdrawal from touring. He told *Newsweek* that after the accident, "I stared at the ceiling for a few months... I haven't been in retreat. I'm a country boy myself, and you have to be let alone to really accomplish anything." Later Dylan was able to tell reporters that the accident "in many ways... was good for me. It really slowed me down... touring had been such a pace to keep up. And I was getting in a rut." Robbie Robertson told the *Saturday Evening Post*, "We did it until we couldn't do it anymore... We were so exhausted that everyone said this was a time to rest."

That rest certainly did them a world of good. Woodstock in 1967 was a calm and creative time for The Band. Helm remembered that Dylan was turning out ten songs a week for months, many written at The Band's house, Big Pink. "Some of the songs... had been cowritten by Bob, Richard [Manuel], and Rick [Danko]," Helm said. "They had a typewriter set up in kitchen, and Bob might sit down and type a few lines. Then he'd wander off, and Richard would sit down and finish the verse." In this way, both Dylan and Rick Danko wrote "This Wheel's on Fire." Richard Manuel and Bob cowrote "Tears of Rage." Helm said that they played him some of these tapes, and he was astonished, saying, "I could barely believe the level of work they'd been putting out... The boys had also discovered how to write songs. Bob Dylan had opened it up for them."

The Band's music was reaching new heights. John Simon, who produced their first album, said that what was important about The Band was that "everybody played something that was meaningful and that meshed. There were hardly any solos, and nothing was gratuitous. The studio had four tracks. We recorded everyone live on two tracks. The horns—Garth on soprano, me on baritone—went on the third track, and the fourth was saved for vocals and tambourine." Reviewers noted that there was a collective, sincere sound to "the band" although it was made up of five distinct individual voices and instruments mixing folk, blues, gospel, R&B, classical, and rock 'n' roll. Critics felt their music was steeped in Americana and historical and mythic American imagery. Their songs were populated with characters like "Crazy Chester," "Young Anna Lee," "Luke," and "Carmen and the Devil," all based on friends from the past, especially from Helm's early years in Turkey Scratch, Arkansas. When the Band's first album *Music From Big Pink* was released in 1968, the public heard "a totally individualistic group," as Robert Shelton noted, not just the back-up band for a superstar. "The Band's music was played at humane volumes with an understated, almost diffident stagecraft. *Big Pink* took rock into serene pathways" the critic wrote. It was during this creative time that what Robertson called "a tape of a tape of a tape of a dub of a tape" slipped out and became Dylan's first bootleg album. The songs became part of what is now known as *The Basement Tapes*, which Columbia released in 1975. The Band's fast ascent into the upper reaches of the rock world was acknowledged by the polite and modest Garth Hudson, who noted who was responsible for their success. "We went from a bar band to the Royal Albert Hall because of Bob," Hudson said, "Any exaggeration would be an understatement when it comes to the help we got from Bob Dylan."

Rock critic Greil Marcus offered elegiac praise for The Band, whose sound in the late '60s was a departure from the over-electrified psychedelic sounds of the popular San Francisco bands like the Jefferson

Airplane, and whose return to country and folk roots conjured up nostalgia for a calmer, simpler America. Marcus said, "Their music gave us a sure sense that the country was richer than we had guessed, that it had possibilities we were only beginning to perceive. In the unique blend of instruments and good rhythms, in the shared and yet completely individual vocals, in the half-lost phrases and buried lyrics, there was an ambiguity that opened up the world with real force. The songs captured the yearning for home and the fact of displacement that ruled our lives; we thought that the Band's music was the most natural parallel to our hopes, ambitions, and doubts, and we were right to think so."

In the late '60s the members of The Band were becoming rich from tours with Dylan and new record deals negotiated by Albert Grossman, who became their manager. Hawkins urged them to take some of their newfound wealth and invest it. "I had begged them to buy that house, Big Pink, and they could have had it for $25,000," said Hawkins, who still maintained a fatherly protectiveness towards his younger friends. "They spent more than that on drugs... The worst thing is they had plenty of money at one time and wasted it all. If they had managed their affairs right, The Band would have been set for life. I begged Rick Danko to buy a house in Canada when I heard about 800 acres for sale. I suggested that he buy it and let his folks live in it until he was ready. He didn't," said Hawkins regretfully.

Hawkins recalled that time. "Bob was hot after The Band got with him... I remember a time they sold out Maple Leaf Gardens. I told them, 'If I had Bob Dylan playing rhythm in my band I'd sell out, too.'" Yet there was a down side to the new life in the fast lane. Hawkins pointed out, "When The Band got with Dylan, there was too much going on. Albert Grossman had a stable of superstars: Janis Joplin, Ian and Sylvia, Gordon Lightfoot. Then they moved to Malibu, and took everyone including their women and a camp of followers. When they went to Malibu, everything changed. Hollywood will change anybody. Drugs messed up so much. Their records were so great."

During the late '60s, of all the Band members, it was Robbie Robertson who was closest to Dylan, and who garnered his great respect. The late esteemed music critic Ralph J. Gleason offered some interesting insights into Dylan to biographer Robert Shelton. "He is a power figure, surrounded by satellites—Grossman, Neuwirth. The only person he can really believe is Robbie." Gleason also frequently compared Dylan to Miles Davis. "Both are little bantam roosters," Gleason said. "Seriously proud. Distrustful, on the surface, of the whole world.

Really aching to trust somebody. Sentimental, and filled with all sorts of good instincts, which they won't, for an instant, admit they have. If you ask Miles or Dylan a question, that's certainly not the way to get an answer. The only way I can have a rational relationship with Miles is to leave him alone. It's like winning the confidence of a scared puppy that has been mistreated. Patience is the only thing. You've got to demonstrate that you are not like all those other people that have been bugging him... You are never proven. You are always on trial."

During the late '60s, while the Band was moving in stellar rock circles, Hawkins was content to play clubs in Canada; he played the Coq D'Or on Yonge Street for 12 years, and another club for four years. He and Wanda had married in 1962 and they had a growing family, so Hawkins liked to stay close to home. "I came out here for adventure and chiseled out a circuit for myself from Windsor [Ontario] to Montreal. I got here before they played rockabilly," he recalled.

In 1974 Hawkins was on hand for Dylan and The Band's performances in Toronto and Montreal during Dylan's first tour in eight years. During the tour, Robbie Robertson talked with Ben Fong-Torres of *Rolling Stone* about Dylan's reception. Fong-Torres noted that the newspapers were saying that Dylan's audience wanted more than music, they wanted "The Word." "I don't understand that attitude," Robertson said. "I don't ever remember him ever delivering what they believed he delivered, or what they think he's going to deliver now... He certainly had a way of saying something that everybody felt, a way of phrasing it and condensing it down. But people have a fictitious past in mind about him." This tour set records among ticket buyers with all 40 shows very nearly sold out. With The Band's impeccable music backing him, Dylan played "Just Like Tom Thumb's Blues," "Ballad of a Thin Man," "The Times They Are A-Changin'," the Band's popular "The Weight," and the Dylan-penned "I Shall Be Released," among others.

To reach this level of musicianship, rehearsals began three months before the tour. Robertson said, "We sat down and played for four hours and ran over an incredible number of tunes. Just instantly. We would request tunes. Bob would ask us to play certain tunes of ours, and then we would do the same, then we'd think of some that we would particularly like to do. And when it was over, we said, 'That's it.'" Robertson said that, even while planning the tour, Dylan and the Band were nervous. "Not a real emotional nervousness, but also a physical endurance nervousness. Like Bob was saying, 'Shit, I haven't done anything in eight years. All of a sudden I'm going to go out there and hit it for 40 concerts?' We're not really outgoing people," Robertson admitted, "We're just not the kind of people that can say—'Sure, turn us loose.'"

They let concert promoter Bill Graham and David Geffen, chairman of Elektra Asylum Records [Dylan's label at the time], work out all the details. Despite Robertson and Dylan's case of nerves, anyone who saw that 1974 tour cannot easily forget it: The anticipation, the energy, the sterling choice of songs. Dylan even admitted to Fong-Torres that, during the past eight years, he had missed being onstage. "There's always those butterflies at a certain point," Dylan confessed, "but then there's the realization that the songs I'm singing mean as much to the people as to me; so it's just up to me to perform the best I can." Years later Bill Graham, recalling the 1974 tour, said, "Dylan had written most of those songs years earlier. The kids were now in the 30-year-old world listening to songs they had first heard when they were 15 and 16. It was a soulful experience because there was a lot of soulful remembrance going on. ... I have great respect for Springsteen. I have great respect for Jagger. But I have always thought Dylan was the ultimate performer of the ethereal kind. Different from Otis Redding. He just had such a profound effect on everybody. He communicated on as strong a level as I have ever seen an artist communicate with his fans."

After their Toronto concert, Dylan and The Band went to Nickelodeon, a casual, comfortable, eat-drink-and-dance place where Hawkins performed. There Hawkins entertained them with his mellow version of Dylan's "One Too Many Mornings" and as he was rolling through "Bo Diddley," Hawkins worked in a couple of verses of "The Ballad of Hollis Brown." Other post-concert parties in their hotel included Hawkins, his wife, and Gordon Lightfoot, among their many Canadian family members and friends.

In addition to being included in The Band's farewell concert in San Francisco during Thanksgiving of 1976, Hawkins was invited to join the Rolling Thunder Revue and be part of Dylan's film *Renaldo and Clara*. It was the film that Joan Baez had called "a monumentally silly project." *Renaldo and Clara* is partly a documentary of Dylan's fall 1975 performances of the Rolling Thunder Revue, which included musicians Roger McGuinn, Ronee Blakely, Ramblin' Jack Elliott, Baez, and others. Paul Williams noted in his book *Bob Dylan: The Middle Years* that shooting the movie occurred from October to December 1975. Dylan chose to work without a script, although he did have writers around to generate ideas—writers like Allen Ginsberg and Sam Shephard. These writers and the professional actors who were brought in—Harry Dean

Stanton, Helena Kallianiotes, Ruth Trangiel—had no idea what was expected of them. Dylan was the director and he worked intuitively.

Hawkins recalled his experience on the shoot in New York. "When Bob came in they were filming with more crew and lights than Cecil B. DeMille. One day the camera crews woke me up at 3 a.m. They said, 'Ronnie, we're gonna shoot now.' I asked for the script. 'There's no script. We're gonna wing it.' I was to play Bob Dylan. My line was to talk this young girl into going to the motel room with him. It was wild." As Hawkins soon found out, most of the dialogue and dramatic situations in the film are improvised, with perhaps a little guidance. (For instance: "I want you to be a rock 'n' roller trying to convince this girl to be your companion for a six-week tour, and I want you to insist that he should come live on the farm instead, and anyway you can't go without Daddy's approval. Say whatever you want, but be sure to mention the following things: God, marriage, Daddy, rock 'n' roll, good times, and the end of the world.")

In *Renaldo and Clara,* Hawkins used some smooth persuasion on a lovely, young brunette, trying to convince her to spend time with him and go on the road with him. "Rock 'n' roll is the answer," Hawkins softly said in his Southern drawl. "Live fast, love hard, and die young." While making the film Hawkins got a taste of how Dylan did business, too. "I would have done the film for nothing. All the people on the Rolling Thunder Revue were supposed to sign something. I forgot to sign the clearance. Then this lawyer calls me and is carrying on, saying, 'You've gotta do this, do that.' The lawyer pissed me off so I said,' Take me out of this!'"

Five minutes later, Dylan called Hawkins himself. "He acted as if he didn't know this guy had called. He said, 'We need you to sign this. You're going to get $25,000.' I came out to L.A. and signed it. Bob put me up at Beverly Hills Hotel, with an eight-door limousine at my disposal... big time. I had two of the biggest mooches in the world with me: Garth Hudson and Mack [Dr. John] Rebannack. But we had a lot of fun."

Hawkins recalled this time with a touch of irreverence. "Bob played in the Rolling Thunder Revue with white paint on his face... He was acting like he didn't want to be noticed. I said, 'If you wash your face and put some decent clothes on, no one will notice you.'" Hawkins doesn't quite understand what he called, "Dylan acting weird, putting white paint on his face. If I dressed up as a clown people would stare at me, too. But he's a genius. Maybe he's putting people on, getting even."

Hawkins may have a point. With all the references to masks and clowns in *Renaldo and Clara*. Dylan seemed to be emphasizing that life is a cabaret and we are all here just playing roles, some comical, some confusing. He was conjuring up Italy's *commedia dell' arte*, its traveling actors. The French singer Charles Aznavour talked about these actors when he introduced one of his signature songs, "Les Comédiens," explaining that "comédiens" is French for actors, and these were performers who went from place to place, from one public square to another, performing in the towns. *Renaldo and Clara* was not a commercial or critical success; it was too dense and long for an audience to follow it. The critics were harsh. Pauline Kael, writing in *The New Yorker,* said that "despite all his masks and camouflage" Dylan is "still the same surly, mystic tease... more tight close-ups than any actor can have had in the whole history of movies. He's overpoweringly present, yet he is never in direct contact with us... We are invited to stare... to perceive the mystery of his elusiveness—his distance."

In 1979 when Dylan released *Slow Train Coming* and was in the middle of his born-again Christian phase, Hawkins went to one of his concerts. "The music was good. I said next tour he's gonna tour as a Communist," chortled Hawkins. "He was hipped up, trying anything. His concerts can be the best you've ever heard, and the worst. With his Christian phase, I loved the gospel back-up singers, great singers [Regina Havis, Helena Springs and Mona Lisa Young]."

Hawkins has also witnessed Dylan's impression of people who don't know him well. "I've been at parties with all these big stars: Jack Nicholson and all. Dylan walks in, and you'd think Jesus walked in ... the atmosphere changes. I'm sure surprised he's still hot. It's a miracle." As for Hawkins' opinion about why Dylan keeps performing, he said, "He likes the action. He likes to show off... like I do. It's his life. And he's makin' history." Hawkins is used to the idiosyncrasies of talented performers. "Kris Kristofferson had to be tricked to do his first album, they told him it was a demo. He had stage fright," said Hawkins, who first met Kristofferson when Kris was playing folk houses in Toronto early in the singer/songwriter's career.

While Dylan's career has extended with astonishing longevity, The Band's later years offer a stark contrast. Several members' lives were severely affected by the excesses of drinking and drugs. Looking back, Hawkins was sad to see The Band break up in 1976, but admitted, "Robbie put up with it a lot longer than I would have. Richard and Rick were out of control. Richard was drinking a bottle of Scotch a day for

13 to 14 years. Ricky later on got heavily into drugs." In March 1986, The Band—without Robbie Robertson—were on a tour playing relatively small clubs in Florida. "A lot of traveling and not much dignity," recalled Helm in his book. On the tour Richard Manuel committed suicide, hanging himself from a shower rod with his belt wrapped around his neck. His fellow musicians, who had endured 25 years of rock 'n' roll's good and bad times with him, were devastated. In December 1999, Rick Danko died in his sleep at home. He had had a heartbreaking heroin habit and was overweight and ill for months before he passed away, although he had been working steadily, out of necessity.

Since 1976, when Robertson broke up The Band to pursue a film career, Hawkins admitted that the handsome, intelligent musician has not had the big career as a film star to which he aspired. He has done well, however, producing music for film scores. "Robbie is a writer. He's now in his 60s, and when you're in your 60s you mellow out. He still absorbs knowledge like a sponge. He knows nine more words than Webster. He is self-educated—has read every book out," said Hawkins with admiration. "I had told him, 'Learn all you can and look after yourself.' He absorbed a lot of business knowledge from Albert Grossman. I said to him once, 'Robbie, I hope you didn't trade your Telecaster for that Armenian suit.' A pun on Armani."

Hawkins has stayed in closer touch with his lifelong fellow Arkansawyer Levon Helm, saying, "Levon is doing well. He has recovered from throat cancer." Helm still lives in Woodstock. Once or twice a month at his home studio, he plays host to the "Midnight Ramble," a night of music played by blues and country singers. Some of the musicians who gather might include Emmylou Harris, blues-harp blower Little Sammy Davis, and former Dylan guitarist Larry Campbell. "Guests pay $100 to cover overhead expenses, and they have a party and Arkansas barbecue," said Hawkins. He admitted that Helm is "still mad about The Band … He thought he should have gotten more credit and money from songwriting. Early on Levon was the boss of The Band; he did everything. He was a gifted musician. There was a streak of redneck in him. But then Robbie took over because no one else was up early in the morning to go to meetings."

Arkansas folks tend to be loyal friends. When Bill Clinton was elected President in 1992, The Band, Ronnie Hawkins, and Dylan were invited to provide entertainment for the "Blue Jeans Bash," an unofficial inauguration barbecue for 2,500 Arkansawyers and Clinton's campaign staff. Hawkins tore the place apart with his familiar Bo Diddley tune, "Who Do You Love?"

During that period, Dylan was prone to wearing a hooded sweatshirt and sunglasses. Despite Dylan's attire, the Washington crowd loved hearing Dylan and The Band play "To Be Alone With You" and then end their set with "I Shall Be Released." Others have mentioned that Dylan looked strange when he performed in a hooded sweatshirt with the hood over his head. "I've seen it," said Hawkins. "When you go to a movie with him, he shifts seats all the time." From the many times Hawkins had been around Dylan, he said, "He was quiet... He's like a chameleon, he changes personality."

Hawkins has befriended many notables in his years in rock 'n' roll, yet he has held his relationship with President Bill Clinton in special regard. Hawkins first met the former President in the early '70s, when he was teaching law at the University of Arkansas. "When Bill became Governor he had a security detail with shoulder-length hair," Hawkins recalled. "I had never seen that before."

Hawkins couldn't resist recounting one of his favorite stories about President Clinton. In 2003 and 2004, Hawkins was very ill with pancreatic cancer, and doctors did not hold out much hope for him. His friends around the country rallied around and held parties for him in Los Angeles and Toronto. After one party hosted by producer David Foster in Toronto, Hawkins and a handful of friends were relaxing in their hotel suite, smoking pot and shooting the breeze. The phone rang, and a man said, "The President is in the lobby. Do you mind if he comes up?" "Nope," Hawkins said, "just give us a few minutes."

Hurriedly, Hawkins recalled, his friends opened the windows and aired the place, hiding the stash and any other reminders of their partying. When Clinton and his security detail came up to the suite, the good ole boys had a welcoming get-together. As Hawkins told it, "After a while Clinton said, 'Can I use your restroom?' I pointed to it, and he was gone for 5 or 10 minutes. I started to worry. I remembered all the feel-good potions I had near my bedside, in addition to the drugs I was taking for my illness. But eventually Clinton came back in the room. He chatted with everyone and then had to leave. I went back into my bedroom, and there, under my pill bottles was a note from him with all of his phone numbers: Little Rock, Harlem, all of them."

A few hours after this interview, Hawkins was on stage again at Ontario's Havelock Country Music Festival in front of several thousand fans, performing his old standbys like "Mary Lou," Carl Perkins' "Honey Don't," and "Forty Days." "He's got the best band I've seen during this entire three-day festival!" said one audience member. Hawkins still had his magic: He could work the crowd; he knew how to make a personal connection; he sang upbeat songs with passion and downhome fervor. After his set and a couple of encores, festival attendants whisked him away to an autograph area. Hawkins didn't admit to being tired, but cracked with his trademark humor, "Hell, this was fun 30 or 40 years ago!"

Is this the way a rockabilly legend spends his golden years? Hawkins recalled that Bob Dylan had once said, "Ronnie Hawkins discovered America and everyone in it." "Yeah," Hawkins cracked, "and if I ever get a job I'm gonna ask for a raise."

ROSANNE CASH

Retna, Inc.

*J*ohnny Cash started corresponding with Dylan after being blown away by his album The Freewheelin' Bob Dylan *in 1963. Later that summer 22-year-old Dylan first met Cash at the Newport Folk Festival. Dylan loved the music of this wide-ly respected country singer of hits like "Folsom Prison Blues," and "I Walk the Line." When they finally got together, Bob and Johnny were so happy that—together with Joan Baez and June Carter—they jumped up and down on the bed in Cash's motel room, "like kids," as Cash described it. Their friendship lasted almost 40 years until Cash's death in 2003.*

Rosanne Cash, the eldest daughter of Johnny Cash and his first wife, Vivian Liberto, was only 14 years old when her father and Dylan recorded songs for Nashville Skyline *together in 1969, six years after they met, but she was already steeped in music enough to be thrilled at the prospect of these two artists recording together.*

Rosanne was born May 24, 1955 in Memphis. [She shares a Gemini birth day with Dylan; he was born in 1941.] She grew up in

Los Angeles and lived there with her mother after her parents divorced in 1966. As a child, her ambition was to become a writer; she wanted to write songs rather than perform and sing them. When she graduated from high school, she joined her father's road show and over a three-year period moved from backup singing to being an occasional soloist. After spending her twenties in Nashville, L.A., and London, she recorded her debut album in 1978. It was produced by Texas singer/songwriter Rodney Crowell. She returned home to Nashville from London and was signed to CBS, the same label her father recorded on. In 1979 her first CBS album, Right or Wrong, *was released. The album included three hits: "No Memories Hangin' Around" (a duet with Bobby Bare), "Couldn't Do Nothin' Right," and "Take Me, Take Me." Crowell, whom Rosanne married in 1979, also produced this album.*

Her follow-up, Seven Year Ache, *was released in 1981. Again produced by Crowell, the album went Gold, reaching the Top 30 of the U.S. pop chart. The title track, which Cash wrote, became the first of eleven Number One country hits for her and remains her signature song. Her beautiful, aching, deep, and sultry voice has a distinctive and unforgettable quality. Since her debut in 1978, Cash has released 12 country-pop albums. She has blurred the line between country, pop, and rock. Critics have hailed her warm vocal style and artistry. The* Dallas Morning News *has said, "Rosanne Cash has one of those familiar voices. The warm, slightly husky tone, the soulful expressiveness, and the earthy delivery of intelligent, accessible lyrics. Her pipes are like old friends. It doesn't matter how long it's been since you've seen each other, you reconnect immediately."*

In addition to writing, recording, and performing songs, Cash has published a short story collection called Bodies of Water *(Hyperion Books, 1996). She has also published a children's book,* Penelope Jane: A Fairy's Tale *(HarperCollins 2000). Her essays and fiction have appeared in the* New York Times, Rolling Stone, New York, *and various other periodicals and collections.*

Her marriage to Rodney Crowell ended in 1992. She has three daughters from that union: Caitlin, Chelsea, and Carrie. In 1995, she married producer and guitarist John Leventhal. They have a son, Jake, who was born in 1999. They make their home in New York City.

Over lunch at a Chelsea restaurant near her New York home, Rosanne talked about Bob Dylan's long and loyal friendship with her father and also spoke about him from the perspective of a singer/song-

writer. She wore a maroon beret over her shoulder-length brown hair,
a gray dress trimmed with black, and black boots. Her hands, which
moved excitedly as she talked, bore beautiful rings; a large antique
diamond sparkled on her left hand.

In the Scorsese documentary *No Direction Home*, Dylan's old friend
Bob Neuwirth said that Johnny Cash gave Dylan a guitar when they
first met. He noted that there is a tradition in country music that when
an older singer gives a younger singer a guitar, it's like passing on a legacy. "My Dad gave a lot of guitars to a lot of young musicians. I never
heard it put that way, that literally, but I'm sure that's the undercurrent
of it. Dad and Bob loved each other. Do you know Bob's quote about
my father? 'Johnny Cash was like the North Star. You could guide your
ship by him,'" Rosanne said with a smile.

"My father and Bob's correspondence spanned many years," she
added. "My brother [John Carter Cash] has all of the letters. Although
I am very interested in this history, I have not read the letters. We would
never publish them without calling Bob. We can't do anything like that
until my father's estate is settled. I think the letters are about songs
because that's where they met."

It is easy to understand why Dylan respected Johnny Cash. With a
strong, seemingly gruff exterior, Cash was a product of a Depression
childhood on an Ozarks farm, but he was also an intelligent, honest,
and uncompromising individual who straddled several music worlds. In
his autobiography, Johnny Cash recalled that he was deeply into folk
music in the early '60s, both the authentic songs and the new "folk
revival" songs of the time, so he took note of the young folksinger as
soon as the *Bob Dylan* album came out in early '62. In 1963, he listened
almost constantly to *The Freewheelin'* album. Cash had a portable record
player that he would take along on the road, and he would put on
Freewheelin' backstage, then go out and do his show, then listen again as
soon as he came off. "After a while after that, I wrote Bob a letter telling
him how much of a fan I was. He wrote back almost immediately, saying he'd been following my music since 'I Walk the Line,' and so we
began a correspondence," Cash wrote in his book, *Cash: The*
Autobiography. "Mostly it was about music: What we ourselves were
doing, what other people were doing, what I knew about so-and-so and
he didn't and vice versa. He asked me about country people; I asked him
about the circles he moved in."

Later, Johnny Cash described a visit he and his wife June Carter Cash made to Woodstock to see Dylan. Ramblin' Jack Elliott drove them up from New York City. They stayed at Albert Grossman's house, and, the elder Cash remembered, "Bob and I, and whoever else was around, were indulging ourselves in lots of guitar picking and song trading. There's nothing on earth I like better than song trading with a friend or a circle of them, except perhaps doing it with my family." Johnny Cash also heaped praise on *The Freewheelin' Bob Dylan* years after its release. "I have to say it's still one of my all-time favorite albums. If I had to answer that old but still interesting question, 'What music would you want with you if you were stranded on a desert island?' I'd say that *Freewheelin'* would have to be on the list."

The 1969 collaboration between Johnny Cash and Dylan on *Nashville Skyline* came about in a rather accidental way. Dylan had been asked to write a song for John Schlesinger's film *Midnight Cowboy* and he wrote "Lay, Lady, Lay." Dylan did not deliver it in time, so instead Schlesinger used Fred Neil's song "Everybody's Talkin.'" Dylan might have let "Lay, Lady, Lay" stay buried, but at the urging of his record producer Bob Johnston and Columbia Records executive Clive Davis, it was included on *Nashville Skyline*. Davis also wanted it released as a single, and in the summer of 1969 it stayed in the Top 40 for eleven weeks.

During the time Dylan was in Nashville recording *Nashville Skyline*, Johnny Cash was at the same studio working on his own album. On the spur of the moment, the friends decided to record together. They recorded about 18 songs, both playing acoustic and using members of Cash's band. Only one of their duets was released on *Nashville Skyline*, a rough-hewn version of "Girl of the North Country," yet one of the most enduring and distinctive features of the album was that it planted in the public's mind the image of two musical legends performing together: Cash and Dylan. As Kristofferson said, "Dylan brought respectability to country music [by performing with Cash]." The flavor of *Nashville Skyline* also brought rock fans over to country.

That May, Dylan overcame his nervousness about TV to appear on the debut of Cash's ABC TV show, which was recorded live at Nashville's Ryman Auditorium, the home of the Grand Ole Opry. There was heavy security around the TV taping, and the show's executive producer, Bill Carruthers, said at the time of the taping, "Bob wouldn't do this unless John had asked him to… Bob was the center of attraction, and he hates it—just hates it. He said to me yesterday, 'Please, no photographers, because I look bad.' Well, he doesn't. Bob looks healthy and suntanned and wants to wear a suit and a tie on the show. … He's such a deep little guy you can tell the moment he's upset because there's a little twitch in his eye or lip." Joni Mitchell was also a guest on the show and she said, "Sometimes the most frightening thing is when everyone loves you too much… Dylan's such a sensitive guy…He used to be better off when he was younger and an angry young man… He would scream at you and diminish you if he thought your questions were stupid or unartistic. Now he knows he can't be an angry young kid anymore. He can't growl. Instead, he stays silent and explodes inside. Instead of taking it out on you, he takes it out internally."

Although it is clear that Dylan had great respect for Johnny Cash, which comes across both in "Girl of the North Country" and scenes from the TV show they did together, Rosanne noted, "My father didn't see himself as the elder statesman. " [In fact, Cash was only nine years older than Dylan.] "He felt like a contemporary of Dylan's, a peer, an equal. They saw themselves doing much the same thing. Bob was as deeply steeped in country music as my father was. His lexicon was also the Carter Family, Hank Williams, folk, the blues—there are no differences there. I don't think my father could have come up with a song that Bob didn't know or vice versa."

Although her father passed on to her a respect for country music and its range, Rosanne did not originally set her sights on becoming a performer. "I wanted to write songs and didn't care about performing, so it's strange that I ended up where I am." When she was starting out, Rosanne said, "My Dad gave me a list of '100 Essential Country Songs' and he said that to be his daughter I had to learn these songs. I went through the list and learned them all. They included a wide variety, from Appalachian tunes to the Woody Guthrie protest songs to history ballads like 'The Battle of New Orleans.' There were songs on the list by Hank Williams and Roy Acuff."

As a musician, Rosanne has always taken inspiration from Dylan. "As a songwriter, the guy is amazing. I definitely studied his songs. I had his *Lyrics* book and went over those songs. I studied how he changed from first person to third person in some songs. It always puzzled me why he did that. Perhaps in changing to the third person he made the song more universal as a songwriter. His work has resonated with me." Using a writer's gift for metaphor, she added, "Dylan has been the cradle I became a songwriter in. He created the playground."

What fascinated her was "the beautiful complexity of his images. He uses very specific images and melds them into his melody so that it all sounds like first inspiration. The greatest artists do that. The song feels like they reflect your own life back to you. It might be their use of an old image in a tune or chords you wouldn't necessarily hear together. I always appreciated that Dylan didn't talk about his songs or explain them. He didn't pre-empt the listener's experience. We want to bring our own life to each song, right?"

Summing up Dylan's originality, she said, "There was no one else like him. There's very few prototypical artists around. My Dad was one, Dylan is one. Frank Sinatra, as great as he was, wasn't one because he came from a great tradition. He was an interpreter." Rosanne continued to emphasize Dylan's influential role. "G.E. Smith lives in my building, and we were talking about the Scorsese film on Dylan. We were so excited by it. We think Dylan is so inspiring and such an important reference point."

While Rosanne did not remember when she first met Dylan, she recalled performing with him in 1992 at the David Letterman 10th Anniversary Special. "Bob played 'Like a Rolling Stone' and Chrissie Hynde, Carole King, Mavis Staples, Emmylou Harris, Michelle Shocked, and I sang back-up. That was so much fun!" Rosanne, Johnny Cash, and June Carter Cash all performed at Madison Square Garden in the fall of 1992 at the Bob Dylan 30th Anniversary Concert, which was recorded on video and CD. "Dylan's office called me and said they wanted me to do a song with Chapin [Mary Chapin-Carpenter] and Shawn [Colvin]. They asked us what song we wanted to do. I suggested 'Sweetheart Like You' but Tom [Petty] was doing it, so we settled on 'You Ain't Goin' Nowhere.'" There were a few days of rehearsals before the event. "It was a big deal. The night of the concert I was terrified until I got onstage, and then I was so happy," Rosanne recalled enthusiastically. "It was one of those transcendent moments when everything is working and you don't want it to end. And it was over like that!" The ebullient performance by Rosanne, Mary Chapin-Carpenter, and Shawn Colvin that was caught on video conveyed that happiness. Rosanne recalled that after the performance, "There was a lot going on backstage because of the Sinéad O'Connor thing." O'Connor had made some ill-received political comments and was booed off the stage. "After she was booed, she threw up backstage. A lot of women were sharing a dressing room—Sinéad, Sheryl Crow was singing back-up to Sinead, this was before her career began; Sophie B. Hawkins was there. A lot of women and a lot of drama in there."

Backstage at the Garden that night Rosanne was asked to come by Dylan's dressing room to say hello. "I think he was flirting a little bit," she said shyly and quietly, a twinkle in her eye. "I was so nervous about the gig. I was almost 40, but I felt like 12. Then I found my Dad, and I said 'I think Bob likes me.' And my Dad said," and she affected a deep baritone, "'Oh, I know he does!' It was a sweet moment. Bob was being nice."

She added another vivid memory. "Dylan showed up at my house one time. Bob called me when I was living on Mercer Street in SoHo. This was about '92 or '93. He said something about an acoustic set he had to do and how would I like to sing backup? He asked if we could we get together, so I said 'How about Tuesday?' and he said, 'How about right now?'" She laughed her throaty laugh, recalling his spontaneity. When Dylan came to her apartment, "He played a lot of really obscure songs, most of them I did not know. I couldn't really tell what to do. So I was sitting there enjoying it, and occasionally I'd throw in a harmony. Then my nanny came in with my daughter and her jaw dropped. There's Bob Dylan in my living room." Rosanne concluded the anecdote by adding that she never got together with Dylan for a gig. "It was so funny, but nothing came of it," she recalled. "I saw him a couple of times after that, and he was always incredibly sweet to me."

Like others, Rosanne has great respect for the way Dylan has conducted himself throughout his long career, especially handling sensitive moments such as an uncomprehending media in the mid-'60's and being booed on his European tour. The Scorsese documentary showed Dylan in the early '60s, being grilled by the press about his music. "The press couldn't get Dylan," Rosanne said. "His contact with the press was almost torturous, so much of the experience involves a visceral feeling; you get inspiration from his art that rings of truth."

Rosanne was also affected by the film's footage of Dylan being booed in the U.K. in 1966 after he went electric. "That whole period was essential to his development as an artist; to run up against disapproval… this was really important for him. It happened at a formative time in his life and career. I'm sure he has no bitterness about it." In the film, people were booing songs from *Blonde on Blonde* and *Highway 61 Revisited,* two of Dylan's greatest albums. "They looked like idiots," she sighed of his detractors.

While there was a critical backlash to Dylan's explorations of different genres—for example, when he recorded the Christian-influenced *Slow Train Coming* and *Saved*—Rosanne said, "I didn't care. What I cared about was the songs. He wrote 'Gotta Serve Somebody' during that time, which is one of his greatest songs. I thought, 'Okay, this excursion is worthwhile… Here's the song he got out of it.'"

As for her father's attitudes about Dylan's Christian forays, Rosanne says, "My father never judged him. He would never judge anybody, especially not someone on a spiritual quest." She mentioned Cash's own disaffection with Nashville and the country-music pressures he had to undergo. "My father was from Arkansas, not Nashville. He started his career in Memphis and then lived in Nashville, but he was not from that scene. My father wasn't part of that Nashville community. Five years before his death, he took out a full-page ad in *Billboard* of himself giving the finger to the entire Nashville music industry. He wasn't part of it. They didn't get him." Rosanne recalled an illustrative example of the disconnect between her father and the Nashville music business. "One time my Dad kicked in all the footlights at the Opry and got disinvited from returning. He was a rebel." This rebellious streak in Cash can also shed light on the Dylan-Cash friendship. Both were very much their own men, not following a trend or feeling they needed to belong to a certain part of the industry, either country music or folk music. Each man wanted to be free to be himself.

As Johnny Cash said about his own musical style, "The way we did it was honest. We played it and sang it the way we felt it, and there's a whole lot to be said for that."

In addition to being influenced by Dylan in her songwriting, Rosanne added, "I was influenced by Lennon-McCartney, Don Gibson, and Hank Williams, my Dad of course, Ray Charles. In my teens I loved the Southern California sound: Buffalo Springfield, Elton John, Jackson Browne, Steve Winwood, The Byrds." Part of Rosanne's interest in these artists was their lyrical expertise. It is an art form she considers worth preserving. "Several years ago I edited this book called *Songs Without Rhyme*. It included 13 songwriters writing prose. They each took a line from one of their songs and wrote a short story around it. Tough going but the end result was great. In the foreword I said that my fear is that great songwriting is going to become an arcane folk art, like divining water with a stick. So much in music is about the image now." *Songs Without Rhyme* included prose pieces by David Byrne, Johnny Cash, Shawn Colvin, Rosanne, and others.

When Rosanne began her career, she had some preconceptions about fame, based on her father's problems with drugs in the 1960s. When Johnny Cash's career began to take off, he became addicted to amphetamines and barbiturates. He shared a Nashville apartment with Waylon Jennings, who was also addicted to amphetamines. She once said, "Fame is the worse thing." She added, "That was what came to mind to me. Fame made you go on drugs, stay on the road all the time, and disrupt your family. It's not necessarily the correct connection, but it's the one I made."

Throughout her career, Rosanne felt that she never wanted to "use" her father. "That was my default position for my entire career. I wanted to be judged for myself, not for my father. It was the background noise of my career, but my Dad was very respectful of my wish to be independent," she admitted. She can understand some of the challenges that have confronted Jakob Dylan, Bob's son. "I think it's a lot harder for Jakob. I'm not a boy. But Jakob is so good. He has retained his dignity, detachment, and patience with it," she observed.

Her attitude about fame also helped her understand Dylan's withdrawal in 1966 after his motorcycle accident. "I understand it and admire it. It was essential. Great fame destroys people. If it doesn't destroy you, a lot of the times it destroys your art. You become addicted to preserving that level of fame that made you famous and start doing parodies of yourself... replicating what you did before. Dylan never did that and my Dad didn't either. I admire that so much. It's like Matisse creating the 'Jazz Dancers' when he was in his eighties. He kept opening up to that sense of the truth and creative energy."

For his part, Johnny Cash's attitude towards Rosanne was one of great fatherly pride. In his autobiography he noted of his six daughters, "Rosanne is my oldest. She's famous, and justly so. As a matter of fact, she's had as many Number One country hits as I have. She's a great singer and a great writer of songs, fiction, journalism, and poetry. Her first book of stories, *Bodies of Water*, got a wonderful review in The *New York Times*, and in *The Illustrated History of Country Music* it says that her music is 'an *auteur* odyssey, a chronicle of songs taken directly from her own life and feelings with very few holds barred, for which there isn't a parallel in modern Nashville.'" Her father also applauded her move from Nashville to New York. "She belongs in a bigger, more cosmopolitan creative community," he once said.

With fatherly insight, Cash continued, "Sometimes I call Rosanne 'the Brain.' She and I operate on much the same wavelength, so there's always been a special closeness between us. It's not a matter of deeper love (or hurt) than between me and the other girls; it's more like a greater degree of instinctive understanding." One of their traditions was to do book-swapping; Rosanne would scout books that she enjoyed and share them with her father.

Rosanne is not the only offspring of Johnny Cash to follow his footsteps into the music business. Her brother John Carter Cash is a musician and record producer. She has three sisters who are not in the business, but her stepsister Carlene Carter is a country singer. Carlene is the daughter of June Carter Cash. [June's other daughter, Rozanna Adams, died in 2003.]

Rosanne's own daughters are following into the family business as well. Her 26-year-old daughter Caitlin runs a record label, and 24-year-old Chelsea is a songwriter. "Chelsea called me recently and asked, 'Mom, how do I become a successful musician without becoming famous?'" Rosanne threw her head back and laughed her throaty laugh. "I said to her, 'I've been asking that question my whole life!'"

The singer/songwriter also lightly brushed off comments that she has achieved a lot by raising a big family while becoming successful in her career. There are many women who feel they can't do both. "Then they can't," said Rosanne emphatically. "You absolutely can have children and have a successful career. Do I believe you can have it all? No. You have to make choices. Maybe you can have it all at 22 but not at 50." She conceded that living in New York makes a lot of it easier: Everything is close, and she doesn't have to drive everywhere as she would in other cities. More than the convenience, however, Rosanne feels very appreciative of the rich culture of the city. "The most important thing to me about New York is the network of really creative people. The other night I was at a dinner party, and everyone sat around singing songs. Ethan Hawke was there singing one of his songs. I haven't done that since the '70s. It was so fantastic."

In the fall of 2005, the film *Walk the Line* about her father's life was released. Rosanne's sister Kathy publicly expressed her displeasure, if not disgust, at the portrait of their mother Vivian Liberto as a weak, demanding shrew, but Rosanne had another take on it. "My mother didn't want a public life. She didn't enjoy it," she said. Her mother died on Rosanne's birthday in 2005. She had been what Rosanne called, "a force of nature, incredibly strong. Mothering was her life. She made chocolates, sewed, was the president of her garden club, and had a wide circle of friends. [She had] a beautiful spirit." Rosanne concluded that the movie didn't help correct the public's misconception about her late mother. It was with a great deal of reluctance that Rosanne saw the film. "I've been avoiding it. There's no reason for me to relive the disintegration of my nuclear family and my father's drug addiction." It was her 17-year-old daughter who helped her put the movie in perspective. Her daughter said, "'Mom, that was a pretty good story.' I let it go at that," Rosanne concluded.

Rosanne also reflected on the complexity of father-daughter relationships in an interview with Jim Fusilli for the *Wall Street Journal* in 2005.

She confessed, "I took great pride in being a dutiful daughter and doing the things I was supposed to do. But I look back and think, 'Why didn't I share more when I was younger? Why didn't I let him in? Why was I so difficult?'"

Her lifelong desire for independence from her father's career also made Rosanne wary of recording a duet with him, but it was her husband, John Leventhal, who persuaded her to record the moving "September When It Comes" with the ailing Cash in 2002. The song, which Rosanne wrote, is about facing one's mortality, "about living with what is unresolved in your own heart," she said. "At first, I didn't want to do the duet. I thought it might be too intense because of the subject matter and also because my relationship with my father was so precious, I didn't want anyone to think it was a gimmick. Then John kept after me. He said, "It's this song... think about it." The results are a beautiful and poignant reflection on life and its inevitable endings. It was released on her 2003 album *Rules of Travel*.

After several years of ill health, her father passed away in September of that year [2003] at the age of 71 from complications from diabetes. His death came four months after that of his wife, June Carter Cash, who died in May from complications following heart-valve surgery. Rosanne's latest CD, *Black Cadillac*, also reflected the fact that in a short two-year period she lost both her parents and her stepmother. Alan Light in the *New York Times* wrote: "With her characteristic sense of craft and precision, Ms. Cash explores a kaleidoscopic range of experiences related to loss and mortality on *Black Cadillac*, reaching from when her parents first met through her responses to their passing, her anger, her regrets." Light wrote that the CD "flows effortlessly from intimate acoustic moments to bluegrass-inflected songs like 'House on the Lake,' mirroring the scope and ambition of the lyrics.'"

Since Rosanne long ago established herself as a talented singer respected in her own right, her fears about riding on her father's coat-tails can now be replaced by a gentler sense of pride at carrying on his legacy. In the *New York Times,* in 2005, Stephen Holden noted of Rosanne's music, "the same qualities that distinguish her father's songs are embedded, though softened, in her own: Her plainspoken tunes, some with country-blues echoes, stay close to the dusty ground." Noting the highlights of a recent performance, Holden added, "It was in three of her vintage songs, 'Blue Moon With Heartache,' 'Seven Year Ache,' and 'The Wheel' that her alchemy of folk, country, and soft rock fused into gold."

Postscript: Dylan on Remembering Johnny Cash

This personal reminiscence of Rosanne's father, Johnny Cash, by Bob Dylan first appeared in Rolling Stone, *October 16, 2003 shortly after Cash's death. It was among the accolades offered by many in the music business about the late country singer.*

Dylan: I was asked to give a statement on Johnny's passing and thought about writing a piece instead called "Cash Is King" because that is the way I really feel. In plain terms, Johnny was and is the North Star; you could guide your ship by him—the greatest of the greats then and now. I first met him in '62 or '63 and saw him a lot in those years. Not so much recently, but in some kind of way he was with me more than people I see every day.

There wasn't much music media in the early Sixties and *Sing Out!* was the magazine covering all things folk in character. The editors had published a letter chastising me for the direction my music was going. Johnny wrote the magazine back an open letter telling the editors to shut up and let me sing, that I knew what I was doing. This was before I had ever met him, and the letter meant the world to me. I've kept the magazine to this day.

Of course, I knew of him before he ever heard of me. In '55 or '56, "I Walk the Line" played all summer on the radio, and it was different from anything else you had ever heard. The record sounded like a voice from the middle of the earth. It was so powerful and moving. It was profound, and so was the tone of it, every line; deep and rich, awesome and mysterious all at once. "I Walk the Line" had a monumental presence and a certain type of majesty that was humbling. Even a simple line like, "I find it very, very easy to be true" can take your measure. We can remember that and see how far we fall short of it.

Johnny wrote thousands of lines like that. Truly he is what the land and country is all about, the heart and soul of it personified and what it means to be here; and he said it all in plain English. I think we can have recollections of him, but we can't define him any more than we can define a fountain of truth, light and beauty. If we want to know what it means to be mortal, we need look no further than the Man in Black. Blessed with a profound imagination, he used the gift to express all the various lost causes of the human soul. This is a miraculous and humbling thing. Listen to him, and he always brings you to your senses. He rises high above all, and he'll never die or be forgotten, even by persons not born yet—especially those persons—and that is forever.

Cash Tribute reporting by Anthony DeCurtis, Matt Diehl, Austin Scaggs and David Wild.

ON THE ROAD TO REINVENTION
1980–2006

BRUCE SPRINGSTEEN

*" **T**he first time I heard Bob Dylan, I was in the car with my mother listening to WMCA, and on came that snare shot that sounded like somebody'd kicked open the door to your mind," said Bruce Springsteen in 1988 at the induction of Bob Dylan into the Rock and Roll Hall of Fame. "'Like a Rolling Stone.' My mother, she was no stiff with rock 'n' roll, she liked the music, sat there for a minute, then looked at me and said, 'That guy can't sing.' But I knew she was wrong. I sat there and I didn't say nothing, but I knew that I was listening to the toughest voice that I had ever heard. It was lean and it sounded somehow simultaneously young and adult." Springsteen ran out and bought the single, but the factory had mistakenly labeled it and a Lenny Welch song played. He ran back to the store and got the Dylan 45, and played it. "Then I went out and got Highway 61. That was all I played for weeks, looking at the cover with Bob in that satin blue jacket and Triumph motorcycle shirt."*

In the summer of 1965 when "Like a Rolling Stone" was released,

Springsteen was a 15-year-old who was growing up in a poor, work-ing-class Catholic family in Freehold, New Jersey. He joined his first band in 1964, and in 1965 his band the Castiles played their first professional gig at the Woodhaven Swim Club. The four band members and manager Tex Vinyard split the evening's take of $35 five ways, according to biographer June Skinner Sawyers.

"When I was a kid, Bob's voice somehow thrilled me and scared me," Springsteen admitted during the Rock and Roll Hall of Fame induction speech. "It made me feel kind of irresponsibly innocent—it still does—when it reached down and touched what little worldliness a 15-year-old high school kid in New Jersey had in him at the time. Dylan was a revolutionary. Bob freed the mind the way Elvis freed the body. He showed us that just because the music was innately phys-ical did not mean that it was anti-intellectual. He had the vision and the talent to make a pop song that contained the whole world. He invented a new way a pop singer could sound, broke through the lim-itations of what a recording artist could achieve, and changed the face of rock 'n' roll forever."

At 15, Springsteen already sought the music of Elvis and The Beatles as a refuge from the lonely, confusing, and disorienting world he lived in, at school and at home. Late at night, Springsteen stashed his radio under his pillow and listened to the songs of Roy Orbison, the Drifters, and Smokey Robinson. "The songs that he heard during those days and nights stayed with him. In their innocence and joyful release as well as their coded paeans to rebellion and forbidden pas-sion, they seemed to promise a better life than the one he understood," Sawyers wrote. Springsteen practiced his guitar with indefatigable energy—up to eight hours a day. From 1965 to 1972, he played in a series of bands on the Jersey shore, adding a saxophone in one to offer a powerful R&B sound. In 1969, he moved to the Jersey Shore town of Asbury Park. His band at the time, Steel Mill, performed in Berkeley, California and the San Francisco Examiner's music critic Phil Elwood wrote a great review of their performance. "I have never been so overwhelmed by an unknown band," wrote Elwood. The crit-ic even singled out the 20-year-old Springsteen when he said, "Springsteen is a most impressive composer."

In March of 1972, Springsteen signed a management contract with local independent producer Mike Appel on the hood of a car in an unlit parking lot. Appel helped Bruce by getting him gigs and things started happening for him. In May of the same year, the *aggressive Appel arranged a meeting with legendary Columbia Records producer John Hammond, who had discovered Dylan.*

Hammond told the story of auditioning Springsteen to *Crawdaddy!* reporters Peter Knobler and Greg Mitchell in 1973. "He walked into my office," Hammond recalled. "He was *led* into my office!" The producer's secretary made the appointment after Springsteen's manager Mike Appel very strongly urged her to do so. "Okay, I have 15 minutes," was Hammond's response.

Hammond recalled, "Bruce, who looked marvelously beat, was sitting over there." He gestured to a chair tucked away in the far corner. "And so Mike started yakking. He said, 'I want you to know that we're just, you know, being nice to you because you're the guy who discovered Dylan and we just wanted to find out if that was luck or whether you really have ears.'" But Hammond interrupted Appel's bold diatribe saying, 'Stop, you're making me hate you!' Hammond said that "Bruce was very quiet, sort of grinning over there in the corner. He told me he played both guitar and piano, and I said, 'Well you want to get your guitar out?' He said, 'Sure.' And he started. I think the first song he played was 'Saint in the City.' And I…" He paused. Hammond was thunderstruck. "You know, I couldn't believe it!"

Hammond asked Springsteen if he had ever performed solo. Springsteen hadn't, having played in bands for the last eight years. Two hours later Hammond had set up a performance for him at the Gaslight café in the Village. Hammond recalled, "By this time he'd played some more songs, and I was just convinced that he really *was…* Just 'cause he was so unassuming and so right. Everything he did."

Hammond ran and got some other people just down the hall at Columbia. They all liked him, but "the initial reaction was, well he looks so much like Dylan, he's a copy of him. But he's not. I mean not even remotely," Hammond emphasized. "You see, when Bobby came to me, he was Bobby Zimmerman. He said he was Bob Dylan; he had created all this mystique. Bruce is Bruce Springsteen. And he's much further along, much more developed than Bobby was when he came to me."

Once again, Hammond was convinced he had found a real talent. "So I went straight to Clive [Davis, president of Columbia Records at the time]. Clive had to check around a bit, but Clive loved what he heard on the tape. He said, 'You know, John, he's very amusing, isn't he?' 'Yeah,' I said,'" Hammond recalled. "'He's more than that, Clive. He's fantastic!'"

Columbia released Springsteen's first album *Greetings From Asbury Park, New Jersey* in 1973. Because Columbia needed an easy hook to promote the new album, they settled on "the new Dylan" designation. The first album contained such Springsteen songs as "Spirit in the Night," "Growin' Up," "For You," and "It's Hard To Be a Saint in the City." Critics bit into the "new Dylan" comparison. Knobler and Mitchell wrote, "His voice flew between Van Morrison and Dylan, but imitation was out of the question. There was influence all right—undenied and rather unconcealed—but the tone was coming out Springsteen." They had seen a performance at Kenny's Castaways in New York and were blown away.

Knobler and Mitchell asked Springsteen about the Dylan comparisons. "You're going to get confronted with the Dylan image sooner or later," said Knobler. "How can you deal with that?"

"I don't know," Springsteen answered. "I don't like it, and it's hard to live with. I mean, I resent it when *I* hear it about anyone." A 24-year-old Springsteen then continued to heap praise on the revered singer/songwriter. "I love Dylan!" he laughed. "What can you say? I think Dylan is great. I listened to all his records. It's *the* greatest music ever written, to me. The man says it all, exactly the right way. Incredibly powerful. You don't get no more intense. Such a great instrumental sound. And he was...." He searched for an exact description. "He was Bob Dylan, you know?"

Then Springsteen expressed his desire for his own individuality. "You've gotta say, I dig the way this cat's doing it; I want to do it like that, but..." He glided his hand on an arc to the left, "...like this."

He elaborated. "I go onstage and feel myself. And I'm not worrying about, 'Oh, man, that note sounds like this dude. Hey man, I heard that word off of 'Subterranean Homesick Blues'!" He laughed and shook his head. "At one time it worried me, but it doesn't anymore, because when I get onstage finally I feel myself. That's who I am."

In September 1973, Springsteen's second album, *The Wild, the Innocent & the E Street Shuffle,* was released. Again he was interviewed by *Crawdaddy!* magazine, this time by the magazine's founder Paul Williams. In this 1974 interview, Williams asked Springsteen which Dylan albums influenced him musically.

"In 1968 I was into *John Wesley Harding,*" Springsteen replied. "I never listened to anything after *John Wesley Harding.* I listened to *Bringing It All Back Home, Highway 61, Blonde on Blonde.* That's it. I never had his early albums, and to this day I don't have them, and I never had his later albums. I might have heard them once, though. There was only a short period of time when I related, there was only that period when he was important to me, you know, where he was giving me what I needed. That was it."

Springsteen continued, "Yeah, it was the big three [Dylan albums]. I never was really into him until I heard 'Like a Rolling Stone' on the radio, because it was a hit. FM radio at the time was just beginning, but even if there was no FM at the time, I never had an FM radio. In 1965 I was like 15 and there were no kids 15 who were into folk music. There had been a folk boom, but it was generally a college thing. There was really no way of knowing, because AM radio was really an incredible must in those days. The one thing I dug about those albums was—I dug the sound. Before I listened to what was happening in the song, you had the chorus and you had the band and it had incredible sound and that was what got me." Springsteen then went on to discuss other music he loved: The Stones' *December's Children (And Everyone's)* and *Aftermath*, the Yardbirds' first two albums, The Zombies, Them. At the time of this interview, Springsteen was writing the lyrics for *Born To Run*.

Fate was about to elevate his career to a new level when, while playing a gig in Cambridge, Massachusetts in April 1974, he met *Rolling Stone* rock critic Jon Landau. When Springsteen returned to Cambridge the next month, Landau reviewed his performance at the Harvard Square Theater. In Boston's *Real Paper*, Landau wrote, "Last Thursday at the Harvard Square theater, I saw my rock 'n' roll past flash before my eyes. And I saw something else: I saw rock and roll future and its name is Bruce Springsteen." Landau asked in amazement, "Can anyone really be this good?" To Landau, Springsteen embodied the ultimate rock 'n' roll hero: "He is a rock 'n' roll punk, a Latin street poet, a ballet dancer, an actor, a joker, bar band leader, hot-shit rhythm guitar player, extraordinary singer, and a truly great rock 'n' roll composer. He leads a band like he has been doing it forever." He also described Springsteen's distinctive appearance: "Bruce Springsteen is a wonder to look at. Skinny, dressed like a reject from Sha Na Na, he parades in front of his all-star rhythm band like a cross between Chuck Berry, early Bob Dylan, and Marlon Brando."

After such effusive praise, Landau made one of the most interesting career transitions in rock history. He soon became Springsteen's producer, then manager. He had input into the musician's next album *Born To Run*, and then took over as Springsteen's manager, a move that resulted in a protracted legal battle with former manager Mike Appel. Landau felt it was imperative for the energy and excitement of Springsteen's live shows to translate into his recordings. Certainly Landau was willing to throw himself completely behind Springsteen. According to Jay Cocks' article in *Time* in 1975, loyalists at Columbia persuaded the company to spend $50,000 to publicize Landau's quote about Springsteen: "I saw rock and roll future and its name is Bruce Springsteen."

Born To Run was an instant hit. The album made it to Number One and the title track became a hit single. Due to Appel's moxie, Springsteen appeared on the covers of both *Time* and *Newsweek* during the same week in 1975. Cocks wrote, "He is the dead-on image of a rock musician: Street-smart but sentimental, a little enigmatic, articulate mostly through his music. For 26 years, Springsteen has known nothing but poverty and debt until, just in the past few weeks, the rock dream came true for him." Cocks went on, "His music is primal, directly in touch with all the impulses of wild humor and glancing melancholy, street tragedy, and punk anarchy that have made rock the distinctive voice of a generation." When Cocks cited influences, he said, "Springsteen's songs are full of echoes—of Sam Cooke and Elvis Presley, of Chuck Berry, Roy Orbison, and Buddy Holly. You can also hear Bob Dylan, Van Morrison, and The Band weaving among Springsteen's elaborate fantasias...."

Springsteen makes demands, Cocks wrote. "He figures that when he sings

Baby this town rips the bones from your back
It's a death trap, it's a suicide rap
We gotta get out while we're young..."

everybody is going to know where he's coming from and just where he's heading."

Other rock critics joined in the chorus of acclaim. The late Lester Bangs (1949 to 1982) wrote in *Creem,* "He reminds us what it's like to love rock 'n' roll like you just discovered it and then seize it and make it your own with certainty and precision." Bangs added, "The music races in a flurry of Dylan and Morrison and Phil Spector and a little of both Lou Reed and Roy Orbison, luxuriating in them and an American moment caught at last, again, and bursting with pride."

Critic Greil Marcus also noted the impact that Springsteen's excellent E Street Band had on the album: "What is new is the majesty Springsteen and his band have brought to this story... For all it owes to

Phil Spector, it can be compared only to the music that Bob Dylan and The Hawks made onstage in 1965 and '66. With that sound, Springsteen has achieved something very special. He has touched the world with glory…" In this review, Marcus paid special attention to the deserving talents of the E Street Band that included Roy Bittan on piano, Clarence Clemons on saxophone, Danny Federici on the organ, Garry Tallent on bass, Steve Van Zandt both guitar and vocals, and Max Weinberg on drums. *Rolling Stone* critic Dave Marsh underscored the talent of the band. After seeing The Bottom Line shows in New York in the summer of 1975, Marsh wrote, "Springsteen is everything that has been claimed for him—a magical guitarist, singer, writer, rock 'n' roll rejuvenator—but the E Street Band has nearly been lost in the shuffle. Which is ridiculous because this group may very well be the great American rock 'n' roll band."

The critics loved Springsteen's '50s rock 'n' roll influence and his powerful storytelling ability: His compassion for the working-class man, his empathy for his struggle for survival, his need for escape. Bangs wrote, "Through all these songs Springsteen's characters… are skating for a long shot in automobiles and beds with the omnipresent roar of the radio driving them on to connect anew, as even in the failure of their striving they are redeemed by Springsteen's vision: Tramps like us—baby, we were born to run."

Bruce had found his own voice. The American public had found him. He was an original. "Like only the greatest rock singers and writers and musicians, he has created a world of his own. Like Dylan and the Who's Peter Townsend, he has a galaxy of full-formed characters to work with. But while he is comparable to all of the greats, that may only be because he is the living culmination of 20 years of rock 'n' roll tradition," wrote Marsh in *Rolling Stone*. Springsteen was a street-smart New Jersey charismatic rocker and mythmaker. His runaway American dream had begun.

Springsteen's protracted lawsuit with Mike Appel delayed the release of his next album after *Born To Run*. In 1978, after they had settled their lawsuit, *Darkness on the Edge of Town* was released. Springsteen began showing a more political side, performing in antinuclear concerts in 1979 and organizing a benefit for Vietnam vets in 1981. In interviews he began to discuss literary influences such as the short stories of Flannery O'Connor and Raymond Carver and the novels of Bobbie Ann Mason, much as Dylan had earlier discussed the inspiration of Kerouac,

Ginsberg, and Rimbaud. Springsteen was self-taught, without a college degree. [He dropped out of community college after one year.] He possessed a self-awareness about how his working-class upbringing had affected him, saying, without apology, "I didn't grow up in a community of ideas—a place where you can sit down and talk about books, and how you read through them, and how they affect you… I think I'm more a product of pop culture: Films and records, films and records, films and records, especially early on. And then later, more novels and reading."

Springsteen's albums *The River* and *Nebraska* continued to cement his reputation as a star singer/songwriter. (*The River* contained the Top 40 single, "Hungry Heart.") During the time he wrote *The River,* "he had been living on a farm in rural Holmdel, New Jersey, watching old John Ford films and listening to the music of Hank Williams, Roy Acuff, and Johnny Cash," wrote June Skinner Sawyers in 1994.

By 1984, Springsteen had become the most famous and popular rock performer in the world. His next album, *Born in the U.S.A.* proved to be "a career-defining turning point," said Sawyers. He had been transformed from a charismatic rocker into a megastar. The album became Columbia's best-selling album ever up to that time. Springsteen was asked about the idealism in his music by *Los Angeles Times* music critic Robert Hilburn in the early '80s. "When you listen to those early rock records or any great rock 'n' roll, or see a great movie, there are human values that are presented. They're important things. I got inspired mainly, I guess, by the records, a certain purity in them," said Springsteen.

"I just know that when I started to play, it was like a gift. I started to feel alive. It was like some guy stumbling down a street and finding a key. Rock 'n' roll was the only thing I ever liked about myself.

"On the new album [*The River*], I wrote this song called 'Out on the Street.' I wasn't gonna put it on the album because it's all idealism. It's about people being together and sharing a certain feeling of joy. I know it's real, but it's hard to see sometimes. You go out in the street and there's a chance you get hit over the head or mugged. The song's not realistic in a way, but there's something very real at the heart of it."

In subsequent albums, *Tunnel of Love* (1987), *Human Touch* and *Lucky Town* (1992) and *The Ghost of Tom Joad* (1995), Springsteen continued to explore the social realism that infused the songs of Woody Guthrie and Dylan with such meaning and history. In 1994 his song "Streets of Philadelphia," written for the film *Philadelphia,* won an Academy Award for Best Song. His 2002 album *The Rising* was written in the aftermath of September 11, 2001, and touches on many things including "faith, duty, love, death, survival, loss, decency, resurrection, redemption, suffering, and hope," according to Sawyers.

Springsteen's personal life was in flux from the mid-80's to 1990, when he finally settled down with his longtime girlfriend, Patti Scialfa, who sang back-up in the E Street Band. Before beginning his relationship with Scialfa, he had very publicly married actress and model Julianne Phillips in 1985. They separated in 1987 and were divorced in 1989. In 1990 Springsteen purchased a four-and-a-half acre $14 million estate in Beverly Hills. He became a father in 1990 when Patti gave birth to their son, Evan, and they married in 1991, soon to welcome two other children into their family: Jessica Ray in 1991 and Sam Ryan in 1994.

Springsteen has continued to be abundantly productive throughout the years, whether writing songs for movies or staging mega-tours at stadiums around the world or producing new albums.

Throughout this time he has also had to navigate the pitfalls of huge celebrity and success but has always been more open than many rock stars. In fact, his personal life has been covered as extensively as any Beverly Hills movie star. He even talked about his therapy in the *New York Times* in 1995. He told reporter Neil Strauss that one of the biggest steps he ever had to take was in 1982 when he decided to undergo therapy, which he said he continues sporadically. "I grew up in a working-class family," Springsteen said to Strauss. "It was very, very difficult for me to ever get to a place where I said I needed some help. I stumbled into some difficult, very dark times where I simply had no other idea of what to do. It's not necessarily for everybody, but all I can say is that I've accomplished things personally that felt simply impossible previously. The leap of consciousness that it takes to go from playing in your garage to playing in front of 5,000, 6,000, 7,000 people or when you experience any kind of success at all can be very, very demanding." Such candor won over the *New York Times* reporter, who wrote, "Mr. Springsteen has made the transition from garage-rocker to arena-rocker better than most rock singers. He doesn't have to try to be sincere; it comes naturally. In the 1970s, at the height of rock-star decadence, Mr. Springsteen set himself apart from his contemporaries by rarely indulging in anything but a sweaty, energetic three- or four-hour show."

Part of Springsteen's appeal is his respect for music history, and his recognition that he is another link in a long chain of innovators. He rightly views Bob Dylan as an incomparable musical pioneer. In his induction speech for Dylan at the Rock and Roll Hall of Fame, he noted how Dylan paved the way for others to follow. "Without Bob, the

Beatles wouldn't have made *Sgt. Pepper*, the Beach Boys wouldn't have made *Pet Sounds*," Springsteen said. "The Sex Pistols wouldn't have made *God Save the Queen*, U2 wouldn't have done 'Pride (In the Name of Love),' Marvin Gaye wouldn't have done 'What's Going On,' The Count Five would not have done 'Psychotic Reaction,' and Grandmaster Flash might not have done 'The Message.' And there would have never been a group named the Electric Prunes. To this day, whenever great rock music is being made, there is the shadow of Bob Dylan. Bob's own modern work has gone unjustly underappreciated because it's had to stand in that shadow. If there was a young guy out there writing the *Empire Burlesque* album, writing 'Every Grain of Sand,' they'd be calling him the new Bob Dylan."

When Springsteen concluded his speech, he referred to the fame that both musicians had worked so hard to attain, and the mantle of which both have found understandably difficult to bear. "About three months ago," said Springsteen, "I was watching the *Rolling Stone* Special on TV. Bob came on and he was in a real cranky mood. He was kind of bitchin' and moanin' about how his fans come up to him on the street and treat him like a long-lost brother or something, even though they don't know him. Now speaking as a fan, when I was 15 and heard 'Like a Rolling Stone,' I heard a guy who had the guts to take on the whole world and who made me feel like I had to too. Maybe some people misunderstood the voice as saying that somehow Bob was going to do the job for them, but as we grow older, we learn that there isn't anybody out there who can do that job for anybody else." Springsteen then turned to address Dylan directly. "So I'm just here tonight to say thanks, to say that I wouldn't be here without you, to say that there isn't a soul in this room who does not owe you his thanks, and to steal a line from one of your songs—whether you like or not—'You was the brother that I never had.'"

BONO

Retna, Inc.

*O*ne of the most popular musicians in the world today, Bono was born Paul Hewson in Dublin, Ireland on May 10, 1960. According to biographers, as a boy he was a "bloody exasperating child" who got a reputation at an early age for being "absent-minded and argumentative." At the same time, he has also been described as "starry-eyed and wickedly curious." Paul suffered an early tragedy; his mother died of a brain aneurysm when he was only 14. [John Lennon and Paul McCartney also each lost their mother around the same age.] During this time, Paul was drawn into the world of music and loved bands like Patti Smith, Thin Lizzy, and The Ramones. During his high school years he got his new name. A high school friend called him "Bono Vox," a phrase he'd picked up at a hearing-aid store. The name means "good voice" in cockeyed Latin. During high school, while he had many female admirers, Bono also met his sweetheart, Alison Stewart, who became his wife.

At a young age, Bono exhibited a love of performing. During high school, he often could be seen singing on stage. One day in 1976, he *answered an ad posted on a bulletin board at the Mount Temple Comprehensive School in Dublin, asking for anyone who was interested in forming a band to meet after school at the house of Larry Mullen, Jr. Mullen served as the drumming catalyst for the formation of one of the most popular bands of the past 20 years. Along with Bono, the other musicians who joined included a guitarist/guitar builder named Dave Evans, later nicknamed the Edge, and bassist Adam Clayton. Together they formed the band U2. They were serious about music and developed a big, self-assured sound. By 1977, the following year, they were performing in clubs, quickly creating a buzz and a large local fan base. The band has been together ever since, and their manager, Paul McGuinness, has been with them since those early days, which is almost unheard-of in rock. Journalist Gary Graff said, "Taking its lead from classic figures like The Beatles and the Rolling Stones and punk heroes like The Clash and Patti Smith, the quartet emerged like a blast furnace out of Ireland, with a new generation of anthems ('I Will Follow,' 'Pride,' 'I Still Haven't Found What I'm Looking For'), an unapologetic dedication to the Christian faith, a keen political awareness, and a fiery passion that more than compensated for occasional indulgences into righteous self-seriousness."*

In 1979 when Bono was 19, U2's first album, Boy, *was released by Island. It began with "I Will Follow," a song that critics called, "the instant classic, a real toe tapper, notable for its great 'in your eyes' midsection." One critic wrote, "The band rocks throughout, something that can't be said for many of their more-refined later releases, and the sheer passion and sincerity that goes into these performances always wins me over."* Boy *began "the band's innocent climb towards rock immortality." Their second album,* October, *contained lyrics that hinted at Bono's future role as an activist: "I can't change the world but I can change the world in me." This was followed by the '80s albums* War, Under a Blood Red Sky, *and* The Unforgettable Fire. *The latter included the work of producers Brian Eno and Daniel Lanois. The band then released* The Joshua Tree *in 1987. This was the album that firmly established U2 in the star-studded pantheon of great rock 'n' roll bands. The band released the album at a time when little in rock, with the exception of Bruce Springsteen, could approach U2's passion and excitement. "The album has a broad, cinematic sweep and is a subdued, subtly beautiful album by a band that had reached full artistic maturity," wrote one reviewer. The album included the three successful singles that helped make U2 the biggest band in the world: "I Still Haven't Found What I'm Looking For," "Where the Streets Have No Name," and "With or Without You."*

The following years saw U2 release the albums Rattle and Hum, Achtung Baby, Zooropa, Pop, *and* All That You Can't Leave Behind. *Their 2005 release,* How to Dismantle an Atomic Bomb, *won the Grammy for Album of the Year and they won the Song of the Year Award for "Sometimes You Can't Make It On Your Own" off the album. [The Album of the Year Award is U2's second; they also won for* The Joshua Tree *in 1987.] These albums, with a passionate mix of love and politics, featured what became known as "the classic U2 sound": Layers of atmospheric guitar, a stellar rhythmic thrust, and Bono's distinctive voice, fiery, intense, sometimes leaping into a falsetto crooning. "As a band, we thrive on discovering new ground," The Edge said in a 2001 interview. "I just hate rules, I hate any sense that there are real absolutes when you're being creative... You have to go with what feels right, and in the end, your ears are the judge." That's the philosophy that has guided their career, says journalist Graff. The Edge also tried to describe U2's influences in a 1989 interview when he said, "It's been said that rock 'n' roll died in 1959, and there's something to that. I think that the music we tend to go back to all the time is something very fragile and hard to pin down. It's in the early Elvis records, it's in some country records, in The Band. You find it in obscure bars in New Orleans and places like that. You'll never hear it on the radio. I couldn't begin to explain what exactly it is, but I know that people like T-Bone Burnett and even Dylan spent their life finding this music. We're just getting a feel for it now."*

U2's tours over the past 25 years have been visually dazzling, powerful, and passionate affairs. The New York Times' *James Traub described a concert at Madison Square Garden. He wrote that after the entire arena went dark, "in a cone of white light through which innumerable bits of confetti fluttered and danced, Bono materialized, twirling slowly, ecstatically, his arms raised to the light as if asking to be drawn up to the heavens. It was a gesture with intimations of the messianic. And yet what you felt, throughout the evening, as Bono pranced and hopped along the catwalk that extended out into the crowd in the pit, inviting girls up to dance with him, was that he was beckoning his fans to join him in the ecstatic place where the music came from." Traub described Bono's voice: "It takes the form*

*sometimes of an arena-enveloping shout, sometimes of a keening wail,
and sometimes of a piercing falsetto."*

*Unlike most other rock stars, Bono uses that voice in arenas other
than musical ones. Since 1997, when an activist approached him
about helping to cancel the debts that the most impoverished nations
owed to the industrialized nations, Bono has been as passionate
about this cause as he has about U2's music. His efforts to spearhead
the debt-relief cause for poor African nations has brought him beyond
stadium stages into the lavish offices of some of the most powerful
people in the world. Bono has met with people like Presidents Bill
Clinton and George Bush, British Prime Minister Tony Blair, UN
Secretary General Kofi Annan, and many others.*

*Bono and Bob Dylan have been friends for more than 20 years. If
anyone can understand his boundless energy and describe Bono's fre-
netic enthusiasm accurately, it is Dylan. And if anyone can understand the Dylan mystique, it's Bono. When Dylan turned 60 in
2001, Bono wrote, "There's a lot of mystery about him, but he does-
n't turn mystery into melodrama. He's dealt with celebrity with a
smirk and a mask of indifference. He's just got on with his life as a
writer and performer."*

In 2005, *Rolling Stone* published a cover story on Bono that included an interview conducted by Jann Wenner. In the interview, Bono told
Wenner about his early rock 'n' roll influences, especially Dylan and
The Beatles. He heard "I Want to Hold Your Hand" when he was 4; he
listened to Tom Jones and Elvis when he was around 8. Later he got into
The Who, the Rolling Stones, and Led Zeppelin. When he was 12,
Bono recalled, "I really remember John Lennon's *Imagine.* That's one of
my first albums. That really set fire to me. It was like he was whisper-
ing in your ear—his ideas of what's possible, different ways of seeing the
world. When I was 14 and lost my mother, I went back to *Plastic Ono
Band."* Bono noted that he was also listening to Bob Dylan's acoustic
albums. He admitted, "I then starting to think about playing those
acoustic songs, trying to teach myself guitar, and him sort of helping."

Bono talked further about how these musicians influenced him. In
talking about The Who, Bono said, "At about age 15, that starts really
connecting. In amongst the din and the noise, the power chords and the
rage, there's another voice. 'Nobody knows what it's like behind blue
eyes…' And the beginnings of what I would discover is one of the essential aspects for me—and why I'm drawn to a piece of music—which has

something to do with the quest. The sense that there's another world to be explored. I got that from Pete Townshend; I got that from Bob Dylan." Wenner asked him whether the album *Imagine* was his first powerful influence. Bono replied, "*Imagine* and Bob Dylan. 'Blowin' in the Wind'—all that stuff—and the folksy things, which is, I suppose, what set me up for John Lennon."

And how did Dylan set him up for John Lennon? "Because it's folk... words and whisperings, that quiet thing," Bono replied. "I was in my room listening on headphones on a tape recorder. It's very intimate. It's like talking to somebody on the phone, like talking to John Lennon on the phone. I'm not exaggerating to say that. This music changed the shape of the room. It changed the shape of the world outside the room; the way you looked out the window and what you were looking at.

"I remember John singing 'Oh My Love.' It's like a little hymn. It's certainly a prayer of some kind—even if he was an atheist... Yoko came up to me when I was in my twenties, and she put her hand on me and said, 'You are John's son.' What an amazing compliment!"

Later in the interview talking about U2's fame after the success of *The Joshua Tree,* Bono said, "I didn't realize that being famous isn't that important. I'm thinking, 'Oh gosh, if I go out there, I don't want to let people down.' Bob Dylan taught me this: You should let people down. You do not have to live up to people's expectations. And if they have them, well, then let them down." When U2 was on the cover of *Time,* and had Number One singles and Number One albums, "I remember him [Dylan] saying, 'You're in a band, you're lucky. I went through this on my own,'" Bono recalled.

In retelling the story of how Bono first met Dylan, Bono told Wenner, "I went to interview him for the *Hot Press,* an Irish music paper in 1984 (that interview is reprinted at the end of this chapter). We talked about playing chess. Van Morrison was there, too." Bono also noted that, "Dylan was responsible for *Rattle and Hum* because he's the one who said, in that interview, that you have to understand the past, where the music comes from.

"He was talking to me about the McPeake family and the Clancy Brothers and then Hank Williams and Leadbelly, none of whom we knew. Bob came out on *The Joshua Tree* tour, played a few songs with us. During *Rattle and Hum,* he came down and played keyboards. We went out to his house in California and wrote a couple of songs together. "I think he was just keeping an eye out for me," Bono said. "I probably didn't realize what this meant, and I may not have respected his privacy the way I should have," Bono admitted. "People say, 'Oh, you've written with Bob Dylan,' and I'd tell them what happened, not realizing that his privacy was sacrosanct. So I don't know why he continued to be my friend. He kind of comes and goes."

In an interpersonal context, Bono explained, "I find him to be the least obtuse person in the world, except when there's more than a few people in the room. He's much better one to one." He continued, "The collision of The Beatles and Bob Dylan gave us the galaxy that our planet is in. I would consider myself to be more of a fan than a friend. He might call me a friend; I would call me a fan. I find him very old-school–ancient values, ancient wisdom. For a man who helped to give birth to the modern era, he's really coming from a very old place. He is a pilgrim, a sojourner, a troubadour. It's almost a medieval way he sees the world, in terms of performing. For a person like myself who's trying to keep my dignity in a very undignified era and trade, where your own opportunism can trip you up, he just reminds me all the time of what's possible."

Bono then cited as his favorite Dylan song and album: "Visions of Johanna" and *Bringing It All Back Home*. "I loved [the album] as a teenager and still love the humor and discovering some of the references as you get older, just realizing what that was about."

At the end of the *Rolling Stone* interview, Bono was asked whether rock 'n' roll contained everything that he wanted to do. The musician and activist replied, "It's so exciting—music. It really is. I believe that old adage that all art aspires to the condition of music….. It is how we speak to God finally—or how we don't. Even if we're ignoring God, it's the language of the spirit... The thing that drives me on is a sort of curiosity about the world and people. When we were in the middle of punk rock I wanted to hang out with Johnny Cash. I wanted to know what was going on under his hat, and I got to. Frank Sinatra—I got to know what was going on under his hat and in his heart—and he shared things with me. The blessing that I was talking about—I've been chasing that blessing all my life from all different sources and places, from Bob Dylan to Willie Nelson to Billy Graham."

Since Bono had described Dylan as a "friend who comes and goes," the Irish singer must have been surprised to find himself in his friend's autobiography. In *Chronicles*, Dylan describes an evening in 1989 when Bono came over to his house for dinner with some other friends:

"Spending time with Bono was like eating dinner on a train—feels like you're moving, going somewhere. Bono's got the soul of an ancient poet and you have to be careful around him. He can roar 'til the earth shakes. He's also a closet philosopher. He brought a case of Guinness with him. We were talking about things that you talk about when you're spending the winter with somebody–talked about Jack Kerouac. Bono knows Kerouac's stuff pretty good. Kerouac, who celebrated American towns like Truckee, Fargo, Butte, and Madora—towns that most Americans never heard of. It seems funny that Bono would know more about Kerouac than most Americans. He seems to know a lot about America and what he doesn't, he's curious about." Dylan recalled that he and Bono talked late into the night about fame and a place Dylan called "the birthplace of America: Alexandria, Minnesota."

Eventually, the conversation got around to music. As Dylan writes, "Out at sea, the lights of a freighter moved by every so often. Bono asked me if I'd had any new songs, any unrecorded ones. It just so happened that I did. I went into the other room and pulled them out of the drawer, brought them back and showed them to him. He looked them over, said I should record them. I said that I wasn't so sure about that, thought that maybe I should pour lighter fluid over them—said that I had been having a hard time making records, making that work out. He said, 'No, no,' and he brought up the name of Daniel Lanois." Bono told Dylan that U2 had worked with producer Lanois for U2's album *The Unforgettable Fire* and he had been "a great partner." Bono picked up the phone, called Lanois, and put Dylan on the phone with him. A Canadian living in England, Lanois told Dylan that if he was ever in New Orleans, where Lanois was currently working, Dylan should look him up.

"I said I would do that," Dylan writes. "To be sure, I was in no hurry to record. Performing was what was on my mind first and foremost. If I ever did make another record, it would have to have something in common with that purpose. I had a clear road ahead and didn't want to blow the chance to regain my musical freedom. I needed to let things straighten out and not get mixed up anymore." Dylan then describes going to New Orleans and recording his album *Oh Mercy* with Lanois.

So this is what rock stars like Bono and Dylan talk about over a case of Guinness. It makes sense. Bono was on top of the world at the time; Dylan was in a career slump and feeling discouraged. The slump followed what Dylan called "an ungodly" injury to his hand that led him to question whether he could ever play guitar again. At the time, Dylan felt, "Wherever I am, I'm a '60's troubadour, a folk-rock relic, a word-smith from bygone days, a fictitious head of station from a place nobody knows. I'm in the bottomless pit of cultural oblivion. ... I can't shake it."

The album *Oh Mercy* was recorded in September 1989 under Lanois' direction. Later, in an interview to promote the album, Dylan recalled his first meetings with Lanois. "We hit it off. We had an understanding of what my music was all about. It was thrilling to run into Daniel because he's a competent musician and he knows how to record with modern facilities... He managed to get my stage voice, something other people working with me never were quite able to achieve." In *Chronicles* Dylan wrote about the creative struggle he and Lanois faced together, recording *Oh Mercy.* Dylan writes, "In the end, there always has to be some compromise of personal interests and there was, but the record satisfied my purposes and his. I can't say if it's the record either of us wanted. Human dynamics play too big a part, and getting what you want isn't always the most important thing in life anyway."

Dylan also admitted that "[Lanois] wanted to understand me more as we went along, but you can't do that, not unless you like to do puzzles." The great singer/songwriter also said, in a tone devoid of self-pity, "I would have liked to have been able to give him the kinds of songs that he wanted, like 'Masters of War,' 'Hard Rain,' 'Gates of Eden,' but those kinds of songs were written under different circumstances, and circumstances never repeat themselves. Not exactly. I couldn't get to those kinds of songs for him or anyone else. To do it, you've got to have power and dominion over the spirits. I had done it once, and once was enough."

Lanois had reported that Dylan had come to the recording sessions for *Oh Mercy* with most of the songs complete, although songs like "Man in the Long Black Coat" and "Shooting Star" were written and rewritten during the sessions. Dylan had said of the songs on *Oh Mercy,* "I was thinking of a series of dreams, where nothing comes up to the top. Everything stays down where it's wounded, and comes to a permanent stop. I wasn't thinking of anything specific, like in a dream when someone wakes up and screams. Nothing too very scientific. Just thinking of a series of dreams." After the album was released, Lanois told an interviewer: "We had four or six songs that we recorded and didn't use. One track 'Series of Dreams,' was a fantastic turbulent track that I felt should have been on the record," Lanois said to the interviewer. "But [Dylan] had the last word."

The song was finally released in 1991 on *The Bootleg Series, Volumes 1–3, 1961–1991.* In his *London Times* review of *Oh Mercy,* music critic

Richard Williams wrote, "Throughout *Oh Mercy*, Dylan's delivery is relaxed and confident. He sounds like a Bob Dylan you could talk to, as opposed to other recent albums where 'he sounds uncomfortable in his own skin.'" Music critic Paul Williams added, "On *Oh Mercy*, Lanois not only manages to get Dylan's "stage voice," but also succeeds in reawakening or making a safe space for Dylan's remarkable intuitive gift for album-building. The two probably go together." No doubt Dylan was very appreciative of Bono for introducing him to Lanois, and the alchemy these collaborators produced is evident in songs like "Political World," "What Is It You Wanted," and "Man in the Long Black Coat."

As Bono said, he first met Dylan when he interviewed him in 1984 at Slane Castle in Dublin, Ireland prior to a concert by the folk-rock legend. While U2 had been shaped by punk rock, the quartet had originally disregarded its Irish roots until this 1984 interview when, as one reporter said, "Dylan sent them excavating." Bono summed up the following interview in this way: "U2 kind of came from outer space, where punk was ground zero and you didn't admit to having roots. Bob scolded me, 'You're sitting on all this stuff. You should check it out.' As we fall over ourselves toward the fast and furious future, Dylan feels like the brakes, reminding us of stuff we might have lost, like our dignity." Bono also admitted that he taught himself guitar while listening to Dylan. "His voice has been a bee buzzing around my ear since I can remember being conscious," Bono said. "It's an unusual voice, not always soothing, sometimes nagging, but it reminds us of the possibilities for music and its place in the world."

As the editors of *Younger Than That Now: The Collected Interviews With Bob Dylan* pointed out, the natural amphitheatre of Slane Castle, where Bono's interview took place, is about 50 miles from Dublin, and is a frequent destination on the international rock festival map. In 1981, the Irish band Thin Lizzy headlined Slane Castle's first ever rock festival. The following year the Rolling Stones drew a crowd of 80,000 to the castle's pile of land near the River Boyne. Since then, the castle has hosted many of rock's biggest acts, including Bruce Springsteen, Queen, REM, and, in 2001, U2 itself.

In 1984 when Bono conducted his interview with Dylan, U2 had not yet achieved their worldwide fame and had yet to win a Grammy. Both Bono and Van Morrison, who appears in the following interview, were later guests at Dylan's show. Morrison did "It's All Over Now, Baby Blue," and Bono joined Dylan on "Blowin' in the Wind." As a longtime admirer of Dylan's music, Bono donned a guest reporter's hat to conduct the following interview, which was originally published in the Irish rock-culture magazine *Hot Press* on July 8, 1984. It was also the beginning of the two musicians' long friendship.

Bono: You have been to Ireland before, haven't you?

Dylan: Yeah, I was in Belfast and in Dublin, and we traveled around a little bit too.

Bono: Have you ever spent any time here? Have you ever been here on holiday?

Dylan: Yeah, well, when I was here, we traveled by car, so we stayed in different places—but Irish music has always been a great part of my life because I used to hang out with the Clancy Brothers. They influenced me tremendously.

Bono: Yeah, they have so much balls as a sound, you know, when they sing, it's like punk rock.

Dylan: Yeah, they were playing clubs as big as this room right here and the place—you couldn't put a pin in it—it would be so packed with people.

Bono: You could smell their breath?

Dylan: Yeah!

Bono: I bet you could. They blow you over with their lungs! God, I'd love to sing like that.

Dylan: Yeah, I spent years with them running around, '61, '62, '63.

Bono: Greenwich Village?

Dylan: All over the place, I played on the same bill with them once.

Bono: Get their autographs? [laughs]

Dylan: No, I didn't get their autograph. But you know one of the things I recall from that time is how great they all were—I mean there is no question, but that they were great. But Liam Clancy was always my favorite singer, as a ballad singer. I just never heard anyone as good, and that includes Barbra Streisand and Pearl Bailey.

Bono: You got to be careful here!

Dylan: He's just a phenomenal ballad singer.

Bono: Yeah, you know what I envy of you is that my music, and the music of U2 is like, it's in space somewhere. There is no particular musical roots or heritage that we plug into. In Ireland there is a tradition, but I've never plugged into it. It's like as if we're caught in space. There's a few groups now who are caught in space...

Dylan: Well, you have to reach back.

Bono: We never did play a 12 bar.

Dylan: You have to reach! There's another group I used to listen to called the McPeake Family. I don't know if you ever heard of them?

Bono: The McPeake Family! I'd love to have heard of them, with a name like that.

Dylan: They are great. Paddy Clancy recorded them. He had a label called Tradition Records, and he used to bring back these records; they recorded for Prestige at the time, and Tradition Records, his company. They were called The McPeake family. They were even more rural than the Clancy Brothers. The Clancy Brothers had always that touch of commercialism to them—you didn't mind it, but it was still there, whereas the McPeake Family sang with harps. The old man, he played the harp—and it was that [gestures] big—and the drums.

Bono: Were they a real family?

Dylan: Yeah, they were a real family; if you go to a record store and ask for a McPeake Family record, I don't know, I'm sure you could still get them in a lot of places.

Bono: Have you heard of an Irish group that are working now in this middle ground between traditional and contemporary music called Clannad? Clannad is Gaelic for family, and they've made some very powerful pieces of music, including a song called "Theme From Harry's Game," it's from a film, and it knocked over everyone in Europe. It didn't get played in the U.S. It's just vocal and they used some low bass frequencies in it as well—it's just beautiful. They're a family, they come from Donegal, and have worked from that same base of traditional music.

Dylan: There's a group you have here, what's it called, Plankston?

Bono: Planxty.

Dylan: They're great!

Bono: Another rock 'n' roll band!

Dylan: Yeah, but when I think of what's happening—I think they're great.

Bono: There's another group called De Dannan. The name De Dannan has something to do with the lost tribes of Dan. You heard of the disappearing tribe of Dan? They say they came from Ireland.

Dylan: Yeah, I've heard that, I've heard that.

Bono: I'm not a musicologist or expert in this area, but it would appear that this is true. Also, you know they say the Irish musical scale has no roots in Europe whatsoever, rather it comes from Africa and India. The Cartesian people, the Egyptian people, what gave them supremacy in the Middle East was the sail they developed. I forget what they call it, I forget the name of the sail, but this sail allowed them to become successful sea farers and traders and they dominated as a result of their reading, and that same sail which was used on those boats, is used on the West of Ireland.

Dylan: Is that right?

Bono: Bob Quinn made a film called Atlanteans in which this theory was elaborated. He suggests that the book of Kells, which is a manuscript, part of it has its roots in Coptic script, not in Europe. It's not a European thing at all—it's linked from Africa, Spain, Brittany, and Ireland, because that was a sea route. I'm not an expert. I shouldn't be talking about it really. But it's of interest when you think of it.

Dylan: Sure it is.

Bono: I might be able to send you over some tapes of that actually.

Dylan: I'd like to have them. You know Planxty? I also like Paul Brady a lot.

Bono: Yeah, he's great. He's a real songwriter. Tell me—have you ever approached a microphone, not with words, but just to sing? I had to do this as a necessity once when some lyrics of mine were stolen—and I learned to sing on the microphone just singing and working the words into it later. I find when I put a pen in my hand it gets in the way! Do you have words first?

Dylan: I do at certain times.

Bono: In Portland, Oregon a number of years ago two pretty girls walked in the dressing room, smiled and walked out with some of our songs in a briefcase. [Inside the briefcase were notes for lyrics for the band's 1981 release *October*.]

Dylan: I used to have that happen to me all the time, except they used to take clothes!

Bono: Is that right?

Dylan: They used to take all my best clothes, but never took my songs.

Bono: After that we had to go in to record our second album, *October* without any songs—there was a lot of pressure, having to sing under that stress without any words. I found out a lot of things about myself that I didn't even know were there. I'd wondered, had some of the things that have come out of you ever been a surprise to you?

Dylan: That usually happens at concerts or shows I'm doing, more than recording studios. Also, I never sit around. I usually play... I'll play my guitar rather than just have something to say, to express myself. I can express it better with my guitar.

Bono: I wondered—had the songs that you were writing ever frightened you in some way?

Dylan: Oh yeah, I've written some songs that did that. The songs that I wrote for the *Slow Train* album did that. I wrote those songs. I didn't plan to write them, but I wrote them anyway. I didn't like writing them, I didn't want to write them. I didn't figure... I just didn't want to write them songs at that period of time. But I found myself writing these songs and after I had a certain amount of them, I thought I didn't want to sing them, so I had a girl sing them for me at the time, and what I wanted to do was... she's a great singer...

Bono: Who is this?

Dylan: A girl I was singing with at the time, Carolyn Dennis her name was. I gave them all to her and had her record them, and not even put my name on them. But I wanted the songs out; I wanted them out, but *I* didn't want to do it because I knew that it wouldn't be perceived in that way. It would just mean more pressure. I just did not want that at that time.

Bono: But are you a trouble maker? Is there something in you that wants trouble that an album like *Slow Train* stirs up? Do you wanna fight? Do you wanna box!?

Dylan: I don't know! I mean, I wanna piss people off once in a while, but boxing or fighting—it would be an exercise to do it. You know, I love to do it, but not with anything at stake.

Bono: Chess, do you play chess?

Dylan: Yeah, I play chess. Are you a chess player?

Bono: I am a chess player.

Dylan: I'm not that good actually.

Bono: I'll challenge you to a game of chess.

Dylan: I don't have it right now actually, I just don't have one on me, but the next time you see me!

Bono: Oh, you can get these little ones you know, that you can carry around.

Dylan: Yeah, I take them on tour all the time, but nobody in the band will play me.

Bono: Really?

Dylan: Yeah, they say it's an ego trip. They say I want to win, I don't want to win, I just like to play.

Bono: When you put out a record that causes trouble—is it part of an overall plan, or do you just do it?

Dylan: No, I don't ever put out a record to cause trouble—if it causes trouble, it causes trouble, that's apart from me. If it causes trouble, that's other people's problem. It's not my problem. I'm just not going to put out a record that I just feel—you know, if I feel like I'm inspired to make a statement, I'll make that statement. But what happens after I do it, I don't care about that.

Bono: What's your opening game?

Dylan: My opening game, you mean king's pawn up two—and all that? I don't know.

Bono: You just takes it as it comes.

Dylan: Yeah. I don't really play that seriously.

Bono: Well, I thought I did until I played Adam's brother Sebastian—he was only about 13 years old and he beat me!

Dylan: Somebody may have a chess game here.

Bono: I'd love to play.

Searching for a chess board... enter Van Morrison

Bono: You haven't used any synthesizers on your records so far?

Dylan: No, I've never used those machines.

Bono: The Fairlight Music Computer—have you heard of that?

Dylan: Fairlight?

Bono: Van, what do you think of electronic music?

Morrison: I like the music Brian Eno plays.

Bono: He speaks very highly of you. He's producing our record right now.

Morrison: Say hello.

Bono: [to Bob] Do you know Brian Eno?

Dylan: Brian Eno? I don't know Brian Eno, but I know some of his work.

Bono: When you're working with a producer, do you give him the leeway to challenge you?

Dylan: Yeah, if he feels like it. But usually we just go into the studio and sing a song, and play the music, and have, you know ...

Bono: Have you had somebody in the last five years who said, "That's crap, Bob"?

Dylan: Oh, they say that all the time!

Bono: Mark Knopfler, did he say that?

Dylan: I don't know, they spend time getting their various songs right, but with me, I just take a song into the studio and try to rehearse it, and then record it, and then do it. It's a little harder now though to make a good record—even if you've got a good song and a good band. Even if you go in and record it live, it's not gonna sound like it used to sound, because the studios now are so modern, and overly developed, that you can take anything good and you can press it and squeeze it and squash it, and constipate it and suffocate it. You do a great performance in the studio and you listen back to it because the speakers are all so good, but, ah, no!

Bono: All technology does is—you go into a dead room with dead instruments and you use technology to give it life that it doesn't have, and then it comes out of the speakers and you believe it. What I've been trying to do is find a room that has life in itself.

Dylan: Yeah.

Bono: A 'living' room.

Dylan: The machines though, can even take the life out of that room, I've found. You can record in St. Peter's Cathedral, you know, and they still make it sound like, eh, ...

Bono: Somebody's backyard.

Dylan: Yeah.

Dylan: That's a good idea. I'd love to record in a cathedral.

Dylan: You know the studios in the old days were all much better, and the equipment so much better, there's no question about it in my mind. You just walked into a studio, they were just big rooms, you just sang, you know, you just made records; and they sounded like the way they sounded there. That stopped happening in the late Sixties, for me anyway. I noticed the big change. You go into a studio now and they got rugs on the floor, settees, and pinball machines and videos and sandwiches coming every ten minutes. It's a big expensive party and you're lucky if you come out with anything that sounds decent.

Bono: Yeah, records haven't got better, have they?

Dylan: No, you go in now, you got your producer, you got your engineer, you got your assistant engineer, usually your assistant producer, you got a guy carrying the tapes around. I mean, you know, there's a million people go into recording just an acoustic song on your guitar. The boys turn the machines on and it's a great undertaking.

Bono: There's a system called Effanel which Mick Fleetwood from Fleetwood Mac brought to Africa. It was built for him because he wanted to get some real African drummin' for "Tusk." We've used that system. It comes in a light suitcase, very small, no bullshit studio, and it just arrives, you can literally bring it to your living room.

Morrison: I think all the same they'll go back to 2-track eventually.

Bono: There's a guy called Conny Plank, who lives in Germany. He's a producer, I think. He produced Makem and Clancy and some Irish traditional bands, also orchestral and funnily enough a lot of the new electronic groups, DAF, Ultravox, and so on. He used to record orchestras by just finding a position in the room where they were already balanced and he applies this in his thinking, in recording modern music: He finds a place in the room where it's already mixed.

Morrison: I don't know, when I started we didn't think about that! You didn't even think about recording... [laughs]

Bono: You didn't even think!

Morrison: You didn't even know what was in the cards. One day you were in the room, they turned the tape on. After about eight hours or so, they'd say, 'OK, tea break, it's over.'

Dylan: Yeah, next song, next song!

Morrison: And that was that—it was an album.

Dylan: Yeah, you'd make an album in three days or four days and it was over—if that many! It's that long now... it takes four days to get a drum sound.

Bono: Do you know the Monty Python team, they're comedians, British comedians, Monty Python and the Holy Grail. They have a sketch that reminds me of you guys—sitting back talking of days gone by: "You tell that to the young people of today and they'd never believe you." But you can't go backwards, you must go forward. You try to bring the values that were back there, you know, the strength, and if you see something that was lost, you got to find a new way to capture that same strength. Have you any idea of how to do that? I think you've done it by the way... I think *Shot of Love*, that opening track has that.

Dylan: I think so too. You're one of the few people to say that to me about that record, to mention that record to me.

Bono: That has *that* feeling.

Dylan: It's a great record, it suits just about everybody.

Bono: The sound from that record makes me feel like I'm in the same room as the other musicians. I don't feel like they're over *there*. Some of our records, I feel like they're over there because we got into this cinema-type sound, not bland like FM sound, but we got into this very broad sound. Now we're trying to focus more of a punch, and that's what we are after, this intimacy... I've never interviewed anybody before, by the way. I hate being interviewed myself.

Morrison: You're doing a good job!

Bono: Is this OK?. Good! What records do you listen to?

Dylan: What records do I listen to? New records? I don't know, just the old records really. Robert Johnson. I still listen to those records that I listened to when I was growing up—they really changed my life. They still change my life. They still hold up, you know. The Louvin Brothers,

Hank Williams, Muddy Waters, Howlin' Wolf, Charlie Patton, I always liked to listen to him.

Bono: I just bought Woody Guthrie's *Bound for Glory.* I'm just a beginner when it comes to America. I mean, it's changed me. When you go the U.S., coming from this country, it's more than a different continent...

Morrison: It's shell shock.

Bono: Yeah, coming from troubled Ireland, it's the real shell shock! I'm just getting acquainted with American music and literature. Do you still see Allen Ginsberg?

Dylan: I run across Allen from time to time, yeah, Gregory Corso's back now, he's doing some readings, I think he's just published a new book.

Bono: I've just been reading this book *Howl.*

Dylan: Oh, that's very powerful. That's another book that changed me. *Howl, On the Road, Dharma Bums.*

Morrison: [to Bono] Have you read *On the Road?*

Bono: Yes I have, I'm just starting that. You have a reference in one of your songs to John Donne, 'Rave On John Donne'. Have you read his poetry?

Morrison: I was reading it at the time.

Dylan: [to Bono] You heard the songs—Brendan Behan's songs?

Bono: Yeah.

Dylan: 'Royal Canal,' you know the 'Royal Canal'?

Morrison: His brother wrote it. His name is Dominic.

Dylan: Oh, Dominic wrote 'Royal Canal'?

Bono: You know Brendan's son hangs out around here in Dublin. He's a good guy, I believe.

Dylan: I know the solo lyrics to the 'Royal Canal.' I used to sing it all the time.

Bono: How does it go?

Dylan: [sings] 'The hungry feeling came over me stealing, as the mice were squalling in my prison cell.'

Bono: That's right, yeah!

Dylan: [continues] 'That old triangle went jingle jangle, all along the banks of the Royal Canal.'

Bono: That's right, when did you read that?

Dylan: [there's no way stopping him now] 'In the female prison there's 70 women. It's all over there that I want to dwell. And that old triangle goes jingle jangle, all along the banks of the Royal Canal.'

Bono: Have you been to the Royal Canal?

Dylan: No I used to sing that song though. Every night.

Bono: Our music—as I was saying earlier—it doesn't have those roots.

Morrison: Yeah, there was a break in the lineage. I sussed that out when I went to see Thin Lizzy years ago, the first night in L.A. and I was watching at the back of the stage and I realized that the music was a complete cut in the connection between the end of the Sixties and the middle of the Seventies—a severing of the traditional lineage of groups.

Bono: I'd like to know more about roots music. I'm hungry for a past.

Morrison: You know you should listen to some of that stuff.

Bono: I will. I've been listening to some gospel music, you know, like the Swan Silvertones, and stuff like that.

Dylan: That's U.S. stuff though.

Morrison: U.S. stuff, but the British stuff you should listen to, you know, like some of the old stuff, like the Yardbirds.

Bono: Yeah, I've got some of their tapes recently, some real good tapes.

Dylan: You can still hear the McPeakes. The next generation may not be able to though. Who knows? I would hate to think that. Listen we're gonna have to get ready to play. Are you gonna stay for the show?

Bono: Certainly, that's what I'm here for actually.

Dylan: To record it, HA!

Note: A few years later Dylan and Bono co-wrote "Love Rescue Me" which appeared on Rattle and Hum, *the U2 album released in 1989.*

Dylan and Bono's mutual interest in many forms of music, including traditional Irish ballads, is evident in this interview. In fact, Dylan appreciated Bono's fascination with the past and interest in music history and later believed it showed in U2's music. No doubt Dylan later also appreciated U2's cover of his song "All Along the Watchtower," which gave U2 fans a glimpse of the Dylan universe. In 1993, music journalist Bill Flanagan asked Dylan what drew him to U2 that he did not hear in other young bands. Dylan replied, "Just more of a thread back to the music that got me inspired and into it. Something which still exists, which a group like U2 holds onto. They are actually rooted someplace and they respect that tradition. They work within a certain boundary which has a history to it, and then they can do their own thing on top of that. Unless you start someplace you're just kind of inventing something which maybe need not be invented. That's what would draw me to U2. You can tell what groups are seriously connected and [laughs] seriously disconnected. There is a tradition to the whole thing. You're either part of that or not. I don't know how anybody can do anything and not be connected someplace back there." With a nod to U2's perseverance, Dylan then summed up his attitude about being a singer, songwriter, and performer. "You do have to have a commitment. Not just anybody can get up and do it. It takes a lot of time and work and belief."

THE BEATLES
AND DYLAN

Paul McCartney, George Harrison, Ringo Starr, and John Lennon.

*O*n May 17, 1964, Dylan performed in London at the Royal
Festival Hall. During the intermission, he received a
telegram from John Lennon. It had been five months since
Dylan had first heard The Beatles' "I Want To Hold Your Hand" and
the group had achieved phenomenal success in the U.S. Although The
Beatles had not yet met Dylan, Lennon had found time to send a
telegram saying they wished they could be at Festival Hall, but they
had a filming commitment.

*There have been many written reports of the meetings between The
Beatles and Dylan. Instead of providing an unnecessary introduction
to The Beatles, it's best for the reader to hear from some of the excellent accounts of these historic encounters.*

One of the best recollections is provided in The Beatles: The
Biography *by Bob Spitz. Spitz's exciting and thorough book on The
Beatles covers the early years of the band in exacting detail. Spitz
describes how their years of struggle, playing clubs, dance halls, and
bars in Hamburg, Germany and Liverpool, and then all over*

England not only rocketed them to unprecedented success in the pop world but developed them into cutting-edge, brilliant musicians who played their immortal music with powerful, raw energy and heart-stopping soul. John Lennon and Paul McCartney set a new standard for pop songwriting. Yet even in 1964, at the height of their fame, they were not immune to the powerful influence and charisma of the 22-year-old Bob Dylan.

Paul had been the first to discover Dylan, buying the *Freewheelin'* album before they'd left for Paris at the beginning of 1964, according to Spitz. He wrote:

> That record hit the turntable the moment The Beatles settled into their suite at the George V. "And for the rest of our three weeks in Paris we didn't stop playing it," John recalled. In fact, George considered the experience "one of the most memorable things of the trip," alleviating the irritation of being cooped up in their rooms…" One can only imagine the impact that Dylan's music had on the boys. The album itself was the first of many watersheds in his long career. That sure command of language might have drifted by unnoticed were it the work of an older, more experienced interpreter, but from a 22-year-old folksinger, this articulation of self-expression had major resonance… "I'm sure this kind of thing found its way into our music, and into our lyrics, and influenced whom we were interested in," Paul explained many years afterward. "Vocally and poetically Dylan was a huge influence." Certainly, in addition to the obvious effect it had on his language and style, Dylan's lyrics served to turn John inward as a songwriter.

Spitz noted that in 10 years, no other artist, not even one as inventive as The Beatles, had been able to cultivate rock's literary essence. "Paul Simon, one of the more articulate young songwriters to tap into that reservoir, understood just how liberating Dylan's contributions actually were. 'He made us feel at a certain time that it was good to be smart, to be observant, that it was good to have a social conscience,'" Spitz quoted Simon as saying. Spitz continued, "As a songwriter, [John's] perspective had expanded, and he was trying to break out of the mold. In Dylan, John had finally found what was, for him, a new direction. It is no coincidence that John began writing 'I'm a Loser' while still in Paris. The song is clearly his attempt at constructing an early self-portrait, with its revealing soft focus on relationships and fame... 'I think it was Dylan who helped me realize that,' John concluded, 'not by any discussion or anything, but by hearing his work.'"

In *The Beatles Anthology* John acknowledged Dylan's influence on 'I'm a Loser,' saying, "The word 'clown' is in it. I objected to the word 'clown,' because that was always artsy-fartsy, but Dylan had used it so I thought it was all right, and it rhymed with whatever I was doing. Part of me suspects I'm a loser, and part of me thinks I'm God almighty." Spitz observed that John reveled in the new possibilities of substance and character that might free his imagination from the "mush" he worked on with Paul.

The Beatles and Dylan met the first time in person in the summer of 1964. According to Spitz, that is when Dylan caught up with The Beatles in their suite at the Delmonico about an hour after their first Forest Hills concert. They were in the midst of having dinner with Brian Epstein, Neil Aspinall, and Mal Evans, when Dylan arrived with his road manager, Victor Maimudes, and *New York Post* columnist Al Aronowitz, who had coordinated the get-together as a favor to the boys. The Beatles found that Dylan was eccentric and intense but cool, very cool, in a way that only another pop phenom could appreciate. There was the usual checking-out process, followed by awkward stabs at conversation, until ultimately everyone discovered that they spoke the same language.

Spitz described how The Beatles retrieved their "communal pillbox" from John's bag and Drinamyls and Preludins were offered "like after-dinner mints to the edgy guests." But Dylan, according to Spitz, suggested: "How about something a little more organic? Something green...marijuana." After Brian hesitated on the part of the boys, thinking they had never smoked marijuana before, Dylan rolled a joint, passed it around, and before long, they were all turned on: Giggling, relaxed, laughing, giddy. According to Spitz, John recalled, "[Dylan] kept answering our phone, saying, 'This is Beatlemania here...' We were smoking dope, drinking wine, and generally being rock 'n' rollers, and having a laugh, you know, and surrealism. It was party time." "That it was: *Party time*. And nothing would ever be the same again," concluded The Beatles biographer.

In *The Beatles Anthology*, Ringo later recalled of the get-together, "Bob was our hero. I heard of him through John, who'd played his records to me. He was just great, he was this young dude with great songs. Songs of the time, poetry, and a great attitude."

Paul agreed with Ringo, adding, "He was our idol. I had seen early programs on Granada TV, when we were in Liverpool, about the New York beat poets' scene, where he had been singing along with Allen Ginsberg. So we were into him as a poet, and we all had his first album with his floppy cap. I'm sure that's where the Lennon cap came from. John was a particularly big admirer. It shows in songs like 'Hide Your Love Away.'"

In *Anthology* John added,

> When I met Dylan I was quite dumbfounded. I'm pretty much of a fan type myself, in a way. I stopped being a 'fan' when I started doing it myself. I never went collecting people's autographs, or any of that jive. But if I dig somebody, I really dig them.
>
> 'You've Got To Hide Your Love Away' is my Dylan period. It's one of those that you sing a bit sadly to yourself. 'Here I stand, head in hand....' 'I'd start thinking about my own emotions. I don't know when exactly it started, like 'I'm a Loser' or 'Hide Your Love Away,' those kind of things. Instead of projecting myself into a situation, I would try to express what I felt about myself, which I'd done in my books.
>
> I had a sort of professional songwriter's attitude to writing pop songs, we would turn out a certain style of song for a single, and we would do a certain style of thing for this and the other thing. I'd have a separate songwriting John Lennon who wrote songs for the meat market, and I didn't consider them (the lyrics or anything) to have any depth at all; to express myself I would write *A Spaniard in the Works* or *In His Own Write*, the personal stories which were expressive of my personal emotions. Then I started being me about the songs, not writing them objectively, but subjectively.

Paul added about Dylan, "Lyrically he is still one of the best. Some of the long rambling poems he set to music are still some of my favorite pieces of work."

Later Spitz noted that The Beatles' songwriting, which had begun to drift away from its simplest pop forms, had accelerated under Dylan's influence. If anything, the seven months of constant travel and fame had given them more perspective on the structure of songwriting, confidently testing new chords and progressions, to say nothing of language, every time they buckled down. "We got more and more free to get into ourselves," Paul explained. "And I think also John and I wanted to do something bluesy, a bit darker, more grown-up. Rather than just straight pop." Spitz said that John's and Paul's fascination with Dylanesque touches—and to some extent the Stones' foray into R&B—cast an edgy enthusiasm over their efforts. There is a definite bridge here to their later albums, discernible in songs such as "I'm a Loser." Spitz also mentioned "Norwegian Wood" and "No Reply" in this context.

When The Beatles played the Paramount Theater in New York on September 20, 1964, Dylan attended and saw Beatlemania in action: Teenagers screaming so loudly the group's music could hardly be heard. Dylan stood on a chair to get a better view of the stage. According to journalist Al Aronowitz, Dylan remarked that the show was the opposite of his concerts, where the audience listened to every word he sang, and he was proud that his concerts were different.

The Beatles' public endorsement of Dylan, in January 1965, triggered Dylan's British breakthrough, according to biographer Robert Shelton. The Dylan tour of England in the spring of 1965 changed him from a folk star into an international pop superstar. To wit, in March, the 7,000 tickets for his May 10 Albert Hall concert sold out within two hours. As Shelton noted, Ray Coleman's article in *Melody Maker* on January 9, 1965 was headlined: "Beatles Say—Dylan Shows The Way." The story—with photos of Lennon, Harrison, and Dylan—was reproduced on the sleeve of the Columbia single of "Subterranean Homesick Blues," whose B-side was "She Belongs to Me."

Shelton recalled that during this tour, Lennon visited Dylan late one night at the Savoy Hotel. Wrote the biographer, "[Lennon] thought those who criticized Dylan for staying at such a plush hotel were fools. Lennon asked, 'What's wrong with staying at the Savoy? Does starving in a garret make his points any more valid? They say to be authentic as a folker you must also be poor and act the part. Absolute rubbish! Especially when you consider that the people he's sometimes having a go at—politicians especially—are probably twice as well off, anyway. If you've got a lot to say, like Dylan has, and if you want to make it heard, you've just got to elevate yourself and make yourself famous so people will listen. Earning a fortune's nothing to do with that side of it, but if he happens to do that as well, good luck to him.'"

Shelton also said that Lennon invited Dylan to dinner at his house in Weybridge, Surrey where the two played records and talked. Shelton quoted John as saying, "He's an interesting bloke with some good ideas. We swapped addresses and said we'd exchange ideas for songs, but it never happened. He said he sent me things, but he got the address wrong and it never arrived. Maybe that's why we get on well—we're both pretty disorganized blokes."

Dylan told Shelton about his visits with Lennon during trips to Britain in 1965 and 1966. "I dug his situation where he lived. It was a 22-room house. Do you know what I did when I got back from England, man? I bought me a 31-room house, can you imagine that? Mine! I bought one just as soon as I got back from England. And it turned into a *nightmare!*" Dylan could be exaggerating the size, but it was indeed an imposing property that he bought for himself and Sara (they married in November, 1965) in the Arts and Crafts colony of Byrdcliffe, a mile from the center of Woodstock. Their sprawling home, built of dark-brown cedar wood, was called Hi Lo Ha. The four-acre property was set back in thick woodland with a mountain stream filling a natural swimming hole, with space for basketball games and a large heated garage. Dylan used part of the garage as a private pool hall.

The friendship between The Beatles and Dylan was always warm and non-competitive. A few years later, when Dylan was interviewed for *Rolling Stone*, he was asked about Lennon and Dylan replied, "Oh, I always love to see John. Always. He's a wonderful fellow."

The *Biograph* liner notes mention an interesting footnote to musical history: During an early English tour, Dylan visited the home of John Lennon and the two penned a song together. "I don't remember what it was, though," said Dylan. "We played some stuff into a tape recorder, but I don't know what happened to it. I can remember playing it and the recorder was on. I don't remember anything about the song."

Lennon said later, "I've grown up enough to communicate with [Dylan]... Both of us were always uptight, you know, and of course I wouldn't know whether he was uptight because I was so uptight, and then when he wasn't uptight, I was—all that bit. But we just sat it out because we just liked being together."

In 1978 when *Playboy* interviewed Dylan, Ron Rosenbaum asked him about influences, and to whom he was listening. Dylan cited some blues players like Lightnin' Hopkins, Robert Johnson, and Memphis Minnie. When Rosenbaum asked him about "more popular stuff," Dylan cited Nana Mouskouri. Rosenbaum asked about The Beatles and

Dylan said, "I've always liked the way George Harrison plays guitar—restrained and good. As for Lennon, well, I was encouraged by his book [*In His Own Write*]. Or the publishers were encouraged, because they asked me to write a book and that's how *Tarantula* came about. John has taken poetics pretty far in popular music. A lot of his work is over-looked, but if you examine it, you'll find key expressions that have never been said before to push across his point of view. Things that are symbolic of some inner reality and probably will never be said again."

The interviewer then asked Dylan whether or not he listened to his own stuff. "Not so much," Dylan replied.

Another fascinating glimpse into The Beatles' and Dylan's relationship comes from Donovan's insightful autobiography. Donovan paints his pictures with a light, sardonic touch, using the same deftness and luminosity that pervade his reflective music. Donovan recalled a visit with Dylan at the Savoy Hotel in London in 1964. When Donovan called Dylan from the lobby, Dylan's sidekick Bob Neuwirth told Donovan to come up to the suite. Donovan described Neuwirth leading the way through the silent apartments to a door that opened into a small room. A television was on in the room, and Donovan heard a voice say, "Hey Don, come in. Siddown." He recalled, "On the floor I sat, beatnik fashion, little Bob in a big soft chair. On the screen, ice-skating. It's late and British TV is nearly in its pajamas. I was a little stoned on hash, and we said nothing." After Donovan and Dylan stared at the TV screen, and Donovan's eyes became accustomed to the dark he became aware that they were not alone. Donovan wrote:

> Shapes appear, on a sofa, on chairs. Four figures emerge from the still corners. The one nearest speaks, 'Hullo, Donovan, hawareya?' The accent is unmistakable, the nasal drawl. It's John and the rest of the band. Bob stands and switches on the light. "Have you met these guys yet?" asks Bob.
>
> It was the four Beatles and they stood also, smiling and nodding to me, amused at my surprise. The four were dressed in identical blue jeans, powder blue, soft and bohemian. I smiled back. There was very little to say. After a smoke of the herb, silence *is* the best way to communicate.
>
> Here I was with five of the most influential musicians and songwriters on the planet, accepted into the

inner circle without fuss, no pop celebrity bullshit. They were all a few years older than me, and I felt like a younger brother.

George Harrison was to say later, "You felt out of your depth, but you weren't, you know." I did feel awestruck a bit. For Christ's sake, it was only a few months earlier that I was sleeping in a pillbox in St. Ives and washing dishes a cardboard wall away from a juke-box jumping with Beatles' hits.

Later, as the get-together ended, George Harrison asked Donovan if he wanted a lift:

> Bob and I said good night, and he invited me around again before he returned to the States. He and I were see-ing a lot of each other. George, John, Ringo, Paul, and I went down the hotel stairs, hoping to avoid any possible fan or media mania, and walked across the Savoy foyer to the parking lot where I was amazed to see four iden-tical custom Mini-Cooper cars ready for 'The Boys.' I guess it was Peter Sellers who had turned The Beatles on to these little cars. The four young blades in blue stood by their four minichariots, and John said to me, 'See ya, Donovan. Let's get together again and play a few songs.' I got into George's mini, furnished inside with leather seats and a fab hi-fi. I did a double take and thought, 'What a flash bloke.' George saw me judge him and understood. He revved up his sporty mini and the natu-ral driver in him zoomed us through the graveyard streets to London to my pad. George and I would become dear friends on the path.

About three years later, The Beatles visited Dylan at his London hotel with their latest album, *Sgt. Pepper's Lonely Hearts Club Band*. Paul recalled, "I remember taking it round to Dylan at the Mayfair Hotel in London; I went round as if I were going on a pilgrimage. Keith Richards was in the outer room and we had to hang around and then went in to meet Dylan. It was a little bit like an audience with the Pope. I remember playing him some of *Sgt. Pepper* and he said, 'Oh, I get it— you don't want to be cute any more.' That was the feeling about *Rubber*

Soul, too. We'd had our cute period and now it was time to expand."

Known as "the quiet Beatle," lead guitarist George Harrison became a good friend of Dylan's. George and his wife Pattie visited the Dylan family at Woodstock during Thanksgiving of 1968. George recalled, "I was hanging out at his house with him, Sara and his kids. He seemed very nervous and I felt a little uncomfortable—it seemed strange especially as he was in his own home." It took about three days until, George said, "we got the guitars out and then things loosened up and I was saying to him, 'write me some words,' and thinking of all this 'Johnny's in the basement, mixing up the medicine,' type of thing and he was saying, 'Show me some chords, how do you get those tunes?'" Overall, George said he "had a great time." During the visit, Dylan and George wrote a song together, "I'd Have You Anytime" which appeared on Harrison's 1970 double album *All Things Must Pass.* The visit was uplifting for George because he had escaped some of The Beatles' difficulties during a time when they were not getting along well and disagreeing on the direction of the band. George returned to record with The Beatles after the visit, and recalled, "For me, to come back into the winter of discontent at Twickenham was very unhealthy and unhappy. But I can remember feeling quite optimistic about it. I thought, "OK, it's the New Year and we have a new approach to recording. I think that the first couple of days were OK, but it was soon quite apparent that it was just the same as it had been when we were last in the studio, and it was going to be painful again. There was a lot of trivia and games being played." During this period, The Beatles were on the way to breaking up.

Yet despite the tensions, The Beatles stayed together long enough to produce the magnificent *Abbey Road,* which was released in the U.S. in 1970. While rock fans in the States were descending en masse onto Yasgur's farm for the Woodstock music festival on August 15, 1969, Dylan and his family were on their way to the Isle of Wight, where he had agreed to play. During the visit the Dylans stayed at the sixteenth-century manor house at Forelands Farm, Bembridge, where they were provided with a housekeeper and a chauffeur-driven Humber. An adjacent barn was available for rehearsing with The Band. Dylan was reportedly nervous about his appearance, which was one of his first big concerts since his 1966 motorcycle accident. During his stay at Forelands, a couple of days before the concert a big limousine pulled up and The Beatles' road manager, Mal Evans, jumped out, marking an X on the lawn. Then a helicopter descended, carrying Ringo Starr, John Lennon, and Yoko Ono. The Beatles played Bob acetates of their new album,

Abbey Road. That night, Bob jammed with members of The Beatles and The Band. Dylan, Harrison, and Lennon sang duets on Beatles songs, but played mostly rock 'n' roll numbers. When Dylan and The Band performed at the Isle of Wight Festival, in front of 200,000 people, Shelton said they "suffered from the festival's vast, impersonal setting and general mismanagement."

George continued to maintain the longest and deepest friendship with Dylan. George joined Dylan's sessions for *Self Portrait* in May 1970. Charlie Daniels played bass on the sessions and recalled, "It was a day I'll never forget. It wasn't Bob Dylan and George Harrison. It was four guys in the studio making music." The musicians called out songs for Bob to sing. "Anything you threw at [Bob], he could sing. It was such a nice thing, such a great day, hour after hour." The tracks did not officially appear on an album, at least not with a credit for Harrison because he did not have a U.S. work permit, but copies of the tapes soon passed into the hands of bootleggers.

In August 1971, Dylan was one of the headliners for George's Concert for Bangladesh to benefit victims of the country's natural disasters and a bloody civil war. George backed Dylan on electric guitar, with Leon Russell playing bass. Ringo Starr played tambourine. Dylan performed five songs and critics noted that his delivery of "Just Like a Woman" was especially powerful. He sang the chorus in harmony with Harrison and Russell, the first time Dylan had ever sung on stage with a Beatle. And as a favor to his friend George, Dylan performed at the concert for free.

Later, Dylan and Sara visited George and Pattie in England when they needed a break during the arduous filming in Mexico of *Pat Garrett and Billy the Kid* in 1973. Over a decade later Dylan and Harrison collaborated on the *Traveling Wilburys Volume 1*. The album became a major commercial success when it was released in the fall of 1988, reaching Number Three in the U.S. album charts, and selling more copies than any Dylan album in that decade. In the spring of 1990, the group recorded a second Traveling Wilburys record, without Roy Orbison, who had died of a heart attack in December 1988 at the age of 52. Around that time, George talked about his appreciation for Dylan's music and the vagaries of fame in an interview with Jenny Boyd, his former sister-in-law (Jenny is his first wife Pattie's sister). George mentioned that musicians can help those who listen to their music.

"I think it's important to share experiences. For instance, if Dylan hadn't said some of the things he did, nobody else was going to say them. Can you imagine what a world it would be if we didn't have a Bob Dylan? It would be awful. There's that side of it. But then there's the other side, where you can start mistaking your own importance. I think I've been in both of those [positions] at various times. You suddenly think you're more groovy than you are and then usually something happens to slap you down a bit, so it all has to be tempered with discretion." George was also quite modest and frank in talking to Boyd about his complete bafflement at the enormous popularity The Beatles achieved in the '60s.

"I thought it was pretty strange why we made the enormous impact that we did—or have still," George said. "It's strange how the chemistry between the four of us made this big thing that went right through the world. There wasn't any country in the world, even the most obscure places, that didn't know about The Beatles—from grandparents to babies. It just blanketed everything, and that amazed me more than anything. We always felt that if we could get the right record contract, we'd be successful. But our tiny little concept of success that we had at the time was nothing compared to what happened. It was just enormous. It does make one think that there's more to this than meets the eye." Ringo Starr agreed with George, "I don't think we were actually there thinking we were tapping into this great God-given consciousness for everybody. I don't know if you think like that when you're a teenager or (in) your early twenties. You're just playing the best you can." The humility and sense of wonder George and Ringo both alluded to says a lot about their personalities, even years after fame had overtaken their lives. They were still amazed by it.

The mutual respect between Harrison and Dylan was very evident to those closest to them. In talking about songwriting, Olivia Harrison, George's second wife—while naturally being biased—said that "George's lyrics were, in my opinion, the most spiritually conscious of our time, although George, in turn, usually referred to the lyrics of Bob Dylan when trying to make a point or elucidate his own feelings of isolation and frustration brought about by things in and beyond this life."

George appeared at Bob Dylan's 30th Anniversary Concert at Madison Square Garden in 1992, where he introduced Dylan, "Some call him Bobby, some call him Zimmy, I call him Lucky! Ladies and gentlemen, Bob Dylan!" to the tumultuous roar of the crowd. A grinning George Harrison playfully romped through "Absolutely Sweet Marie." To watch George play with Dylan and friends like Eric Clapton and Neil Young on "My Back Pages" and "Knockin' on Heaven's Door" was as happy a memory as one can have, underscoring the warm friendship and rapport between this former Beatle and the often-elusive Dylan. It was a concert for the history books.

Nine years later, George was dead. He lost his long battle with throat cancer and died in Los Angeles on November 29, 2001, with his wife Olivia and son Dhani at his side. He was 58. In 1980 John Lennon had been murdered by a deranged fan outside his apartment building in New York. The December 8 anniversary of his death is still commemorated with great mourning and tributes throughout the world. In light of these tragedies, the magic of The Beatles' joyful music in the early '60s, their effusive public endorsement of Dylan in 1965, Beatlemania, and the cultural change these four working-class lads from Liverpool wrought on an unsuspecting world seemed a precious and fading memory.

When George died, only two of the beloved Beatles remained alive. Ringo had once said of The Beatles, "They became the closest friends I'd ever had. I was an only child and suddenly I felt as though I'd got three brothers. We really looked out for each other and we had many laughs together. In the old days we'd have the hugest hotel suites, the whole floor of a hotel, and the four of us would end up in the bathroom, just to be with each other." In his tribute to George, a heartbroken Paul echoed Ringo's feelings when he said, "I am devastated and very, very sad… He is really just my baby brother."

George's early death from cancer while he was in the prime of life and Lennon's murder testified to the vulnerability of the Beatles and other stars, like Dylan, whose work has elevated them to such stellar levels. Dylan once said he was mystified by what he considered the "deification" of John Lennon following his tragic death. If Lennon and Dylan shared anything, it was that anti-establishment feeling, a cheeky and cynical distrust of idols, heroes, or as Dylan put it "Don't follow leaders/Watch parking meters." What must he think, then, when critic Richard Goldstein notes of Dylan, "He's the emblem of his generation's splendor. Beatified in his youth, he's cruising toward sainthood today." Dylan has dusted off that faded halo, and signed up for a DJ spot on XM satellite radio, where he illuminates musical gems by a wide range of performers: from Fats Domino to Stevie Wonder, from the Carter Family to the Staple Singers; from Frank Sinatra to Jimi Hendrix. The irreverence of his youth has been replaced by a reverence for the past. In theme-oriented radio shows (the weather, whisky, mother) he is using his lofty pulpit to support what he loves best: the music.

AFTERWORD

*I*n the course of twenty crowded years, one parts with many illu-
sions. I did not wish to lose the early ones. Some memories are
better than realities, and are better than anything that can happen to one again.

—Willa Cather, *My Antonia*

This journey into Bob Dylan's life and his friendships has illuminat-
ed some of the great excitement involved in Dylan's achievements. He
holds an unparalleled status in American culture. He has forged revolutionary changes that have transformed folk-rock and the craft of songwriting. Thoughtful friends have also reflected on what is missing from
Dylan's life. He tours constantly. Unlike peers like Paul McCartney,
Bruce Springsteen, or Bono, who have had celebrated marriages, Dylan
keeps quiet about his personal life. The writer of great love songs like
"Sad Eyed Lady of the Lowlands" and "Lay Lady Lay" seems to be
spending his later years as a wandering troubadour, serenading others
with songs of love then leaving the stage alone to write or draw in his

journal in a colorless hotel miles from home.

Why does he keep performing? Friends have noted that, like his peers McCartney and Clapton, he performs because it is what he knows. It is more than a job; it is what he *loves* to do. No one told Picasso or Matisse to stop painting after their sixty-fifth birthdays. No one complained when Pablo Casals played cello as beautifully at 70 as he did at 55. Robert Frost was 87 when he recited his poem "The Gift Outright" at John F. Kennedy's inauguration. There is a timelessness to great art, and inspiring music, poetry, and art outlast pedestrian restraints such as age. Artists know how to transcend such limitations. Perhaps it is because rock 'n' roll has always been synonymous with youth that we find it incongruous to be lining up for concerts performed by musicians who are in their mid-'60s, gray-haired, and grizzly. But could it be time for reevaluation? Forty years ago rock was the exclusive province of the young, and we've all grown up together. Now it is twentieth-century music: Ageless, wearing the shiny, worn patina of good copper. For the '60s generation, it is also our legacy to pass on to those coming after us. We may not have achieved racial equality or stopped wars, but we still have the music.

This journey into the friendships and musical relationships that contributed to the unique shape of Dylan's career also may resonate personally with each reader. I was about 11 years old and living in the oil camps in the jungles of Venezuela, where my father worked for an Exxon subsidiary, when I began my love affair with rock 'n' roll. We had parties at the golf club in the center of the oil camp there, and we played records we brought down from the States like Elvis' "It's Now or Never" and Del Shannon's "Runaway." To the sounds of Bobby Vee's "Take Good Care of My Baby" we did the gentle dancing of the day, rocking back and forth on our heels, holding hands. A little spin here. A twirl there. The boys, in their button-down shirts and khakis, smelled of Canoe. Our parents had long, animated dinner parties fueled by rum, bourbon, and scotch and listened to Johnny Mathis. Acacia trees lined the wide streets of the manicured camp, with its identical stucco houses installed with ceiling fans to cool the tropical heat. Families owned parrots as well as dogs and cats, and grew exotic orchids on their patios. The distant thunder of Vietnam, of Birmingham, of Selma, seemed far, far away. "Why must I be a teenager in love?" crooned Dion as we danced. Then the drums rolled, a deep chortle came over the P.A system. and we heard "Wipe out…" and the irresistible rhythm riff of the surf guitars.

Later, I was in a strict boarding school in eastern Canada where no television or radio was allowed and where we were only permitted to listen to records for one hour on Saturday afternoons. A spill during a ski trip fortuitously put me in the hospital in February of 1964 when The Beatles first appeared on the Ed Sullivan Show. Since I was in the hospital I was able to watch. I instantly fell in love with the joyful sounds of "She Loves You" and my lifelong passion for rock 'n' roll was exalted to a near-obsession. I remember the first time I heard Dylan's *Freewheelin'* album and wondered where he would take folk rock. He had such authority and presence. Later, this obsession of sorts placed me at the Monterey Pop Festival where I far preferred the bone-chilling blues of Janis Joplin to Jimi Hendrix's pyrotechnics and The Who's explosive finale. I saw Janis again in 1969 at her last concert at Harvard Stadium, and then made my way to Yasgur's farm with 300,000 others for the Woodstock Festival, covering it for *The Harvard Crimson*. But already, a change was in the air. Even before Altamont, we knew that this euphoria could not continue. We would have to grow up...*someday*.... But it was always the music that tied us to our ephemeral, fleeting youth and all the music, love, hope, and idealism it embodied. The music also embodied a new language that was sweeping the culture: A new way of speaking, thinking, caring. Its messages were universal messages: "All You Need Is Love," "Universal Soldier," "A Change Is Gonna Come," "Respect." And with these messages inspiring us, our generation felt omnipotent, invulnerable, both wise and young at the same time, seeking a new union, a greater communion, a higher spirituality. We would right the old wrongs. We stood for justice.

"We could have played all night," is what Dylan said to me when we met at the post-concert party at The Last Waltz, The Band's farewell concert in San Francisco in 1976. About 15 years later, when he performed a free concert spontaneously at a small college in the Boston area, I had a front row seat just three yards from the small stage. Dylan had abandoned his normally impassive stage persona and was winking and laughing with the audience in between playing his guitar, harmonica, and singing. He was joyful. The highs Dylan gets from an enthralled, rapturous audience and the thrill he feels from playing with a tight, rhythmic band may well make long days on the road pale in comparison. This is *his life*—it is a self-defined creative life. *He is his own man.*

As an artist he has inspired millions with the simplicity and power of his timeless songs. In this book his friends have been unanimous in offering expressions of gratitude for his gifts. They have shared treasured memories that made us all feel young again, helped us remember hearing a certain Dylan song for the first time, and rekindled our belief that indeed, for an adventurous soul, anything is possible. So Dylan continues to lead his life on the road as the outsider, a picaresque hero on the run, painting vivid pictures, singing ageless songs, and drawing dreams of an unforgettable American landscape. No matter what path you have chosen since the '60s, you have had the music as your steady companion. It has comforted and uplifted you. It has made your journey swifter and your burden lighter. For all of you—including those born after the '60s—you have appreciated the music of Bob Dylan and that of all of his friends, and I thank you for taking this journey with me. With that, I think it is fitting that I close with Bob's own lyrics.

This is for Bob, and for you, dear friend:

> *May God bless and keep you always*
> *May your wishes all come true,*
> *May you always do for others*
> *And let others do for you*
> *May you build a ladder to the stars*
> *And climb on every rung*
> *And may you stay*
> *Forever young.*

—"Forever Young"
B. Dylan Copyright © 1973 by Ram's Horn Music.

ABOUT THE AUTHOR

Photo by John McDermott

Kathleen Mackay has co-authored several nonfiction books and contributed to the anthology *The Anne Rice Reader.* A Harvard graduate, her writing on arts and culture has appeared in *Time, People, Rolling Stone, Los Angeles Times, Washington Post,* and many other publications. She lives in Concord, Massachusetts. Her Web site is *www.kathleenmmackay.com.*

ACKNOWLEDGEMENTS

Heartfelt thanks to my friends and trusted colleagues: Agent Elisabeth Weed of Trident Media; Omnibus Press managing editor Andrea Rotondo; and attorney Christine Cuddy of Kleinberg, Lopez, Lange, and Cuddy. I also want to thank Sarah Mitchell for her excellent research and editing, and Merrin Layzan and Stephanie Tung for other research assistance.

A warm thank you of course to all the musicians who took the time to be interviewed for this book. In addition, thanks to Jeff Rosen, of Special Rider Music; my former *Rolling Stone* editor Ben Fong-Torres; Jim Henke of the Rock and Roll Hall of Fame; Michael Smith and the late Harold Leventhal of Woody Guthrie Archives; Betty Stookey, Joyce Hall, Denise Levy, Jeff Velline, Lisa Kristofferson, Mary and Wanda Hawkins, Danny Kahn, Elizabeth Freund, Jonathan Taplin, Thom Mackay, and Ike Williams. The incomparable Lourdes Blanco published my first articles on music in *The Daily Journal* in Caracas, Venezuela in the summer of 1966, and treated the criticism offered by a 17-year-old seriously and professionally. In the '60s and '70s music critic Ralph J. Gleason, *San Francisco Chronicle* columnist John Wasserman and promoter Bill Graham were warm and encouraging friends, and it was difficult to see their lives end too soon. More recently, steadfast friends like Janet Bailey, Priscilla McMillan, Margot and Eric Hawke, and Harry Gittes also offered support, encouragement, and appreciation for the music history contained here, as did my husband, David Garcelon, in abundance.

Oriana Fallaci deserves a special acknowledgment. Years ago she broke down barriers for women journalists and recorded inspiring, passionate interviews with history that stand the test of time.

SOURCE NOTES

Foreword

"More confessional than professional": Dylan in the *Songtalk Interview* with Paul Zollo, 1991 in *Younger Than That Now*, p. 270.

"The Times They Are A-Changin'": Baez, p. 92.

Donovan's description of Dylan: Donovan, p. 86.

"I was there to find": *Chronicles*, p. 9.

1961–1965 Greenwich Village and Beyond

1. Noel Paul Stookey of Peter Paul and Mary

Grossman creates PP&M: *Goldmine*, April 12, 1996.

Dylan living at Van Ronk's: *Chronicles*, p. 92.

PP&M's recording milestones: PP&M web site, accessed July 15, 2005.

Dylan Town Hall concert: *Sounes*, p. 129–130.

2. Liam Clancy

Clancy's Irish childhood: *The Mountain of the Women,* jacket copy.

Elvis Presley's influence: *Biograph Liner Notes,* p. 5.

Protégé of Pete Seeger and Woody Guthrie: *Bob Dylan: The Early Years,* p. 17

Dylan on Clancy, *No Direction Home.*

Bar at Gerde's Folk City: *The Mountain of the Women,* p. 257

Robert Shelton pushing Dylan: Bauldie, *Wanted Man: In Search of Bob Dylan,* interview by Patrick Humphries, London, 1984.

Dylan at *30th Anniversary Concert: Bob Dylan,* Sony/Columbia Video.

Times change, but Dylan leaves a lasting imprint": Judy Collins, quoted by Edna Gunderson, *USA Today,* May 17, 2001.

French poets and beat writers' influence: *Biograph Liner Notes,* p. 5.

Paul Clayton's suicide: *Mountain of the Women,* p. 258.

Dave Van Ronk quote: *No Direction Home.*

Clancy's father on being an actor: *Mountain of the Women,* p. 72.

3. Pete Seeger

Mike Baker's records: Sounes, *Down the Highway,* p. 47.

Seeger on Wyclef Jean's "Guantanamera,": Rogovoy, *Pete Seeger.*

Music could shape society: Seeger's father in Dunway, *How Can I Keep from Singing?* p. 15.

Folk music and politics go hand in hand: interview with Jeffrey Pepper Rodgers *of Acoustic Guitar magazine* in Dunway.

Influence of Woody Guthrie: *Acoustic Guitar.*

Seeger's singing moved people: Dunaway, p. 221.

Visit to Mississippi: Sounes, p. 134.

Medgar Evers' murder, Wikipedia online, Sept. 7, 2005.

"The songs are there…" *Sing Out!*

An entertainer should always be happy: *No Direction Home.*

I look upon myself and other songwriters, Zollo, *Songwriters on Songwriting,* p. 12.

Rock and Roll Hall of Fame Induction Speech, Hall of Fame Web site, September 7, 2005.

Woody Guthrie "opened up a whole new world,": *Younger Than That Now,* p. 116.

"Old songs–people have always been changing them": *No Direction Home,* Scorsese film.

4. Joan Baez

"The Queen of Folksingers, that would have to be Joan Baez," to "made your teeth drop," *Chronicles,* p. 254–257.

"He was not overly impressive" Baez, p. 83.

Dylan and Joan meet, Hajdu, p. 77

She had a hit album, Hajdu, p. 89–90.

"Everything was happening too fast," Hajdu, p. 89.

Monterey Folk Festival, Hajdu, p. 159–160.

"His humor was dry, private and splendid." Baez, p. 85.

Newport Folk Festival, Hajdu, p. 166–167.

"They were the King and Queen," Sounes, p. 136.

Biographers have noted, Sounes, p. 136.

A variety of photographers, Williams, *Bob Dylan: Performing Artist 1960–1973,* p. 84

"I was getting audiences" Baez, p. 90.

Dylan on Baez's tour, Williams, p. 84.

"On August 28, 1963" Sounes, p. 140.

"Nothing could have spoken" Baez, p. 92.

When they were in New York, Sounes, p. 141.

Dylan came out to California, Sounes, p.141.

"mumbled something about marriage" Baez, p. 94.

"I loved the fame" Baez, p. 94.

"I left happily with memories" Baez, p. 93.

"It never calmed down" Baez, p. 96.

"That sold-out concert" Baez, p. 97.

Although Joan had not been asked to his room, Baez, p. 98.

Dylan married Sara Lownds, Sounes, p. 193

Dylan and Sara divorce, Sounes, p. 306.

Joan thought the project was a silly one, Baez, p. 239.

1984 tour in Europe, Sounes, p. 361.

5. Bobby Vee

Dylan on Bobby Vee: *Chronicles*, p. 79–80.

Vee recollections of Dylan with The Shadows: Bobby Vee website copyright 2005. Accessed August 11, 2005.

John Kangas quote: *No Direction Home.*

Dylan at The Shadows concert in Long Island: *Wanted Man—In Search of Bob Dylan,* p. 18–19.

Growing up in Fargo, N.D.: Interview with Gary James, *www.classicbands.com.*

Dylan relied on instinct and intuition: *Chronicles,* p. 149.

6. Maria Muldaur

Dylan quote: *No Direction Home.*

Bruce Langhorne quote: *No Direction Home.*

"Folk music was strict": Dylan in *Biograph,* p. 6.

Dylan's writing process, *The Early Years,* p. 50.

Dylan playing harmonica on Victoria Spivey's album in 1961: *The Early Years,* p 24–25.

Theodore Bikel quote: Shelton, p. 306.

Review of *Maria Muldaur:* Landau *Rolling Stone,* June 6, 1974.

Review of *Waitress in the Donut Shop,* Maria Muldaur: Landau *Rolling Stone,* December 19, 1974.

Back-up singers in San Francisco in 1979: Williams, *The Middle Years,* p. 153.

Guest performers at Warfield shows: Williams, *The Middle Years,* p. 178.

Bloomfield joined the band at the Warfield: Sounes, p. 337.

7. Johnny Rivers

Dylan on Johnny Rivers: *Chronicles,* p. 60.

Rivers' biographical information: *www.johnnyrivers.com,* August 15, 2005.

Rivers meets Elvis: Tianen, *Milwaukee Journal Sentinel on line.*

"It was pretty exciting...", "Conversation with Rivers," Hazen, *Vintage Guitar* magazine.

1966–1976 Woodstock, Nashville and Beyond

8. Kris Kristofferson

Biographical material: Morthland, *Singer/Songwriter.*

Ron Rosenbaum interview: from *Playboy* in *Younger Than That Now.*

Pitched songs to everybody: Skanse, *Rolling Stone,* November 5, 1999.

Wrote "Me and Bobby McGee" in the Gulf of Mexico: Skanse, *Rolling Stone.*

Bob Neuwirth introduces Janis Joplin to Kristofferson: *Buried Alive,* p. 209–211.

Kristofferson's compositions in high demand: *Wikipedia.org, Kris Kristofferson site.*

On the set of Pat Garrett and Billy the Kid: Sounes, p. 271 from Weddle, *If They Move…Kill 'Em*; as quoted in Sounes, *Down the Highway.*

Pat Garrett filming: Dylan in Crowe, *Biograph Liner Notes*, p. 13.

Composing music for Pat Garrett: Dylan, Sounes, p. 272.

Ron Rosenbaum *Playboy* interview: *Younger Than That Now.*

A songwriter's songwriter: Skanse, *Rolling Stone,* November 5, 1999.

9. Ronnie Hawkins (with The Band)

"We'd grown up with Ronnie Hawkins": Helm, *This Wheel's on Fire*, p. 165.

Hawkins' camel walk: Helm, *This Wheel's on Fire*, p. 46

Ronnie could work a crowd: Helm, *This Wheel's on Fire*, p. 48.

Ronnie Hawkins had molded us: Helm, *This Wheel's on Fire*, p. 9

Music the Hawks played: Eder, *All-Music Guide.*

Robbie Robertson, "It was a rowdy life…to secured by one another": Marcus, *Mystery Train*, p. 72.

Bob's lack of experience: Sounes, *Down the Highway*, p. 188.

On European tour: Robbie Robertson in Crowe, *Biograph Liner Notes.*

"Dylan was compelled to justify his withdrawal…": Shelton, p. 376.

"Some of the songs…," Helm, p. 155–156.

John Simon: Helm, *This Wheel's on Fire*, p. 164.

Basement Tapes released: Crowe, *Biograph*, p. 12.

"We went from a bar band": Sounes, p. 215.

On The Band's music: Marcus, *Mystery Train*, p. 44.

"He is a power figure": Ralph J. Gleason in Shelton, p. 333.

1974 tour "Knockin' on Dylan's Door": Fong-Torres, *Rolling Stone,* February 14, 1974.

Graham quote on 1974 tour: Graham and Greenfield, p. 360.

Renaldo and Clara: Baez, *And a Voice to Sing With*, p. 239.

Shooting Renaldo, Clara, and improvisation: Williams, *The Middle Years.*

Pauline Kael on Renaldo and Clara: Shelton, p. 471.

Richard Manuel's suicide: Helm, *This Wheel's on Fire*, p. 295.

10. Rosanne Cash

Johnny Cash first meets Dylan: Cash, *Cash: The Autobiography* p. 266.

Johnny Cash gave Dylan a guitar: *No Direction Home.*

Cash on Dylan's album *Freewheelin'*: Cash, p. 267.

Cash on Dylan's music: *Cash: The Autobiography*, p. 266.

Cash on visiting Dylan in Woodstock, Cash, p. 267.

Dylan wrote "Lay Lady Lay": Sounes, p. 237.

Dylan and Cash recording together: Sounes, p. 238.

Dylan on Cash's television show: Sounes, p. 241.

Quote from Bill Carruthers: Shelton, p. 402.

Quote from Joni Mitchell: Shelton, p. 402.

"The way we did it was honest:" Cash in *Cash: The Autobiography*, p. 104.

Cash's attitude towards his daughter: Cash, p. 354.

Rosanne on the film *Walk the Line*: Fusilli interview, *Wall Street Journal.*

Reflecting on her father, "Why didn't I let him in?" Fusilli interview, *Wall Street Journal.*

Review of Black Cadillac: Light, *New York Times.*

"From Country to Show Tunes": Holden, *New York Times.*

Remembering Johnny: DeCurtis, *Rolling Stone.*

1980–2006 On the Road to Reinvention

11. Bruce Springsteen

Bruce Springsteen: Rock and Roll Hall of Fame, Dylan induction speech, 1988. Hall of Fame Web site, February 10, 2005.

He joined his first band, Sawyers, *Racing in the Street*, p. 3.

Late at night....Sawyers, *Racing in the Street*, p. 3.

Elwood quote: Sawyers, *Racing in the Street.*

John Hammond auditioning Springsteen: Knobler, *Crawdaddy* reprinted in *Racing in the Street.*

Comparisons to Dylan: *Crawdaddy*, March 1973.

Interview with Springsteen: Williams, *Crawdaddy* October 1974. Reprinted in Racing in the Street.

Landau on Springsteen: Marcus, *Racing in the Street*, p. 7

Review of Springseen, "Rock's New Sensation": Cocks, *Time.*

Lester Bangs on Springsteen: Creem, November 1975. Reprinted in *Racing in the Street.*

Marcus on the E Street Band, *Racing in the Street*, p. 8.

Dave Marsh, *Rolling Stone*, September 25, 1975.

"I didn't grow up in a community": "Rock and Read: Will Percy Interview Bruce Springsteen," *DoubleTake*, Spring, 1998. Reprinted in *Racing in the Street*.

"When you listen to those early rock records," "Out on the Streets," Robert Hilburn, *Los Angeles Times*, 1985. Reprinted in *Racing in the Street*.

Chronology of Springsteen marriage, children born, Sawyers, xxii.

Neil Strauss on Springsteen: Straus, *New York Times*, May 7, 1995.

12. Bono

Biography of Bono: Kevin Byrne, U2 Web site, January 20, 2006.

"Taking its lead from classic figures like...": Graff, *Launch*. June 7, 2001.

"U2 Album Reviews": *www.geocities.com*, February 21, 2006.

Quote from The Edge, Graff, *Launch*, June 7, 2001.

"It's been said that rock & roll died...": *The U2 Reader*.

Concert at Madison Square Garden: Traub, *New York Times Magazine*. September 18, 2005.

Bono's voice: Traub, *New York Times Magazine*. September 18, 2005.

Bono on Dylan, "There's a lot of mystery about him..." by Caspar Llewellyn Smith, *The Observer*, Sunday, October 3, 2004.

Interview with Bono: Wenner, *Rolling Stone*, November 3, 2005.

Dylan on Bono: *Chronicles*, p. 174.

Dylan on Lanois promoting *Oh Mercy*: Williams, *Dylan: Mind Out of Time*, p. 173.

Dylan on Lanois: *Chronicles*, p. 218.

I would have liked to been able to give him: *Chronicles*, p. 218.

Lanois on "Series of Dreams": Williams, *Dylan: Mind Out of Time*, p. 208.

"Dylan sent them excavating.... to... place in the world," Gunderson, *USA Today*, May 17, 2001.

Bono Vox Interview: *Hot Press*, July 8, 1984.

What drew Dylan to U2: Williams, *Dylan:Mind Out of Time*, p. 56.

13. The Beatles and Dylan

Dylan received a telegram from the Beatles: Sounes, p. 155.

"That record hit the turntable…" to "as a songwriter": Spitz, *The Beatles*, p. 533–534.

Paul Simon quote to……"hearing his work," Spitz, *The Beatles*, p. 534.

"I'm a Loser": *Anthology—The Beatles,* p. 158.

Dylan caught up with the Beatles: Spitz, *The Beatles*, p. 534.

Beatles retrieved their "communal pillbox": Spitz, *The Beatles*, p. 535.

Ringo later recalled: *Anthology—The Beatles*, p. 158.

"He was our idol": *Anthology—The Beatles*, p. 158.

"I'm pretty much a fan": *Anthology—The Beatles*, p. 158.

"Lyrically he is still one of the best": *Anthology—The Beatles*, p. 158.

"The Beatles' songwriting accelerated under Dylan's influence": Spitz, *The Beatles*, p. 538.

Beatles played the Paramount Theater: Sounes, p. 162.

Beatles' endorsement of Dylan: Shelton, p. 288.

"Lennon visited Dylan…" to "nightmare": Shelton, p. 294.

Dylan bought a sprawling property: Sounes, p. 177.

"I always love to see John": Wenner interview, *Rolling Stone.* November 29, 1969.

A footnote to musical history: *Biograph Liner Notes*, p. 10.

"Lennon also said later": *Biograph Liner Notes*, p. 10.

"Blues players like Lightnin' Hopkins": Rosenbaum, *Playboy*, reprinted in *Younger Than That Now.*

Visiting with Dylan: Donovan, *Autobiography of Donovan*, p. 88–89.

Beatles visited Dylan with Sgt. Pepper: *Anthology—The Beatles*, p. 197.

George's quote on visiting Dylan: Harrison, p. 164.

George visited Dylan: *Anthology—The Beatles*, p.

George and Dylan wrote a song together: Sounes, p. 236.

"Dylan at the Isle of Wight…" to "played mostly rock & roll numbers": Sounes, p. 252.

Isle of Wight was a "vast, impersonal setting": Shelton, p. 318.

George joined Self Portrait sessions: Sounes, p. 258.

Dylan played the Concert for Bangladesh: Sounes, p. 266–267.

Traveling Wilburys sold more than any Dylan album of that

decade: Sounes, p. 384–385.

George talked about Dylan's music: Boyd, p. 138.

George and Ringo talk about the Beatles: Boyd, p. 112.

Olivia Harrison on George's lyrics and Dylan: Harrison, p. 3.

"They became the closest friends I'd ever had": *Anthology—The Beatles*, jacket copy.

"I am devastated": CNN.com News, December 1, 2001.

Richard Goldstein quote," He's the emblem of his generation," *The Nation*, May 15, 2006.

Afterword

Dylan... writing or drawing in hotel rooms, Sounes, p. 409–410.

BIBLIOGRAPHY

Baez, Joan. *And a Voice to Sing With.* 1ˢᵗ Ed. New York: Summit Books, 1987.

Bangs, Lester. "Hot Rod Rumble In The Promised Land." *Cream.* November 1975.

Bauldie, John, ed. *Wanted Man: In Search of Bob Dylan.* New York: Citadel Press, Carol Publishing Group, 1990.

Bono Vox Interview: "Bono, Bob and Van." *Hot Press.* Slane Castle, Dublin, Ireland: July 8, 1984.

Bordowitz, Hank. *The U2 Reader: A Quarter Century of Commentary, Criticism and Reviews.* Milwaukee: Hal Leonard Corporation, 2003.

Borodowitz, Hank, ed. *The U2 Reader: A Quarter Century of Commentary, Criticism,* and *Reviews.* Milwaukee: Hal Leonard Corp., 2003.

Boyd, Jenny, Ph.D. *Musicians in Tune.* New York: Fireside Books, 1992.

Byrne, Kevin. "Biography: Bono." Web site. *www.atu2.com/band/ bono,* accessed January 2006.

Cash, Johnny with Patrick Carr. *Cash: The Autobiography.* New York: HarperPaperbacks, 1997.

Clancy, Liam. *Mountain of the Women.* New York: Doubleday, 2002.

CNN News. "Beatle George Harrison Dies." CNN online, December 1, 2001. *http://archives.cnn.com/2001/SHOWBIZ/Music/11/30/harrison.obit,* accessed January 2006.

Cocks, Jay. "Rock's New Sensation: The Backstreet Phantom of Rock," *Time,* 1975.

Crowe, Cameron. *Biograph Liner Notes.* Copyright 1985 Special Rider Music.

DeCurtis, Anthony, Matt Diehl, Austin Scaggs, and David Wild. "Remembering Johnny." *Rolling Stone,* October 16, 2003.

Dunaway, David King. *How Can I Keep From Singing: Pete Seeger.* Columbus, OH: McGraw-Hill, 1981.

Dylan, Bob. *Chronicles, Volume One.* New York: Simon and Schuster, 2004.

Dylan, Bob. *Writings and Drawings.* New York: Alfred A. Knopf, 1973.

Eder, Bruce. "Music the Hawks Played." All music guide: *www.thebandforever.com,* January 2006.

Erlewine, Stephen Thomas. *All Music Guide. www.vh1.com,* accessed July 11, 2005.

Feinstein, Barry, Daniel Kramer, and Jim Marshall. *Early Dylan.* Boston: Bulfinch Press, Little, Brown and Co. 1999.

Fleming, Renee. *The Inner Voice.* New York: Viking Penguin, 2004.

Floman, Scott. "U2 Album Reviews." Scott Floman Music Reviews Web site. *www.geocities.com/sfloman/u2.html,* accessed February 2005.

Fong-Torres Ben. "Knockin' on Dylan's Door." *Rolling Stone,* February 14, 1974.

Friedman, Myra. *Buried Alive: The Biography of Janis Joplin.* New York: William Morrow & Co., 1973.

Fusilli, Jim "Rosanne Cash Turns Her Sorrow Into Music." *Wall Street Journal,* December 22, 2005.

Gill, Andy and Kevin Odegard. *A Simple Twist of Fate: Bob Dylan and the Making of Blood on the Tracks.* Cambridge, MA: Da Capo Press, 2004.

Goldstein, Richard. "Satellite Dylan: First an Icon, Now a DJ," *The Nation,* May 15, 2006.

Goodman, Fred. *Mansion on the Hill.* New York: Vintage Books, 1997.

Graff, Gary. "The Unforgettable Fire Still Burns." *Launch*. Launch Media, Inc. June 7, 2001.

Graham, Bill and Greenfield, Robert. *Bill Graham Presents: My Life Inside Rock and Out*. New York: Delta Books (Dell Publishing), 1992.

Gunderson, Edna. "Times change, but Dylan leaves a lasting imprint." *USA Today*, May 17, 2001.

Hajdu, David. *Positively 4th Street, The Life and Times of Bob Dylan, Joan Baez, Mimi Baez Fariña and Richard Fariña*. New York: Farrar, Straus and Giroux, 2001.

Harrison, George. *I, Me, Mine*. San Francisco: Chronicle Books, 1980 and 2002.

Helm, Levon with Stephen Davis. *This Wheel's on Fire. Levon Helm and the Story of The Band*. New York: William Morrow & Co., 1993.

Holden, Stephen. "From Country to Show Tunes." *New York Times*, February 15, 2005.

Knobler, Peter and Greg Mitchell. "Who is Bruce Springsteen and Why are we Saying All these Wonderful Things about him?" *Crawdaddy*, March 1973.

Landau, Jon. "Review of *Maria Muldaur.*" Warner Archives: *Rolling Stone,* June 6, 1974.

Landau, Jon. "Review of *Waitress in the Donut Shop, Maria Muldaur.*" Warner Archives: *Rolling Stone,* December 19, 1974.

Leitch, Donovan. *The Autobiography of Donovan: Hurdy Gurdy Man*. New York: St. Martin's Press, 2005.

Light, Alan. "Rosanne Cash Walks a Line of Her Own." *New York Times,* January 22, 2006.

Marcus, Greil. *Invisible Republic: Bob Dylan's Basement Tapes*. New York: Henry Holt & Co., 1997.

Marcus, Greil. *Like a Rolling Stone: Bob Dylan at the Crossroads*. New York: Public Affairs, 2005.

Marcus, Greil. *Mystery Train: Images of America in Rock 'n' Roll Music*. London: Omnibus Press, 1977.

Marsh, Dave. "Bruce Springsteen: A Rock 'Star is Born.'" *Rolling Stone*, September 25, 1975.

Marsh, Dave. *Bruce Springsteen: Two Hearts, The Definitive Biography, 1972– 2003*. New York: Routledge, 2004.

Mico, Ted. "Hating U2." *Spin Magazine*, January 1, 1989.

Percy, Will. Interview with Bruce Springsteen. *Double Take Magazine*, Spring 1998. Reprinted in *Racing in the Street*.

Ricks, Christopher. *Dylan: Visions of Sin.* New York: HarperCollins Publishers, 2003.

Riley, Tim. *Hard Rain: A Dylan Commentary.* New York: Da Capo Press, 1999.

Sawyers, June Skinner. Ed. *Racing In the Street: The Bruce Springsteen Reader.* New York: Penguin Books, 2004.

Scaduto, Anthony. *Bob Dylan.* Rev. ed. London: Abacus, 1973.

Scorsese, Martin. *No Direction Home.* American Masters. PBS, Fall 2005.

Scorsese, Martin. *Racing in the Street: The Bruce Springsteen Reader.* New York, NY: The Penguin Group, 2004.

Seaman, Donna. "Review of *Bodies of Water,*" *Booklist,* 1996.

Seeger, Pete. *Where Have All the Flowers Gone?* Bethlehem, PA: A Sing Out Publication, 1993.

Shelton, Robert. *No Direction Home.* New York: Beech Tree Books, 1986.

Smith, Caspar Llewellyn. "Bob on Bob–but do we really know where's he's at?" *The Observer,* October 3, 2004.

Sounes, Howard. *Down the Highway The Life of Bob Dylan.* New York: Grove Press, 2001.

Spitz, Bob. *The Beatles: The Biography.* New York: Little, Brown, 2005.

Strauss, Neil. "Springsteen Looks Back but Keeps Walking On." *New York Times,* May 7, 1995.

The Beatles. *Anthology—The Beatles.* London: Apple Corps. Ltd., 2000.

The Rock and Roll Hall of Fame. Bruce Springsteen's Bob Dylan Induction Speech. The Rock and Roll Hall of Fame and Museum, Inc. Web site. *www.rockhall.com,* accessed February 2005.

Thomson, Elizabeth and Gutman, David, editors. *The Dylan Companion.* New York: Da Capo Press, 1990.

Traub, James. "The Statesman: Why, and how, Bono matters." *New York Times Magazine,* September 18, 2005.

Wenner, Jann. S. "The *Rolling Stone* Interview: Bono," *Rolling Stone,* November 3, 2005.

Wikipedia contributors. "Kris Krostofferson." *Wikipedia: The Free Encyclopedia.* http://en.wikipedia.org/wiki/Kristofferson, accessed March 21, 2006.

Wikipedia contributors. "Medgar Evers." *Wikipedia: The Free Encyclopedia. http://en.wikipedia.org/wiki/Medgar_Evers,* accessed March 21, 2006.

Williams, Paul. "Lost in the Flood." *Crawdaddy,* October 1974.

Williams, Paul. *Bob Dylan: Performing Artist, 1960–1973, The Early Years.* New York: Omnibus Press, 1990.

Williams, Paul. *Bob Dylan: Performing Artist, 1974–1986, The Middle Years.* New York: Omnibus Press, 1992.

Williams, Paul. *Bob Dylan: Performing Artist, 1986–1990 and Beyond, Mind Out of Time,* Omnibus Press, 2004.

Younger That That Now. The Collected Interviews with Bob Dylan. New York: Thunder's Mouth Press, 2004.

Zollo, Paul. *Conversations with Tom Petty.* New York: Omnibus Press, 2005.

Zollo, Paul. *Songwriters on Songwriting.* 4th Ed. Cambridge, MA: Da Capo Press, 2003.

WEB SITES
FOR MUSICIANS

1. 1961–1965 Greenwich Village and Beyond
Paul Stookey of Peter, Paul and Mary *www.noelpaulstookey.com*
www.peterpaulandmary.com
Liam Clancy *www.liamclancy.com*
Joan Baez *www.joanbaez.com*
Bobby Vee *www.bobbyvee.com*
Maria Muldaur *www.mariamuldaur.com*
Johnny Rivers *www.johnnyrivers.com*

2. 1966–1976 Woodstock, Nashville and Beyond
Kris Kristofferson *www.ohboy.com/kris.html*
Ronnie Hawkins *www.ronniehawkins.com*
Rosanne Cash *www.rosannecash.com*

3. 1980–2006 On the Road to Reinvention
Bruce Springsteen *www.brucespringsteen.net/news*
Bono *www.u2.com*
www.atu2.com/band/bono
www.bonoonline.com/bono_version22.html

4. Let Me Hear Some of that Rock & Roll Music
The Beatles *www.beatles.com*
Paul McCartney *www.paulmccartney.com/main.html*

PERMISSIONS

INDEX